After 9/11

This is an incisive and readable analysis of American foreign policy and international politics since the end of the Cold War. The book is organized around two key themes: the role of culture in international politics and the changing nature of American power. It argues that cultural perspective is vital to an understanding of recent American foreign policy and also the reactions of others to America.

Taking a distinctive and challenging viewpoint on Samuel Huntington's 'clash of civilizations' thesis, Richard Crockatt endorses the claim that culture and values have become central battleground of international relations since the end of the Cold War.

In a series of linked studies, this book examines such themes as

- America's relations with the Islamic world, with particular focus on the war in Iraq and its aftermath
- the rhetoric of Bush's speeches
- the history and rebirth of 'Americanism'
- ideas of global order and the rise and fall of neoconservatism.

Combining an international relations approach with an American studies perspective, *After 9/11* is a much-needed balanced account of the most significant political questions of the twenty-first century.

Richard Crockatt is Professor of American History and Head of the School of American Studies at the University of East Anglia, where he specializes in US foreign policy and contemporary international relations. He is author of *The Fifty Years War* (Routledge, 1995) and *America Embattled* (Routledge, 2003).

After 9/11
Cultural dimensions of American global power

Richard Crockatt

Routledge
Taylor & Francis Group

LONDON AND NEW YORK

First published 2007
by Routledge
2 Park Square, Milton Park, Abingdon, Oxon OX14 4RN

Simultaneously published in the USA and Canada
by Routledge
270 Madison Avenue, New York, NY 10016

Routledge is an imprint of the Taylor & Francis Group, an informa business

© 2007 Richard Crockatt

Typeset in Joanna by
Taylor & Francis Books
Printed and bound in Great Britain by
Antony Rowe Ltd, Chippenham, Wiltshire

British Library Cataloguing-in-Publication Data
A catalogue record for this book is available from the British Library

Library of Congress Cataloging-in-Publication Data
Crockatt, Richard.
    After 9/11 : cultural dimensions of American
  global power / Richard Crockatt.
      p. cm.
    Includes bibliographical references and index. [etc.]
      1. United states–Foreign relations–2001. 2. Politics and culture.
    3. Nationalism–United States. 4. United States–Foreign public
    opinion. 5. World politics–1989-I. Title. II. Title: After nine-eleven.

JZ1480.C76   2007
303.48′273–dc22   2006039493

ISBN 978-0-415-39284-6 (hbk)
ISBN 978-0-415-39285-3 (pbk)
ISBN 978-0-203-95693-9 (ebk)

To my father
John L. Crockatt

Contents

Acknowledgements

Many institutions and individuals have helped in the making of this book. All but one of the chapters began life as lectures, and the reactions of audiences have helped greatly in the redrafting for publication. I am grateful to the following institutions for the opportunity to present my work: the Royal Institute of International Affairs, Chatham House; the University of Luxembourg (where I was privileged to be present at one of a series of conferences celebrating the founding of the institution); the Department of American Studies, University of Birmingham; the Rothermere America Institute, Oxford University; the Centre for International Studies, Cambridge University; the Mershon Centre, Ohio State University; the Public Affairs Forum, University of New Orleans; the Department of History, Rice University, Texas; the University of Trento; the University of Bologna, Forli; Oxford Brookes University; the Institute for the Study of the Americas, University of London; and last, but by no means least, the University of East Anglia which, as always, has provided me with a most supportive setting in which to teach and research. Special thanks to the American Studies Research Seminar and all my colleagues.

Certain individuals have read and commented on one or more of the chapters, either as editors of collections of essays or simply as interested colleagues. I am most grateful to them all for giving their time and their expertise: Chris Bigsby, David Ellwood, Sergio

Fabbrini, Stephanie Lawson, Lee Marsden, Brendon O'Connor, Mario Del Pero, and Nicola Pratt. For support, conversation, and insights I would also like to thank Günter Bischof, Alexander Stephan, and Roger Thompson. Many thanks to Ellen Berg for the loan of a book at a crucial moment. Successive years of students in my MA course on 'American Interventions' have proved a great source of energy and ideas. Conversation over the years with my wife Julia, especially about the Middle East, has been essential to my attempts to make sense of contemporary international politics. Needless to say, no blame attaches to any of the above for any shortcomings in this book. I am indebted finally to my father, to whom this book is dedicated, for unstinting support and encouragement over the years.

I am grateful to Greenwood Press, Intellect (publishers of the *European Journal of American Culture*), and Routledge (Taylor & Francis) for permission to reprint revised versions of essays previously published as follows:

Chapter 1   'Anti-Americanism and the Clash of Civilizations', in Brendon O'Connor and Martin Griffiths (eds) *The Rise of Anti-Americanism* (Routledge, 2006), pp. 121–39.

Chapter 3   'No Common Ground? Islam, Anti-Americanism and the United States', *European Journal of American Culture*, 23, no. 2 (2004), pp. 125–42.

Chapter 4   'Americanism: A Short History', in B. O'Connor (ed.) (under the title of 'Americanism as a Source of Anti-Americanism'), *Anti-Americanism: Historical Perspectives*, vol. 2, Greenwood Press, 2007.

Chapter 5   'What's the Big Idea? Models of Global Order in the Post-Cold War Era', in Sergio Fabbrini (ed.) *The United States Contested: American Unilateralism and European Discontent* (Routledge, 2006), pp. 69–91.

Introduction

In the summer of 2006 the *Guardian* (London) published a brief letter which spoke volumes about attitudes in certain British circles towards the United States. The writer referred to an advertisement by a British university for a lectureship in 'American thought and culture' and invited the reader to share his view that this was a laughable notion, indeed a contradiction in terms. America, the correspondent assumes we will agree, has no thought or culture.[1]

One can take it that the letter-writer was not a deep student of the United States and also that he was opposed to everything the Bush administration stood for. In fact the letter gathers up a whole bundle of implications to produce a composite image of the United States as crude, undeveloped, and anti-intellectual yet also powerful, dangerous and very right-wing. How, the letter-writer seems to be saying, could a country with whose policies one disagrees so profoundly possibly have a culture worth admiring? How could it have any culture at all? How could a country which elected George W. Bush, the very antithesis of the philosopher king, have any thought worthy of consideration? Perhaps also the letter-writer was congratulating himself on the conclusion that he wouldn't have to exert any effort to understand America because there was really nothing to understand.

Any first-year student of American studies could put the letter-writer right on the question of America's cultural and intellectual tradition. America has both produced a great deal of thought and culture and has been a cause of thought and culture in others. America has its novelists, poets, playwrights, philosophers, its music and art; it was the virtual inventor of the motion-picture industry and of jazz. American science leads the world. (As I write, it has been announced that American scientists have won Nobel Prizes in Physics, Medicine, and Chemistry.) With its Constitution, including the commentaries which surrounded its ratification, the United States was a pioneer in what might be called political mechanics. It is often forgotten that America possesses the oldest national written constitution in continuous operation. Without entering into a detailed discussion of the various meanings of the word culture – a subject discussed in Chapter 2 of this book – it should be obvious that whatever one's estimate of America's contribution to 'culture' (in the sense of high art), America certainly has 'a culture' (in the anthropological sense), and a potent and distinctive one at that. A culture is composed not only of books and plays and symphonies but a complex of values, beliefs, habits of feeling and behaviour, and institutions – everything that is implied by the term 'way of life'. We fail to understand the American way of life at our peril because it is of such importance to our own and that of many other countries and continents. But Americans too need to understand how others see their country and in particular the huge gap which often exists between their own sense of themselves and the images which others have of them. It is not so much that these images are sometimes negative but that they are as often as not the product of raw emotion. Such reactions arise in part out of the way America projects itself on the world stage and not merely from the prejudices of others.

This is no more than to say that the American way of life, or what used commonly to be called 'American civilization', is a factor in international relations as much as the specific decisions and policies of the US government. Indeed the re-emergence of the word 'civilization' in public discourse is the theme of Chapter 1. It seeks to show that the policies of the Bush administration are rooted in assumptions which underpin

American culture, even if Bush's America represents a narrow and somewhat rigid version of those assumptions. The leading premise of all the following essays is that a cultural perspective is a necessity in understanding American foreign policy in particular and international relations in general.

It is important to note that culture is not opposed to power but is an ingredient of it. Joseph S. Nye has famously and usefully distinguished between the 'soft power' of culture and the 'hard power' of economic and military strength.[2] But there is nothing necessarily 'soft' about the projection of cultural power. Culture is dynamic especially when allied to hard power. It can be a potent force of persuasion, and all the more effective for being associated with intangible beliefs and values as compared with the apparently more tangible instruments of political and economic power. As Nye notes, soft power 'rests on the ability to set the agenda in a way that shapes the preferences of others'.[3] But it is a mistake to think of soft power as necessarily attractive or appealing to others. Nye urges Americans to rely less on hard power and to cultivate the employment of soft power, which is presumed to be benign. He observes that governments must act in ways that 'reinforce rather than undercut American soft power' since 'the arrogance, indifference to the opinions of others, and narrow approach to our national interests advocated by the new unilateralists are a sure way to undermine our soft power'.[4] But the 'arrogance' and 'indifference to the opinion of others' of the new unilateralists of the Bush administration are themselves manifestations of soft power; they represent particular versions or readings of American culture, values and history. There is ideological force behind the attitudes of the Bush administration; it is not just a matter of tone or behaviour. Indeed, there may be some justification for George W. Bush's comment that 'they [the terrorists] hate our freedoms', though not for the reason he supposes. 'They' may hate the assumption that the freedoms Bush is referring to are precisely the ones that they want or that what Bush and they mean by freedom is the same thing.

There is no denying the attractiveness of American culture. The United States remains the destination of choice for large numbers of immigrants, including Muslims, whose numbers, after a dip following 9/11, have risen to new heights.[5] But one should not underestimate the capacity of American culture to provoke alienation. Perhaps no encounter with American culture had greater or ultimately more violent repercussions than that of the Egyptian intellectual Sayyid Qutb during his visit to the United States in the late 1940s and early 1950s. Coming to study American education in the expectation that he would enjoy close up what he had admired at a distance, he was in fact repelled by American life – its sexual permissiveness, use of alcohol, what he took to be its lack of respect for human life, and its godlessness. America remained an image of decadence and corruption, even evil, for him. Returning to Egypt he joined the Muslim Brotherhood, was imprisoned and tortured by the Nasser government, and became further radicalized, being eventually executed in 1966. His tract *Milestones*, written in prison, presented a vision of a new Islamic order which he believed could only be established through *jihad* against the West and also recalcitrant Muslims. Qutb's example and his writings subsequently helped to shape the ideas of a generation of radical Islamists, including Osama bin Laden.[6] For all the claims by bin Laden that his *jihad* against America was provoked by the Palestinian issue, the presence of American troops in Saudi Arabia, and American policy towards Iraq, he was primed to react to these events by a prior profound alienation from Western culture.

This, of course, is an extreme example but nevertheless a telling one. It demonstrates, among other things, that foreign relations are not always under control of governments. There is an existential and not merely a political dimension to such encounters. At other times governments themselves embody and project aspects of their national cultures, though not always consciously or with awareness of their possible impact on other nations and cultures. Nye's policy-oriented approach to soft power doesn't really help here in so far as it assumes that

American soft power is generally regarded as benign by others. It is surely wrong to say, as Nye does, that 'power in the global information age is becoming less tangible and less coercive'.[7] Less tangible maybe (or at least less visible), but there is much evidence to show that power in the information age can be as coercive as ever, perhaps increasingly so. Is there any reason to doubt that terrorism and the bewildering levels of violence between peoples, ethnic groups, and faith groups are at some profound level wars of religion, ideas and values as well as arms? What is it that drives individuals to kill others by killing themselves if not the pull of a conviction so powerful as to blank out or all other considerations? There is nothing more potent, whether for creative or destructive ends, than a man or woman with an idea, whether religious or secular, which will not be denied expression and enactment. Ideas, it has been rightly said, are weapons. They can also, as Blake said, imprison us; we create our own 'mind-forged manacles'.

In the chapters that follow an implicit and perhaps unanswerable question is how a culture can get out of its skin, see itself as others see it, and thereby reach accommodations which would otherwise be impossible and, moreover, do this without losing its sense of itself, its identity. This question is raised with particular force in the case of the United States since its culture is so dominant, so self-reinforcing, so apparently complete and self-sufficient. Aspirations to the universality of American values and claims to greatness – regarded as self-evident truths by many Americans, boastful and irritating rhetoric by many others – are staples of American public discourse. In this book the focus is on the Bush administration, but it should be borne in mind that Bush represents simply a heightened form of a practice common among American public figures of talking up America in the most grandiose terms. In his acceptance speech as Democratic presidential nominee in the election of 1992, Bill Clinton recounted the influences which had led him into politics. Among them was the example of a professor at Georgetown University who had said that 'America was the greatest nation in history because our people had always believed in two great ideas: that tomorrow can be better than today, and that every one of us has a personal, moral responsibility to make it so'.[8] It is a mistake to think that American politicians do not believe the rhetoric they employ or that it is simply for 'domestic consumption'. The ideas expressed in such speeches are vital clues to American culture. The conviction of American greatness and American goodness, furthermore, is integral to the way in which many Americans conceive of their role in the world. In response to a question about why people 'hate' America, George W. Bush responded that he could not understand it because 'I know how good we are'. To understand that response, we must employ a cultural perspective.

In the chapters that follow, I return on a number of separate occasions to the ideas of Samuel Huntington, whose theory of the 'clash of civilizations' has been the most discussed model of international relations since the end of the Cold War. His theory that cultural conflict has overtaken other forms of conflict as the prime motor of international national relations in the aftermath of the Cold War is frequently regarded as both provocative and wrong. Provocative it is, yes; partly wrong, yes, but wholly wrong, no. In the rush to condemn his theory, which many have on political as well as intellectual grounds, critics have failed to see what is valuable in his arguments. Furthermore, many have used their dissatisfaction with his ideas as an occasion for dismissing out of hand the importance of cultural factors in international relations. In Chapters 1 and 2 I seek to redress this balance.

A second theme of the book is the upsurge of nationalism in the Bush presidency. Many regard the theme of empire as having supplanted that of nationalism, particularly in the light of America's supreme international position since the demise of the Soviet bloc. This is, I believe, to exaggerate not only American power but also America's will to power. Americans by and large do not have the habit of empire even if some of their leaders and some house intellectuals (including some outside the

United States) do and wish the rest of America did too. A number of commentators in recent years have described the growth of nationalist sentiment in America but less has been made of its significance in international relations. In Chapters 5 and 7 I explore the grounds for regarding America's devotion to national sovereignty as a guiding theme of the Bush administration's foreign policy. In this connection, and linking with the first theme, the cultural dimension of American nationalism is critical to an understanding of both American policy and the foreign reactions to it. Chapters 2 and 3 suggest, in contrast to the tendency of commentators to explain anti-Americanism exclusively in political terms, that the Bush administration's projection of a particular brand of cultural nationalism bore a large responsibility for overseas reaction against America. Chapter 4 traces the history of 'Americanism' – a curiously unexplored theme for all the commentary on anti-Americanism – through the nineteenth and twentieth centuries as a clue to the generation of a certain image of America which turns out to be not unlike the one implied by the letter to the *Guardian* referred to above. Indeed, this chapter may go some way towards explaining the narrowness of the image which America often projects of itself and the virulent reaction that image has often aroused.

The third theme of the book, closely related to both the other two, is that history matters in understanding the contemporary world and especially America, that supposedly most unhistorical of nations. Nothing could be further from the truth. In actuality, it could be argued that Americans are prisoners of their own history and no one more so than George W. Bush. Chapters 6 and 7 examine the ideological sources of the so-called 'Bush revolution in foreign policy' which I prefer to see as a counter-revolution since it relies on ideas and assumptions which go back to the roots of American nationhood. In important respects, Bush is a throw-back, an anachronism. Chapter 4 on the history of 'Americanism' and Chapter 5 on 'big ideas' about global order cover a good deal of material which predates 9/11 but the point is to show its relevance to an understanding of today's issues. The premise here is that history – which is to say the stories and myths we tell each other about the past, not necessarily the 'real' past' – is not merely a collection of useful analogies and examples but, particularly at times of crisis, a living influence in the present. It is also an ambiguous presence – a source of strength and stability for those Americans seeking comfort in a violent and unpredictable world but also a potentially distorting lens.

Hovering over these chapters inevitably is the brute fact of the terrorist attacks of 11 September 2001 and their sequel, the war on terror, especially the war in Iraq. The volume of commentary on these momentous events is huge and growing. I have not sought to add to it directly but rather to come at these subjects at a tangent in the hope that by indirection certain less obvious features will be clarified. However, the larger context for these essays is the sense that the world is at a turning point which is defined by the changing structure of the international system. In part it has to do with the shifting status of the nation-state in global politics and in part with new forms of violence and disorder, both of which are associated in complex ways with globalization. This book is centrally concerned with how America has responded to these challenges and the resources from the present and the past it brings to them. In ways which are all too familiar from the pages of our daily newspapers and news broadcasts, the world is characterized by turbulence and rapid change. In such circumstances it is not surprising that politicians should seek to revive old nostrums in efforts to deal with the new realities. Chapter 7 explores the Bush administration's efforts in this direction and questions whether his leadership has equipped America to cope with the future. It should be clear, finally, that, despite the American focus of these essays, I do not believe that America is the cause of all the bad or the good in today's world. American power in all meanings of the word, however, does matter hugely and deserves strenuous attempts to comprehend it.

The chapters stand alone individually but circle round the themes outlined above. Some are developments of subjects such as anti-Americanism, discussed in an earlier book, *America Embattled: September 11, Anti-Americanism and the Global Order* (Routledge, 2003). Others, such as the themes of culture and nationalism, have clarified themselves only since that book was written. I do not pretend to have exhausted the possibilities of any of the topics covered in this book. I offer these essays as a set of explorations which, it is hoped, will stimulate thought and discussion.

1 Anti-Americanism and the clash of civilizations

America is a nation with a mission and that mission comes from our most basic beliefs.

(George W. Bush, State of the Union Address, 20 January 2004)

'Civilization' resurgent

Among the most striking features of post-Cold War debate about international politics has been the revival of talk about 'civilization' and 'civilizations'. Much of it has been stimulated by the publication of Samuel Huntington's 'Clash of Civilizations?', first in article form in 1993 in the influential periodical *Foreign Affairs* and three years later as a book.[1] His argument was both simple and provocative. 'It is my hypothesis', he wrote, 'that the fundamental source of conflict in this new world will not be primarily ideological or primarily economic. The great divisions among mankind and the dominating source of conflict will be cultural.' Nation-states would continue to be important but 'the principal conflicts of global politics will occur between nations and groups of different civilizations'.[2] Commentary on Huntington's argument has reached almost biblical proportions. There are few studies of post-Cold War international politics which do not address Huntington's views, and discussion of his theory has extended well beyond the academy.[3] The authors of the Bush administration's 'National Security Strategy', for example, felt it necessary to point out that 'the war on terrorism is not a clash of civilizations', indicating that Huntington's formulation had become common currency.[4]

Civilization-talk has also appeared in other guises, however, which are not related directly to the Huntington debate. Since September 11 George W. Bush has repeatedly declared that 'this [the war on terror] is the world's fight. This is civilization's fight.' 'The civilized world', he observed in a speech to Congress on 20 September 2001, 'is rallying to America's side.' In his 2002 State of the Union Address he declared that 'the civilized world faces unprecedented dangers' and, speaking of Iraq's weapons of mass destruction (WMD), that 'this is a regime that has something to hide from the civilized world'. In his introductory statement to the 'National Security Strategy' issued in September 2002, Bush noted that that 'the allies of terror are the enemies of civilization'. 'America's purpose', the president declared in his 2003 State of the Union Address, 'is more than to follow a process – it is to achieve a result: the end of terrible threats to the civilized world'. A year later he reminded his audience that 'families and schools and religious congregations' were 'unseen pillars of civilization' which must remain strong in America and be defended.[5] Such rhetoric is to be found in many of president Bush's major speeches since September 11 and is associated with a heavily freighted moral and religious rhetoric.

Moral and religious rhetoric in itself is nothing new in American history. The sense of mission expressed in the epigraph to this chapter can be matched by reference to any number of presidential speeches over the last two centuries. However, the moral dimension of the Bush administration's approach to policy is particularly explicit and salient, exceeding arguably even that of the Reagan administration in intensity and consistency. Furthermore, the explicit invocation of 'civilization' and 'civilizations' appears to strike a novel note, suggesting a heightened sense of crisis and of a shift in the very categories of thinking about global politics. Significantly, such rhetoric was also current in the first years of the Cold War at the beginning of a historical phase which ended in the early 1990s. Arnold Toynbee's *Civilization on Trial* (1948) captured a widespread sense of being at a momentous historical turning point and also of being challenged by new forces which were at once ideological, moral, and political. Among these the spectre of communism loomed large. Toynbee's *Study of History*, an abridgement of which had appeared to great acclaim the previous year, was widely regarded as a warning of the likely fate of Western civilization, should it fail to rise to the challenge of communism. The vogue for Toynbee occurred at a time of maximum tension and anxiety. *A Study of History* appeared the year 'Cold War' entered the vocabulary and Truman's doctrine of 'containment' was announced.[6] While Huntington's essay predated the year of greatest crisis in post-Cold War global politics – 2001 – his formulation was widely held to define the unfamiliar outlines of the post-Cold War world, and for many, the terrorist attacks of 2001 fully confirmed his thesis of the primacy of cultural conflict. For the moment the issue is not the correctness or otherwise of his thesis but rather the unusually wide currency it gained. In this respect, the reception of his writings was comparable with that of Toynbee. A further point of comparison is Huntington's adoption of 'civilizations' as the basic unit of analysis. In this, both Toynbee and Huntington were working in a well-established grand tradition of historical theorizing going back at least to the eighteenth century. 'Civilization' is one of those words bequeathed to us by the Enlightenment, though the idea goes back much further, having roots in any situation in which one society claimed superiority over 'savages' or 'barbarians'.[7] Huntington's scheme of analysis draws heavily on Toynbee and one can assume that the popularity of both was due to the sense they were able to convey, in part through the language they employed, of a depth of historical perspective and weightiness of theme.[8]

It will be clear from the above examples that there is an important distinction to be made between different usages of the terms civilization and civilized. At one end of the spectrum of meaning civilization is a neutral, scientific term indicating a certain kind of society or stage of growth which a society has reached; it is employed in the main by historians and historical sociologists as a means of categorizing various forms of social organization. In such instances the reference is to a particular civilization or civilizations.[9] At the other end of the spectrum civilization is a politically and ideologically charged abstract noun conveying a partial and self-interested notion of what constitutes 'civilization'. As Huntington himself observed, 'every civilization sees itself as the centre of the world and writes its history as the central drama of human history'.[10] To the extent that the West is dominant in today's world, there is always the suspicion among non-Westerners that the West equates 'civilization' with 'Western civilization'. Such terminology in the mouth of an American president can hardly therefore be regarded as being value-neutral. In between these two extremes of usage are any number of intermediate positions, but it is easy for apparently value-neutral uses of the term to spill over into loaded or normative usages. The opening sentence of Charles and Mary Beard's seminal *The Rise of American Civilization* (1929) neatly encapsulates both meanings: 'The history of a civilization may, if intelligently applied, be an instrument of civilization.'[11] Civilization is evidently, as the social scientists like to say, an 'essentially contested concept' whose meaning will always be a subject of debate and controversy, depending on who is using it and how it is being used.[12]

There are several reasons for being interested in this phenomenon. My concern here is with the degree to which it indicates shifts in attitudes in America since the end of the Cold War and in the way America is viewed from abroad. I am less interested in Huntington himself and the fate of his thesis than in the wider phenomenon of 'civilization-consciousness' in the United States.[13] To anticipate my conclusion, I propose the following: that the international conditions of the post-Cold War world in general and the post-September 11 world in particular have inclined many Americans to accentuate their 'American-ness', to enhance and even exaggerate their sense of the nation as unique and exceptional. The times have reinforced a reasser-tion of America's core values and a heightened sense of the nation's distinctive destiny and global role. More particularly, the American right has promoted civilization-consciousness as part of its armory in the effort to reshape American foreign policy. The anti-Americanism which we see around the world is in part a response to this heightened 'civilization-consciousness' and the political and military actions which are prompted by it.

Events, furthermore, it will be argued, have served to reinforce the argument Huntington put forward: that cultural conflict is a major and increasing source of global conflict. It is not necessary, however, to follow Huntington the whole way. There are, as we shall see later, certain serious criticisms to be made of his thesis, but they are not sufficient to reject out of hand the notion that culture was a major source of conflict in the post-Cold War world, even if the conclusions he draws from the prevalence of cultural conflict are not the only conclusions which can flow from his premise. The task here is to rescue a cultural inter-pretation of global conflict both from those who have attacked it and from those who have most forcefully advocated it.

Before proceeding it is necessary to address the meaning and usage of the terms 'culture' and 'cultural conflict'. Is it useful or even possible to distinguish cultural from other sources of con-flict? How precisely does cultural conflict differ from political, ideological or economic conflict? In most definitions culture is associated with language, ethnicity, 'way of life' and above all religion and shared meanings and values.[14] Cultures may, but often do not, coincide with national boundaries. A defined cul-ture may be as small as a village or locality or as large as a 'civilization', which Toynbee defined as 'the largest intelligible field of historical study' and Huntington called 'the highest cultural grouping of people and the broadest level of cultural identity people have short of that which distinguishes human life from other species'. A civilization is, then, 'a culture writ large'.[15] Another way of distinguishing between cultural and other forms of conflict is according to the ways in which conflict is expressed. Characteristically cultural conflicts revolve round issues of identity rather than interests, values rather than material needs, and arise from non-rational levels of experience and behaviour. Furthermore, cultures generally change and develop at a slower rate than do ideologies or political systems. Needless to say, such distinctions cannot be hard and fast; they help to identify family resemblances between different fields of human experience rather than rigid boundaries. It is important, for example, to avoid the trap of assuming that cultures are unchanging essences or that the differences between cultures are always or necessarily more important than common features which they share. Cultures, like political systems, change and evolve; some apparently primordial cultural institutions were created or invented at particular moments in time for particular purposes. Furthermore, fruitful cultural interaction, no more so than in the global age, is at least as important as cultural conflict.[16] The necessity of making such qualifications, however, is not a reason for abandoning the attempt to distinguish between cultural and other forms of conflict or interaction. Often in any particular situation the ascription of one term or another will be a matter of emphasis rather than of absolute difference. Nevertheless, it is important to maintain such distinctions. To collapse all facets of human experience into each other is no less distorting than to separate them from each other.

Civilization-consciousness and its meaning

What is meant by 'civilization-consciousness'? I believe that three claims are being made by those who invoke civilization, not all of them obviously compatible. The examples given here are illustrative only and are in keeping with the exploratory nature of this inquiry. The first claim rests on the identification of civilization with America and is therefore an act of appropriation by America. It expresses a sense of America's distinctive identity as a nation and a culture. This is as old as America and is often called 'American exceptionalism' or 'Americanism' or in its more strident forms '100 per cent Americanism'. But more than this is implied. These ideas rest on the notion that America has the capacity to be a world unto itself, that America itself constitutes a 'civilization'. Historically such notions have been as common on the left as on the right. Charles and Mary Beard's history of the United States, as we have seen, was called *The Rise of American Civilization*. Max Lerner's magisterial study of the United States, published in 1957, was entitled *America as a Civilization*. 'Like a person', he wrote, 'a civilization is more than the sum of its parts. ... When you have described its people, armies, technology, economics, politics, arts, regions and cities, class and caste, mores and morals, there is something elusive left – an inner civilizational style.' In answer to the question 'Is America a civilization?' he answered resoundingly yes: 'to be American is no longer to be only a nationality. It has become, along with communism and in rivalry with it, a key pattern of action and values.' Furthermore, he concluded, 'America represents ... the naked embodiment of the most dynamic elements of modern western history'.[17]

The argument for an American civilization as distinct from Western civilization has received a great fillip recently in the hands of the New Right in America and in particular in the context of strained relations between America and 'old' Europe. In Robert Kagan's eyes 'it is time to stop pretending that Europeans and Americans share a common view of the world, or even that they occupy the same world'. On major strategic and international questions 'Americans are from Mars and Europeans from Venus: They agree on little and understand each other less and less.' Nor was this a superficial or transitory phenomenon: 'when it comes to setting national priorities, determining threats, defining challenges, and fashioning and implementing foreign and defense policies, the United States and Europe have parted ways'.[18] Kagan presents an array of arguments which explain the outcome he identifies, but it is worth pointing out that the notion that Europe and America were different worlds is as old as the United States itself. Indeed, the perception that the Old World and the New were incompatible, most forcefully presented by Tom Paine in *Common Sense* (1776), was what tipped the scales in favour of the argument for a declaration of independence. 'It is evident', Paine wrote, 'that [England and America] belong to different systems. England to Europe: America to itself.'[19] What is clear is that since the end of the Cold War such perceptions have become prevalent on both sides of the Atlantic. Will Hutton's *The World We're In* makes another powerful argument, in this case from the point of view of the liberal left, for regarding America and Europe's 'inner civilizational styles' as being distinct.[20]

What these arguments come down to is the view, shared by many outsiders as well as Americans, that America is a special kind of nation, a nation of nations as Whitman termed it, granted a special destiny stemming from its uniquely fortunate situation, with claims to be a civilization on its own terms, whether or not the word itself is used. As George W. Bush put it in his 2004 State of the Union Address, 'America is a nation with a mission, and that mission comes from our most basic beliefs.'[21] Civilization-consciousness at one level is thus America's peculiar version of nationalism.[22] It expresses claims both to uniqueness and universalism of values, and promotes the argument that America contains within itself all the world's possibilities because it contains elements of all the world's populations and because of the nature of its founding revolution which was at once unique and exemplary. America is, as one scholar has put it, the 'universal nation'.[23] With such claims to specialness came assumptions of special responsibility. That American exceptionalism is a central feature of the Bush administration is evident in the writings of neoconservatives whose ideas have been such an important influence on his policies. In calling during the mid-1990s for a 'neo-Reaganite' foreign policy, leading neoconservatives William Kristol and Robert Kagan observed that 'it is worth recalling that the most successful Republican presidents of this century, Theodore Roosevelt and Ronald Reagan, both inspired Americans to assume cheerfully the new international responsibilities that went with increased influence and power'. Moreover, 'both celebrated American exceptionalism'.[24]

This posture is at once inclusive and exclusive, outward-looking and deeply chauvinist, internationalist and nationalist. Furthermore, this stance expresses something of the effort involved in asserting an American consensus. To make a single entity of all that diversity inevitably involves doing some violence to diversity, setting some limits to difference. One would think that the United States would be well placed to deal with ethnic and cultural diversity, but in fact the opposite has often proved to be the case. 'Nativism' has a long history in the United States, particularly at times when American society is perceived to be under pressure from external threats or large-scale immigration.[25] Precisely because it is so diverse, a premium has been placed on unifying institutions, values, and symbols, no more so than at times of national crisis such as the early years of the Cold War and the terrorist attacks of September 11. The expression of those unifying elements has characterized much governmental rhetoric and policies from the passage of the Patriot Act to the key political and military moves in the war on terror. Significantly, Samuel Huntington followed up The Clash of Civilizations with a study of the challenges to American national identity resulting from new waves of immigration from Latin America and Asia.[26]

The second claim implicit in 'civilization-consciousness' has to do with leadership and in particular the sense that, in all meanings of the term, America is 'bound to lead':[27] bound in the sense that it is the natural role for a nation of America's size and power and bound in the sense that the role is forced on America whether it wants it or not. America is, from this point of view, inevitably leader of the civilized world.

This is a much more complicated issue for Americans than most non-Americans acknowledge. Outside observers of America in the last half century have often assumed that America has been determined to spread its influence and to intervene overseas wherever and whenever it had the opportunity to do so. In fact, American policy has been more cautious than such views would suggest, and American public opinion was and still is ambivalent about most overseas ventures.[28] Indeed, for some, America is not decisive enough in the international arena. For all the discussion of 'American empire' at the turn of the millennium, there are those like British historian Niall Ferguson who note, and bemoan the fact, that 'America has acquired an empire but Americans themselves lack the imperial cast of mind. They would rather consume than conquer.'[29] As leader of the 'civilized' world the United States is generally expected and expects to assume certain responsibilities, and the range of economic and strategic interests has increasingly extended the net of commitments. Intervention, however, is rarely automatic, not least because of the well-documented reluctance in the post-Vietnam years of the American taxpayer to accept costly open-ended commitments of substantial number of American troops, to say nothing of possible casualties. Indeed, this constraint was present during the Vietnam War itself: witness the stealth with which Johnson increased the number of troops and his reluctance to admit the true cost of the war to the American people, which would have meant raising taxes and/or taking funds from his cherished Great Society programme, neither of which he was prepared to contemplate. However, the biggest constraint on large-scale overseas actions prior to 1989 was the possibility of direct confrontation with the Soviet Union or China. The deployment of several hundred thousand troops to the Gulf in 1991 and of lesser but still substantial numbers in Afghanistan and Iraq in the on-going conflict there would have been all but inconceivable during the Cold War.

Some traditional constraints still exist on American interventions, but the context has changed radically since 1989 and especially after the United States was the target of a direct attack on September 11, 2001. With it the issue of leadership has changed. In one sense the situation has become clearer. The United States has no rival globally, whether one is talking about overall size of the economy, defence budgets, sophistication of weapons systems, global military reach, global economic influence, and so on.[30] Not that America is flawless. There are weaknesses as well as strengths in American society and the economy. There is too much domestic debt and too great a gap between rich and poor; growth areas in employment are generally in low-paid casual or temporary service jobs; and deregulated capitalism has spawned corporate fraud on a massive scale. There appear also to be signs of social decay in extreme forms of crime and social violence and what one commentator has called 'the collapse of the public realm'.[31] In the short to medium term, however, these weaknesses do not seem likely to affect America's global position. Some of them have long been features of American life, not least levels of social violence, corruption in business, trade imbalances and so on. The basic ingredients of American power remain intact, and with the Cold War enemy removed America is apparently more free to act on the global stage than at any time since the Second World War. Hence the continuing relevance of the suggestion that America is 'bound to lead'.

On the other hand, the end of the Cold War complicated matters as far as American global leadership is concerned. It is not only the often-remarked absence of a clearly defined enemy so much as the absence of a ready set of rules and justifications for overseas interventions. Rather than the blanket justification of containment of communism, each intervention has to be justified on its own terms or in relation to some as yet not clearly formulated programme – Bush Sr's 'New World Order' or Clinton's 'democratic enlargement'.[32] If Cold War 'realism' had supplied the necessary basis for policy choices in the period of East–West confrontation, in the more fluid world that followed the collapse of communism various elements of idealism came more to the fore. To put it another way, the promotion of cultural values featured more prominently than before. The growth of international terrorism in the 1990s, reaching a climax on September 11 and putting the war on terror at the top of the agenda, served to enhance the cultural and idealist dimensions of policy. Since the enemy was now not a nation-state but shadowy sub- or transnational organizations, conceptions of realism apparently had limited relevance. If realism assumes a rational actor model, operating on the basis of sovereign nation-states, then clearly it could not easily encompass the new threat of terrorism. This is not to say that realism goes entirely out the window. There is not and never has been a simple either/or – realism or idealism – in the making of American foreign policy, but rather various complex mixtures of the two. Crucially, a world in which terrorism was the chief threat simply did not accord with the familiar patterns of conflict and policy choices, to the extent that it was necessary to reinterpret that threat to accord more clearly with realist precepts. Hence the 'war' on terrorism and the war on Saddam Hussein's Iraq.

Furthermore, the increasing use of cultural justifications for policy choices lies in the nature of the enemy's agenda, which contains a large cultural and religious element. 'Bin Laden's grievance with the United States', the authors of the 9/11 *Commission Report* observed,

> may have started in reaction to specific U.S. policies but it quickly became far deeper. To the ... question, what America could do, Al Qaeda's answer was that America should abandon the Middle East, convert to Islam, and end the immorality and godlessness of its society and culture.

The Report then quotes bin Laden's 2002 'Letter to America' to the effect that 'it is saddening to tell you that you are the worst civilization witnessed by the history of mankind'.[33] Even more pointed is bin Laden's response to the question of whether he agreed with the 'clash of civilizations' thesis. 'Absolutely', he replied. 'The [Holy] Book states it clearly. Jews and Americans invented peace on earth. That's a fairy tale. All they do is chloroform Muslims while leading them to the slaughter-house.'[34] For his part George W. Bush noted in his 2002 State of the Union Address that the challenge posed by al-Qaeda terrorism to the United States was in large part moral. 'Our enemies', he said, 'believed America was weak and materialistic, that we would splinter in fear and selfishness. They were wrong as they were evil ... [and] evil is real and it must be opposed.'[35]

The chances of al-Qaeda actually destroying America are slim. September 11, 2001 had numerous and complex effects but its effects on the American economy were modest, comparable, it has been suggested, with a very severe natural disaster but much less damaging than the stock-market collapse of the previous year.[36] The trauma of September 11 arose from the brutally unexpected nature of the attack; its effects were psychological as much as material. The challenge of terrorism is to America's conception of itself rather than to the actual fabric of its institutions, though the effects of the attacks on those directly affected can never be underestimated. It is the nature of terrorism that it seeks to and often achieves an impact far out of proportion to its physical effects and it does so by breaking all the rules of 'civilized' behaviour. One rational response to such a challenge is to reaffirm one's commitment to civilization and civilized values. More specifically, in relation to the issue in question here, the response is to assert American leadership in the fight against barbarism and on behalf of civilization.

The third claim implicit in 'civilization-consciousness' in some ways runs counter to the first two. Though treated last here, it is perhaps the most obvious application of the term. It relates to the identification of the United States with the 'civilized world' which is larger than the United States physically and more extensive culturally. Traditionally the identification has been with Western civilization. Rarely in the contemporary world is it restricted to the 'West', since the United States takes pains to include under the rubric of 'civilized' all those nations and cultures which are willing to join the United States in the war against terror, wherever they are geographically and whatever their religion or culture. That includes Muslims who reject the attempt of bin Laden and others to identify their cause as that of Islam as a whole. America's fight, it has been reiterated by members of the American administration from Bush downwards, is not with Islam but with extremists who have hijacked Islam for their own murderous purposes. For its part, the American Muslim community has declared its allegiance to the United States. The American Council for Islamic Affairs, along with other Islamic bodies in the United States, has taken pains to dissociate itself from 'Islamic terrorism' and to stress the Americanness of American Muslims.[37]

The most obvious manifestation of this aspect of civilization-consciousness lies in the effort to build a coalition against terror and more broadly to associate that effort with the defence of civilization. It is presented as a collective effort, admittedly led by the United States but operating on behalf of the larger whole, indeed the largest possible whole which includes all those who lay claim to the term 'civilization'. Inclusivity is the goal here, with the aim of drawing the clearest possible line between friends and enemies, a line which invokes social and ethical as well as political values.

It would seem that the first and third claims of civilization-consciousness are at odds with each other. In the first aspect the invocation of civilization is an act of national appropriation which lays down a challenge to potential friends and enemies of the United States alike. Can you measure up to our values? Will you support our fight? In the third claim the emphasis lies on collective, cooperative values and is more a matter of the United States reaching out to like-minded nations, drawing the net wide, accentuating supposedly commonly held values. This might be regarded as a contradiction. How can a nation or a culture be both unique and representative of universal values? The answer could be that however contradictory these claims might appear in theory, they are resolved by means of the second claim: in the *practice* of American leadership. There is in practice no fundamental contradiction between the assertion of American nationalism in the name of civilization and the invocation of a world community in the name of civilization. In short, claim number one represents the American argument for the uniqueness of its culture – its 'civilization'; claim three expresses the American argument for the universalism of its values, while claim two is the bridge between them. It is the means by which claim one can give reality to claim three. They are both strategies which rest on the overwhelming given of American dominance and American leadership. Which strategy is employed at any particular time depends on the needs of the moment.

We can link all three aspects by reference to a document which also illustrates some of the political and other difficulties raised by such emphatic and naked assertion of cultural values: the September 2002 *National Security Strategy*. This remarkable document does for the war on terror what *National Security Document 68* (NSC-68, 1950) did for the Cold War: sets out the political, military and ideological basis for a grand strategy.[38] NSC-68 was an in-house document, not made public until a quarter of a century later, while the 2002 *National Security Strategy* was a very public document, designed to enlist public support for the war on terror. NSC-68, however, was no dry-as-dust position paper but a powerfully rhetorical and ideological effort designed no less than the 2002 strategy to persuade, except that in the case of NSC-68 the audience was government rather than the people. Significantly, there are close parallels in rhetoric and content between the two documents, not least the conclusion reached in both cases that a transformation of military doctrine was necessary to fight a worsening global threat.

The 2002 *National Security Strategy* notoriously spells out the doctrine of pre-emption. The concern here is not with that doctrine, important though it is, but with the rhetoric of freedom with which the document is peppered. In itself this is nothing new in American history and foreign policy; it is perhaps America's core value and is regarded as the basis on which all other values are founded. What is particularly significant is first, the context of war followed by nation-building in Afghanistan followed by the same in Iraq; and second, the association of this value with what is called the 'non-negotiable demand of human dignity'. Claims are made here on behalf of America's own history and values, on behalf of American leadership in the current crisis and on behalf of the civilized world whose values are taken to be at one with those of the United States. Crucially it is being claimed that these things are all essentially coterminus. American universalism has rarely been more plainly or more comprehensively expressed; to find comparable claims one has perhaps to go back to Woodrow Wilson, though his are in a somewhat different key. Crucially, America's core demand is 'non-negotiable'. This is doubtless intended in a benign sense to convey the deep, self-evident nature of the value of human dignity — self-evidence being central theme of American discussion of values from the Declaration of Independence onwards — but it conveys also a questionable assumption about the applicability of America's interpretation of 'freedom' and 'human dignity' to other nations and situations; it betrays indeed a potentially coercive and illiberal insistence that America's values are or should be those of all nations. The issue is not whether one believes in freedom — freedom is like food in that you can't be against food — but what freedom means in different cultures. (We don't all need to eat the same food.) The formulation in this document scarcely leaves open the possibility of debate about what freedom means to different peoples. Much of what we call anti-Americanism is a reaction to the sorts of assertions contained in this document. To this we now turn.

Anti-Americanism as a response to American 'civilization-consciousness'

Anti-Americanism is one consequence of the growth of America's civilization-consciousness. Having said that, it is necessary to point out that 'anti-Americanism', like all the terms involved in this discussion, refers to a complex of attitudes and admits of many definitions and explanations. Indeed the term itself is highly political, employed as it often is as a label for attitudes that the user dislikes rather than as a neutral analytical term. Like 'civilization', it is an essentially contested concept. Not least of the difficulties involved is where to draw the line between anti-Americanism and legitimate or rational criticism of American policies. Such decisions are inevitably based on political presuppositions rather than widely agreed canons of evidence. Anti-Americanism is a complex of attitudes towards the United States whose sources are varied according to the nature of the relationship of particular nations, cultures and individuals with the United States.[39]

What cannot be denied, however, is that public consciousness of negative attitudes towards the United States has been powerfully stimulated by the events of September 11 and after. Americans and others want to know 'why people hate America'.[40] It is the disposition to label, as much as the meaning of the label which demands explanation. Thus for the purposes of discussion we shall employ an element of short-hand, defining anti-Americanism first as a predisposition to doubt whether US power can ever be used for good, and second, a distaste for the way in which America goes about expressing its will and asserting its power. Anti-Americanism thus represents a reaction to the exertion of American power and also to the expression of American culture. Here the focus is on the latter, but clearly it is because American power is so great that the nature of its culture matters to so many others.

Anti-Americanism has often attached itself to such apparently trivial matters as the way in which president Bush expresses himself, in particular the (to many non-American eyes) incongruously folksy terms in which he discusses the search for bin Laden and other terrorists. 'We'll smoke 'em out', 'keep those folks on the run', and so on. Behind the reaction to such language in many of the older nations of Europe lie two centuries or more of denigration of American democratic culture combined with growing resentment of American power.[41] The result is that curious amalgam of superiority and inferiority complexes which often characterizes the Old World's perception of the New. The American reaction to September 11 in all its political, military, and cultural ramifications has reminded us how different America is from other cultures. The political complexion of the Bush administration has undoubtedly served to intensify this perception. The American right – and this is arguably the most consistently right-wing administration in post-World War II history – is generally more nakedly patriotic, more nationalist in complexion, more emphatic in its assertion of traditional American values (especially those associated with the founding period) than Democratic administrations. Policy seems to be forged in the American heartland where 'real' Americans live rather than among the more sophisticated 'European' east coast elites. The current 'culture war' between these two Americas recalls the face-offs during the early Cold War between Alger Hiss and his accuser Whittaker Chambers and between secretary of state Dean Acheson and senator Joseph McCarthy. There has justifiably been extensive media and academic commentary on the agenda of the New Right and its influence on the Bush administration.[42]

We shall look at reactions to the three aspects of civilization-consciousness in turn, though inevitably there will be some overlap in the treatment. It is easy to see why those who are already firmly opposed to America will react strongly against America's post-9/11 assertiveness. More significant perhaps are the reactions of those who have no automatic opposition to America but who find themselves embattled in the new climate of the war on terror. The problem here is not simple hatred of the United States but the difficulty of living with a United States which makes such grandiose claims on behalf of its own 'civilization'. This applies, for example, to many in the Muslim world, including American Muslims, who fear that the cost of total identification with the war against terror will be the dilution or even suppression of their own national, religious or cultural identity. Even gestures of friendship by members of the American administration towards Muslims may be regarded with suspicion by Muslims. Such anxieties predate the attacks of September 11. One Muslim observer noted that the Clinton administration tended to divide Islam into two polarized camps: at one end were the extremists who advocated a militantly 'political Islam' and were regarded as terrorists or supporters of terrorism; at the other end of the spectrum was 'Islam' itself 'represented by the faith that is confined to personal belief and ritual practices'. But while apparently affirming respect for Islam, this latter version of the religion was 'a disembowelled Islam that has no input into the human, social, economic and political values, which some Islamists have dubbed "American Islam"'.[43] As many Muslims see it, the price of friendship with America, or for citizenship of the United States, is denial of the full expression of Islam. To put it another way, American civilization does not appear to have a place for Islam.

Under Bush, and especially since September 11, the dilemma for American Muslims, indeed Muslims everywhere, has deepened. Despite efforts to insist that the war against terror is not a war against Islam, despite speedy correction of some earlier *faux pas* in the war against terror such as terming it a 'crusade', and despite efforts by members of the Bush administration – among them Condoleezza Rice – to reach out directly to the Muslim community, scepticism about the administration's attitude to Muslims remains. The passage of the Patriot Act, with its threat to constitutional rights, is one source of concern, as is the general climate of suspicion of individuals with Middle Eastern connections or even appearance.

In this connection America's deep military and political entanglements in the Middle East complicate matters for Muslims in America and elsewhere. Failure to make progress on a settlement of the Palestinian–Israeli conflict is doubly damaging: damaging to the parties directly involved and damaging to Muslims everywhere, who suspect that the American administration's failure to push more strongly for a settlement reflects its true estimation of the significance of the Palestinian issue for them and also tends to reinforce the association of Islam with terrorism. As long as the news about Islam is mainly about terrorist incidents, the deeper will the general suspicion of Islam go and the more vulnerable will individual Muslims be. If such scepticism and anxiety is present among Muslims who are basically sympathetic to America and who deplore al-Qaeda *et al.* as perverters of the Muslim faith, how much more alienated will be those Muslims who have no natural sympathy with the United States and regard it simply as an agent of imperialism?

Similar issues apply *pari passu* to Europe, which in the post-Cold War world has gained new perception of the differences between European and American 'civilizations'. The same applies, of course, in reverse. Anti-Americanism has its counterpart in anti-Europeanism in America. Cultural differences, needless to say, have been part of the long history of European–American relations, and anti-Americanism is part of that history. The collapse of the Cold War, however, has allowed for fuller expression of such sentiments because the tight geopolitical tie promoted by the Cold War no longer underpins the relationship. Writing in 1996, a German scholar and convinced Atlanticist, Werner Weidenfeld, noted with alarm that

> the relationship between Germany, Europe and America is no longer based on certainties of the kind that have existed for fifty years. ... In terms of communications theory, what is happening is a disintegration of the stabilizers and filters required for information-processing. The dominance of world politics by large blocs and their confrontational relations has gone and with it the antagonisms, stereotypes and political rhetoric that used to provide collective orientation for the 'West'.[44]

In short, in the post-Cold War world, there is more fluidity, less obvious need for coordinated policies especially on defence, more scope for conflict in the relationship, and more opportunities for cultural differences to find expression. American unilateralism has provided a target for these concerns, just as it expresses America's own cultural and political imperatives.[45] Following September 11 such expressions heightened European sensitivities to American culture as well as American policies. One significant finding of a Pew public-opinion survey conducted in 2004 was that, although Europeans continued to make a clear distinction between the Bush administration and the American people, favourable opinion of the American people declined in line with opinion about the Bush administration, in the case of France from 71 per cent to 53 per cent. (In Muslim countries there was little difference between attitudes towards Americans and towards the US government, and they were predominantly negative.)[46]

Of particular significance has been the emphasis in discussions of European attitudes towards America of differences in values. A Marshall Fund study conducted in 2003 reported that, when asked whether Europeans and Americans have different social and cultural values, majorities on both sides of the Atlantic overwhelmingly agreed (83 per cent of American and 79 per cent of European respondents). A detailed analysis of American-German relations has concluded that 'the recent tension demonstrates that US–German relations are characterized by a mutual incomprehension of each other's political culture and deeply held political values'. At the root of the difference, which was sharply foregrounded in the aftermath of the September 11 attacks, were 'vastly differing views of nationalism and flag-waving patriotism. ... Because the exaggerated nationalism of the Nazi years led to such disastrous results, post-1945 Germany has been characterized by strongly antinationalist and antipatriotic sentiments.' By contrast, such displays are common in the United States and indeed were integral to the morale-building efforts which followed September 11. Not least among the causes of the difficulties were issues of language, especially the use of the term 'war' in 'war on terror', terminology which is forbidden in German politics and society.[47]

If anti-American feeling attaches itself to heightened expressions of Americanness, it attaches also to America's leadership role; indeed the two areas are obviously closely linked. The awareness that the war on terror is to be fought on America's terms, that America defines these terms, that America supplies the bulk of troops and means to fight the war, and dictates the strategy, promotes resentment even among those who share the goals of the United States. The Marshall Fund survey of 2003 showed sharp declines between 2002 and 2003 in most European countries in the approval ratings of American global leadership, the only increases coming in countries (the UK and the Netherlands) where opinion was already predominantly negative. The Pew survey of 2004 showed an erosion of belief in the trustworthiness of the United States and in its commitment to promoting democracy.[48] The best apparently that could be hoped for among those who wished to influence the way the war on terror was fought – and this was seemingly the basis of Tony Blair's strategy – was to adopt America's goals as their own in the hope that they might be able to influence the direction and pace of American policy. This is not to say that Tony Blair was insincere in his support of President Bush, nor even that he may not have succeeded to some degree in his aim, but it is to say that he has had to go further in Americanizing his approach than normal alliance politics would seem to dictate. To an unusual degree, which was scarcely matched in the Cold War years, with the possible exception of the Thatcher/Reagan axis, Blair adopted the American reading of global events, and more to the point has adopted an American style of international politicking, including an unusual level of rhetorical inflation.[49]

It seems clear that the dissociation of countries such as France, Germany and Russia from the American way of fighting the war on terror had partly to do with style. One cost of support for the United States' political goals was a degree of subordination to the style in which they were couched. Evidently resistance on the part of many Europeans had to do with a lot more than style, but the tenor of the debates in the UN Security Council on the proposed second resolution on Iraq indicated that that Colin Powell and Dominic de Villepin were not only speaking different languages but were expressing different cultures, voicing different assumptions. Such exchanges were eloquent testimony to the fact that American leadership of the war against terror was both inevitable – in the sense that it could not be resisted – and problematic. From the American point of view (shared by Tony Blair), the idea that a strong Europe should act as a counter-balance to US power was tantamount to obstructionism. Indeed, there was no place in the American scheme of things for that old realist nostrum: the balance of power.

Finally, anti-Americanism attaches also to the third aspect of civilization-consciousness: the effort to enlist all nations in an enterprise which transcends the scope and interests of any one nation, that enterprise being civilization itself. At one level there is resistance to the idea that the United States truly represents the ideals of civilization which it claims to uphold. The legal black hole into which the prisoners at Guantanamo Bay were placed, and the treatment of them, is commonly cited in this connection but the revelations about the treatment of detainees by American soldiers at Abu Ghraib prison in Iraq exposed the moral gap most starkly. Under the heading 'Clash of Civilizations', liberal *New York Times* columnist Maureen Dowd observed that

> after 9/11, America had the support and sympathy of the world. Now awash in digital evidence of uncivilized behaviour, America has careered into a war of civilizations. The pictures [of sexual humiliation of Iraqi prisoners] were clearly meant to use the codebook of Muslim anxieties about nudity and sexual and gender humiliation to break down prisoners.

'If somebody wanted to plan a clash of civilizations', senator Diane Feinstein declared, 'this is how they'd do it. These pictures play into every stereotype of America that Arabs have: America as debauched, America as hypocrites.'[50] In short, it was easy to doubt whether the United States could really claim to speak on behalf of global 'civilization'.

Second, there was the belief on the part of critics that the fight for 'civilization' was loaded towards America's interests and that it was no more nor less than a fight for America's national interest dressed up to look like a cooperative venture. The 'coalition of the willing' from this point of view was really a coalition of power based on America's ability to exert pressure on other nations. The coalition was in fact, one observer noted, 'an exercise in unilateralism, with a few friends'. It was, wrote another critic, 'inch deep, in large measure a figment of American imagination, energy and money'.[51] American tactics at the UN during the build-up to the war in Iraq were, from this standpoint, the perfect illustration of special pleading, arousing the suspicion among sceptics that America had already made up its mind about Iraq and was merely going through the motions. Once this conviction was established in the minds of unsympathetic observers, it could only become further entrenched as the rhetoric became further inflated. The more insistent was the president on the necessity for war to defend civilization, the greater the scepticism with which these claims were regarded. Anti-Americanism, to the extent that attitudes went beyond criticism of policy, fed on a sense of the gap between the nature of the claims being made on behalf of war and the actual motives which were conceived to be the advancement of American interests, whether for oil, a dominant role in the Middle East, or the defence of Israel. The slogan adopted by opponents of the war in Iraq on both sides of the Atlantic, 'Not in our name', indicated more than a disagreement with the policy but also a dissociation from the larger collectivity being invoked by the United States. Once again, it was easy to doubt whether the United States could claim to speak on behalf of global 'civilization'.

Conclusions

Huntington's clash of civilizations thesis has been the target of some justified criticisms. What he called civilizations are not the discrete entities he imagined. True, he allows for various forms of conflict within civilizations and countries, but the larger thesis would fail if he were to allow intra-civilizational cleavages to predominate over those between civilizations. But the fact is that in the age of globalization the boundaries between nations and cultures are increasingly porous and, as many of Huntington's critics have pointed out, there are as many clashes inside civilizations as between them. There is thus a real problem with his use of civilization as his main unit of historical study.

Huntington was not wrong, however, to see cultural, especially religious and ethnic, conflict as having increased saliency in the post-Cold War world. In many parts of the world where Cold War pressures had reduced these to a state of suspended animation, the end of the Cold War gave them new life. The task, then, is to adapt Huntington's ideas and make them work for us. If he has done a service, it is to expose the degree to which ethnocentrism can be a source of conflict. He has reminded us that, as Robert Cooper has put it recently, 'foreign policy is not only about interests'. 'At moments of crisis', Cooper continues, 'it is likely that a nation will return to its roots and its myths and respond as the heart urges rather than as the head advises.'[52] The danger is of failing to perceive that this applies to ourselves and not just our adversaries. In Huntington's analysis it is generally other cultures' assertiveness which is the problem, not least Islam, which is said to have 'bloody borders'. Huntington takes less account of how other nations and cultures might regard America's way of acting in the world, and in this he reflects the larger problem of ethnocentrism in the American policy-making process. The greatest challenge in this more fluid, globalizing world is for nations to develop awareness of how their actions and belief systems impinge on others. For America, because it is so powerful, this means being conscious of the power of culture as well as the culture of power.

There is a second limitation in Huntington's thesis which also gives rise to a challenge. His analysis assumes that cultural difference tends always to produce conflict. In response it can be said that it may do but need not. If you assume that cultural difference will always give rise to conflict, then it is very likely that it will. The challenge is to develop ways of cooperation between cultures and nations which mean different things by words which appear to have self-evident meanings: freedom, democracy, human rights, justice. Rather than assume that we know exactly what these things mean and dismiss those who interpret them differently, it will pay to develop dialogues. At least this may open the possibility of isolating those for whom difference will always and only imply conflict.

2 The role of culture in international relations

The cultural 'turn'

The role of culture in international relations, and in politics generally, has become a pressing issue for both immediate and longer-term reasons. The immediate cause is the upsurge of international terrorism carried out in the name of the religion of Islam. The attempt to understand the motives of the terrorists who carried out the September 11 attacks and those which followed them has led to extensive discussion and debate about the role of religion in driving extremist politics. Where once there was talk in intellectual circles about the shadings of difference between various brands of Marxism, attention now focuses on the varieties of Islamic sects and doctrines, including their political manifestations. We have all perforce become cognizant of, even if not experts in, aspects of Islam. Beyond that there is a more general recognition, provoked as much by the 'war on terror' as by the terror itself, of the 'values gaps' between nations and groupings of nations. Among all nations which have been targets of terrorism there has been a reaffirmation of the need to defend cherished 'ways of life' in the face of attack. For many Americans, albeit in the context of official insistence that the war on terror is not a war on Islam, the sense of America's Christian heritage has lain at the core of the country's response to terrorism. Surveys have shown, for example, that the support for the war in Iraq among Christian evangelicals in the United States was considerably higher than that of the general population.[1] Presidential speeches, in particular the inaugural and State of the Union addresses, are saturated with religious rhetoric.

The longer-term reason for the renewed emphasis on culture in discussions of international relations relates to the changes brought about by the end of the Cold War, among which were, according to the influential argument of Samuel Huntington, the replacement of political ideology and economics by culture as the chief source of international conflict. There was and is huge room for argument about all the terms of the arguments referred to here. 'Politics', 'ideology', 'culture' and 'civilization' are all susceptible to multiple and complex definitions, to say nothing of the relations between them. Is there really a distinction between politics and culture or ideology and culture? Does not the term culture include the other two? For the moment, however, we shall take as our premise that the upsurge of talk about culture does represent a significant departure in discussions of politics and international relations.

Despite, or perhaps because of, the growing resort to cultural explanations of international politics, many academics and commentators, especially those on the liberal side, are deeply sceptical of the 'cultural turn' in political analysis. One reason is simply the wide currency of Huntington's ideas. In a situation which has numerous parallels elsewhere – for example in the reception of Arnold Toynbee's works in the 1940s and 1950s – Huntington sells massively, and simplified versions of his ideas are in wide circulation while, according to his critics, more respectable, measured studies are pushed to margins. In the face of Huntington's elevation of culture as an explanatory factor, many international relations specialists have rushed to reaffirm traditional 'realist' ideas of the importance of the nation-state and rational concepts of the national interest. Marxists, or former Marxists, while making nods in the direction of culture, reinstate materialist motives as the driving force of politics. Both realists and Marxists insist upon the 'historicity' of cultural as well as political phenomena and warn against the error of 'essentialism' – the ascription of an essence or inner being to a religion or nation or other cultural manifestation which is treated as if it were detached from the real history which produced it. 'Islam' is one such essentialist concept to the extent that it is taken as a self-contained explanatory category. 'The West' is another essentialist concoction which evidently serves both its friends and enemies as a tool or weapon in intellectual wars and debates of various sorts. Beyond that, discussion of politics in terms of culture apparently privileges the irrational or at least the non-rational, and to that extent serves the purposes of those who do not wish to seek solutions to difficult conflicts via rational means such as discussion, debate, diplomacy, and compromise. To argue for cultural explanation, from this standpoint, is to privilege the inexplicable, to give credence to mysticism, and to provide ammunition to the enemies of order and rationality. Above all, it is to abandon the search for true explanations which are based on evidence and reasoning and hence in turn to give up on rationally based solutions to difficult problems. There is thus a huge amount at stake in seemingly remote and academic debates, nothing less than the possibility of an ordered and principled future.

There is a further explicitly political feature of this debate which deserves mention. With some notable exceptions, cultural explanations tend to be associated with conservative and even reactionary positions, while suspicion of cultural explanations is most prevalent among liberals and the left. A full historical explanation of this would take us back at least to the debate between Edmund Burke and Thomas Paine on the consequences of the French Revolution. The Burkean emphasis on tradition and the 'inheritance from the past', his hatred of 'speculative right', and his insistence on 'following nature, which is wisdom without reflection, and above it' is firmly countered by Paine's embrace of a world which is 'continually changing', in which it is the living who must decide what is right and who can, if they have the will, remake their world according to their own needs.[2] A version of this seminal debate has taken place in recent years between Samuel Huntington and the late Edward Said. While both inhabited the American Ivy League – Huntington at Harvard and Said at Columbia – they occupied wholly different ideological and cultural spaces. For present purposes the significant point is that, taken together, they constitute a double warning to liberal scholars about the dangers of cultural explanations of politics and international affairs. Putting it schematically, Huntington's work, particularly *The Clash of Civilizations*, is taken as an object lesson in all the errors to which cultural explanations can fall prey, while Said's work, particularly *Orientalism*, is said to constitute, by means of its persuasive demolition of a central 'essentialist' cultural concept, the ultimate critique not only of 'Orientalism' itself but of cultural explanations of politics more generally. While that may not have been Said's intention – and given that the bulk of his work was concerned with explaining the relations between culture and politics, it seems unlikely that it was – this was arguably the effect. Perhaps it would be more accurate to say that his approach ruled out of court all but a particular approach to culture and politics – namely, his own. Elements of this approach which will be discussed later. The aim of the following pages is not to offer a comprehensive discussion or critique of Huntington and Said but to clear the ground for a more positive discussion of how we might construct a cultural explanation of international politics which avoids the pitfalls revealed by the work of Huntington and Said.

Huntington v. Said

What, then, is so 'wrong' about Huntington's analysis and what is so 'right' about Said's? In terms which have become almost routine in dismissals of Huntington, one critique, which attacks the 'clash of civilizations' thesis in the light of September 11, argues that the fallacy of this thesis is clear in that the attacks were motivated by specific political, security, and human rights grievances against the foreign policy of the United States, rather than by an irrational, generalized Islamic hostility to so-called 'Western Civilization' as such. ... What is happening everywhere is simply the politics of power as usual and not the manifestation of a clash of civilizations.[3]

A similar realist critique has it that 'in responding to September 11, states acted more as states than as civilizations'.[4] Again in the work of a respected specialist in Islamic studies, 'the causes which drive alienated forces into the arms of terrorists such as Bin Laden are strongly political in character and emanate from specific historical circumstances rather than from broad "civilizational" identity'.[5] In relation to the Gulf War of 1991, which for Huntington was a signal instance of the clash of civilizations, one critic observes that

in his [Huntington's] urge to find that relentless war across Islam's 'bloody borders', Huntington buys Saddam Hussein's interpretation of the Gulf War. It was for Saddam and Huntington a civilizational battle. But the Gulf War's verdict was entirely different. For if there was a campaign that laid bare the interests of states, the lengths to which they will go to restore a tolerable balance of power in a place that matters, this was it.

'Let's be clear', this critic concludes: 'civilizations do not control states, states control civilizations. States avert their gaze from blood ties when they need to; they see brotherhood and faith and kin when it is in their interest to do so.'[6] A more generalized statement of the same point asserts that 'the world remains fractured along political and possibly geopolitical lines; cultural and historical determinants are a great deal less vital and virulent'.[7] Edward Said concluded a stinging critique of Huntington with the view that these are tense times, but it is better to think in terms of powerful and powerless communities, the secular politics of reason and ignorance, and universal principles of justice and injustice, than to wander off in search of vast abstractions that may give momentary satisfaction but little self-knowledge or informed analysis. The 'clash of civilizations' thesis is a gimmick like *The War of the Worlds*, better for reinforcing defensive self-pride than for critical understanding of the bewildering interdependence of our time.[8]

Clearly there are many possible objections to Huntington's thesis and these have been well rehearsed by many commentators. The difficulty of aligning the major current world conflicts with boundaries between so-called 'civilizations' is one. Are there not as many conflicts inside as between civilizations? Is it even possible to establish that there are recognizable 'civilizations'? The current debate over this issue is a re-run, though without much awareness of the repetition, of the same debate which greeted the publication of Arnold Toynbee's *Study of History*.[9] For present purposes, however, the significant feature of these critiques is the common theme of the primacy of power over culture as an explanatory term, of interests over ideas and beliefs, of nation-states over civilizations, of the politics of realism over that of cultural identities. Indeed, thinking in terms of these and similar polarities is of the essence in many discussions of these questions. In the minds of many of his critics, Huntington's sin is not merely insufficient knowledge of many of the cultures he deals with, nor the excessively high level of generalization he indulges in, nor even that embracing his thesis seems to involve embracing also the politics of the American right wing – though all of these are identified as serious problems by his critics. His sin is also a more purely intellectual or conceptual error of abandoning a broadly realist paradigm in explaining international political behaviour. To the extent that Huntington is the most influential advocate of a cultural explanation of international politics, at least in recent times, his work has thus served to discredit such approaches. The claim is not that Huntington has single-handedly persuaded a generation of scholars against cultural approaches but that the high profile given to his work has reinforced an existing predisposition on the part of many scholars to be suspicious of culture as an explanatory concept.

It would be a mistake to argue, however, that culture, including religion, has been wholly ignored by students of international relations; it is rather that there is a reluctance to ascribe to culture an *explanatory* role. An important and influential example of such an approach lies in the work of Fred Halliday, Professor of International Relations at the London School of Economics. In a recent book, *The Middle East in International Relations: Power, Politics and Ideology* (2005), Halliday restates in a comprehensive fashion positions developed over a number of previous works.[10] Noting that explanation of Middle Eastern politics in terms of culture, especially following the Iranian Revolution of 1979, 'has become prevalent again', he asserts that

> such terms as 'Islam', 'Bedouin', 'Arab' certainly have some relevance in regard to discourses of legitimation and forms of solidarity with others, but *not* as substantive explanations of state structure or general policy. What cultural categories tell us a great deal about is how states legitimate themselves, and appeal to their own subjects.

'It is important', Halliday concludes, 'to distinguish ... cultural or religious terms as forms of *self-image* from cultures as forms of *explanation*' (emphasis in the original).[11]

Later we shall look more closely at the dichotomies developed here between culture and politics, legitimation and explanation. For the moment it is enough to point out that wherever such pairings of terms appear, one is privileged at the expense of the other. Culture, it is implied, is essentially an epiphenomenon which on its own explains very little. When considered in conjunction with what are taken to be the questionable conservative political views of Huntington and those who think like him, there are evidently powerful reasons for liberal-minded scholars and commentators to reject out of hand not only the political agenda but also the conceptual approach. The problem, as we shall see, is that such a move comes at the cost of understanding precisely how cultural values and institutions bear on political realities. It also rules out the possibility that culture may indeed have some explanatory value.

If the work of Huntington and others provides powerful negative examples for liberal scholars, illustrating the dangerous uses to which cultural explanations can be put, the work of Edward Said constitutes an equally powerful reinforcing stimulus. Though his life's work has been the exploration of the connections between politics and culture, especially literature, his most influential contribution to scholarly and public debate – *Orientalism* (1978) – also constitutes a damning critique of the West's most deep-lying cultural assumptions. *Orientalism* has special resonance several decades after publication because of the continuing and increasing preoccupation with Islam; indeed it could be said that Said's thesis has been confirmed in the events following the end of the Cold War to the extent that the West's relations with Islam have become a central axis not only in international affairs but in domestic affairs in many countries too. Said's study focuses on literary history and scholarship rather than political events and institutions, but it is perhaps precisely for that reason that his thesis has had such wide application and such an enthusiastic reception in many quarters. His analysis probes the roots of the concepts we use to understand the world and his conclusions are apparently generalizable beyond the fields in which they were originally applied.

Said posits that 'the Orient' was an invention of Europeans which was both a place and a concept associated with 'romance, exotic beings, haunting memories and landscapes, remarkable experiences'. It was a place which was colonized by Europeans in recent centuries but also originally a source of Europe's civilization and languages, 'and one of its deepest and most recurring images of the Other'. Orientalism as a style of thought and a form of 'discourse' became prevalent at a time when Europe assumed effective dominance over the countries of the Orient. In short, 'Orientialism emerged as a Western style for dominating, restructuring, and having authority over the Orient.' Moreover, to a considerable extent Europe came to define itself in relation to the Orient. Nor was Orientalism simply 'imaginative': 'the Orient is an integral part of European *material* civilization and culture. Orientalism expresses and represents that part culturally and ideologically as a mode of discourse with supporting institutions, vocabulary, scholarship, imagery, doctrines, even colonial bureaucracies and colonial styles.' America's Orient was originally less 'dense' and was based more on its relations with China and Japan, with whom it developed relations earlier than with the European Orient of the Middle East and South Asia. However, since the Second World War the United States' Orient has become more consonant with that of Europe since it has assumed much of Europe's role as a hegemonic, even if not strictly as a colonial, power.[12]

The bulk of Said's book is a historical study of the growth of Orientalism, especially in literary and scholarly works, and the uses to which it was put. It is a study of ideas, or rather of a single idea which informed thought across a range of fields and indeed penetrated, so it is claimed, to the roots of Western conceptions of its own society. It is thus no surprise to find Said's analysis being applied to the study of international relations, where it is a staple of discussion of relations between Islam and the West but also more generally of post-colonial relations.[13] The same applies, though to a lesser degree, to Said's later work *Culture and Imperialism*. This appeared coincidentally the same year as Samuel Huntington's *Foreign Affairs* article 'The Clash of Civilizations?' (1993) and they have at least this in common: that they both see conflict as endemic to relations between the rich and the developing worlds. For Huntington, 'conflicts between groups in different civilizations will become more frequent, more sustained and more violent than conflicts between groups in the same civilization ... [and] ... the paramount axis of world politics will be the relations between "the West and the rest"'.[14] For Said the conflict emerges in the resistance of the colonized to the colonizers, an element which he had left out of his study of Orientalism. In the later, as in the earlier, study, the focus is on the cultural forms in which the experience of the colonizers and colonized were expressed. His point is that many key works of literature which are generally regarded as being situated 'squarely within the metropolitan history of British fiction' in actuality 'belong in a history both more inclusive and more dynamic than such interpretations allow'. That wider story is the history of imperialism. 'As we look back at the cultural archive', Said observes, 'we begin to re-read it not univocally but *contrapuntally*, with a simultaneous awareness both of the metropolitan history that is narrated and of those histories against which (and together with which) the dominating discourse acts.'[15]

Said is a cultural historian and critic, not a student of international relations as generally defined, though he wrote extensively about politics, including bi-monthly commentaries on Middle East politics for the Egyptian *Al Ahram* and other publications – later collected and published in book form[16] – and several books about Islam. Said's writings about culture have exerted influence on the field of international relations, however, because he is centrally concerned with the relations between national cultures and because he has included in his approach concepts which are of vital interest to students of international relations. The concept of Orientalism aims to make sense of the manifest gulf of understanding which exists above all between the West and Islam, a task which is all the more urgent in the light of events from the Iranian Revolution to al-Qaeda terrorism of the twenty-first century. *Culture and Imperialism* similarly addresses issues which are increasingly at the centre of discussion of international relations; witness the intensive debate about imperialism, especially American imperialism, since the 1990s.[17]

If, then, Said's work has proved so fertile, and given that the concept of culture lies at the root of his analysis, why include him in a discussion of the suspicion with which culture is viewed by liberal-minded scholars of international relations? First, it seems clear that liberal-minded scholars, especially those who are not themselves Middle Eastern specialists, are much happier to see culture interpreted politically, as Said does, than to see politics interpreted from a cultural point of view, particularly if, as is the case with *Orientalism*, the politics fits liberal predilections. For those looking for a stick with which to beat the Western establishment, 'Orientalism' is an ideal construct. It lays blame firmly where it is held to be due and provides an explanation of what has gone wrong. Meanwhile, 'Orientalists' such as the Princeton historian Bernard Lewis continue to picture the Islamic world as aggressive and fanatical, while Huntington talks of 'Islam's bloody borders', effectively laying the blame for the woes of the Middle East and Islam at Islam's door, confirming the conclusions reached by Said about the outlook of 'Orientalists'.[18] In short, the cultural stereotype which is Said's chief target touches a nerve in Western liberals sensitized to the ravages of colonialism in their past, with the result that they are disinclined to apply the same 'deconstructive' approach to Oriental cultures which they are happy to apply to their own. It is much easier and safer to explain the problems of the Middle East in terms of conventional and more obviously universal categories – ideas of national interest, material need, political realities and so on – than to traffic in suspect cultural categories which could render one vulnerable to accusations of cultural chauvinism – or 'Orientalism'. While this may tell us as much about Said's readership as about Said himself, the clear consequence has been to reinforce a predilection in favour of political and broadly material explanations over cultural approaches.

In a sense Said succeeded too well, particularly with *Orientalism*. This concept proved a powerful deterrent against the risk of being tarred with the brush of 'essentialism' or more damagingly chauvinism. Said's writing proved to be a peculiarly effective and persuasive argument against the tendency to think in terms of stereotypes of the 'Orient'. In the final chapter of *Orientalism*

Said concludes that Orientalism is as prevalent in the late twentieth century as in earlier centuries, if often in modified forms. 'The principal dogmas of Orientalism', Said declares, 'exist in their purest form today in studies of the Arabs and Islam.' Since Said's conclusions bear directly on the present preoccupation with Islam and the Middle East, and since this passage contains the essentials of Said's whole argument, it is worth quoting at length:

> One [dogma] is the absolute and systematic difference between the West, which is rational, developed, humane, superior, and the Orient, which is aberrant, undeveloped and inferior. Another dogma is that abstractions about the Orient, particularly those based on texts representing a 'classical' Oriental civilization, are always preferable to direct evidence drawn from modern Oriental realities. A third dogma is that the Orient is eternal, uniform, and incapable of defining itself; therefore it is assumed that a highly generalized and systematic vocabulary for describing the Orient from a Western standpoint is inevitable and even scientifically 'objective'. A fourth dogma is that the Orient is at bottom something either to be feared (the Yellow Peril, the Mongol hordes, the brown dominions) or to be controlled (by pacification, research and development), outright occupation whenever possible.[19]

These dogmas, Said believes, have proved highly resistant to change. They constituted the received wisdom of the Middle Eastern areas studies establishment. The occasional challenge to this consensus has made little discernible difference. A quarter of a century after the publication of *Orientalism*, as the United States geared itself up for a war on Iraq to remove Saddam Hussein, Said made it clear in a newspaper article that he regarded the conclusions he had reached in *Orientalism* as still fully applicable to American and Western attitudes to Islam and the Arabs. The media and the academic community continued to conspire with governments to keep Orientalism alive.[20]

There are some, however, who broadly share Said's political opinions but who are critical of the thesis of *Orientalism*. Fred Halliday, for example, as an 'Orientalist' himself (a specialist on Iran and the Middle East) regarded the 'the term "Orientalism" itself [as] contestable: we should be cautious about any critique which identifies such a widespread and pervasive *single* error at the core of a range of literature'. In addition, Halliday notes, the category 'Orient' is 'rather vague, since in *Orientalism* its usage implies that the Middle East is in some ways special, at least in the kind of imperialist or oppressive writing produced about it'. In fact, Halliday concludes, Said produces, in the idea of Orientalism, precisely the sort of mythical and stereotypical conception which is the target of his most trenchant criticisms in the book. As Halliday points out, 'the thesis of some enduring, transhistorical hostility to the Orient, the Arabs, the Islamic world, is a myth, albeit one ... which many in the region and in the West find it convenient to sustain'.[21] In short, Said, the great destroyer of myths, has produced a potent one of his own. In doing so, Said has created a powerful tool for those in the West who share Said's critique of the history of Western imperialism and racism. 'Orientalism' gathers up into one unitary conception a whole bundle of arguments and it is all the more persuasive for its focus on cultural attitudes and mindsets which lie deep in the social and cultural fabric of the West. That Said feeds 'liberal' prejudices makes his conceptions no less prejudicial than the ones he is supposedly attacking.

There is some irony in the fact that the great slayer of stereotypes should be accused of creating one of his own. A corollary of Said's argument is that the 'Orient' is actually much more complex and diverse than the Orientalists would have us think. In fact, it is implied, the Orientalists never really see the Orient but only projections of their own prejudices and preconceptions. But nor do we, as readers of his book, really see the Orient since Said is not really concerned with the Orient but with Western representations of it. There is plenty of evidence in Said's life and other works of his acute awareness of the complexity of the Orient, based as much on his own life experience as on acquired knowledge and reflection.[22] The mythologizing associated with his term 'Orientalism' is as much a result of the readiness of his readership to seize on a conception which suits their purpose as of his own intention.

Culture as explanation or legitimation?

How, then, can one build a case for a cultural approach to international relations which avoids the trap of, on the one hand, 'essentialism' and, on the other, a realism which resists attending to the specificities of cultures and the importance of ideas? We must first reject an approach which fails to acknowledge that culture and politics interact with each other. Any adequate explanation of political behaviour will include a cultural component; any adequate understanding of a culture or cultural form requires an acknowledgement of political context – of power. Discussion of culture in relation to politics is bedevilled by a preoccupation with polarities: either we are confronted with a 'clash of civilizations' or with a clash of politics or economic interest; either the chief factor is religion or it is a more or less rationally conceived interest; conflicts are driven either by dimly remembered but highly potent and symbolic historical memories or by urgent present needs. When, as is often the case in discussions of Islam and Middle Eastern politics, reference to religion is unavoidable, recourse is often made to the argument, referred to earlier, that the language of religion and tradition is a legitimation strategy rather than the essence of the matter. Religion is the clothing in which conflict is expressed but at bottom the issues are explicable in terms of secular political conflict – economic need, relative deprivation, social dislocation, and so on. Culture, it seems is always a secondary phenomenon; it lacks explanatory power.

Further objections to cultural explanations are frequently expressed. Cultural explanations, it is assumed, must necessarily involve recourse to large abstractions and generalizations. But while this may be true of some interpretations, of which Huntington's writings are often cited as a case in point, it is possible for cultural explanations to be as detailed, empirical and nuanced as any others. There is no necessary connection between cultural interpretation and excessive generalization. To posit such a connection is to create a straw man.

One of the difficulties of talking about culture is the multifaceted nature of the term. An initial distinction has to be made between culture as 'high culture' – art, literature, music – and the wider anthropological sense of culture as the way of life, habits of thought and behaviour, social customs and system of meaning of a whole society. It is this latter sense which is involved in the present discussion, but even here there is an embarrassing range of reference, from mindsets at one end of the scale to institutions at the other. Perhaps the core meaning of the term lies in the concept of meaning itself: the collective ways in which societies ascribe meaning and value to their lives. Hence the central role of religion in discussions of culture, since religion is the most comprehensive expression of efforts to achieve such understandings.

There remains the question of how far culture can explain events or relations between societies and nations. It is easier to ascribe causation to something apparently harder, deeper, more 'real' such as economics or political power. In fact in most discussions of international relations, as we have seen, power trumps culture. There is, however, an established literature which takes as its premise that 'a nation ... is a "cultural system" and international relations are interactions among cultural systems'.[23] Indeed until the writing of history was firmly established in national moulds it was common to write history in terms of 'civilizations' whose essences lay in different cultural assumptions and practices, 'the broadest construction of cultural identity ... [being] a civilization'.[24] It is plausible to argue that as the nation-state adjusts to the challenge of globalization, cultural differences and interactions will be of increasing significance and traditional concepts of power based on national interest less so. Certainly there is an increasing number of studies which take as their premise that globalization is a cultural as much as an economic or political phenomenon. 'McWorld,' writes Benjamin Barber in his *Jihad vs McWorld: Terrorism's Challenge to Democracy* (1995), 'is a product of popular culture driven by expansionist commerce. Its template is American, its form style. Its goods are as much images as material, an aesthetic as well as a production line.' In the globalized world 'ideology is transmuted into a kind of videology that works through sound bites and film clips'. Furthermore, while Jihad is McWorld's 'most formidable rival ... the information revolution's instrumentalities are also Jihad's favored weapons'.[25]

It is not necessary, however, to restrict application of cultural approaches to inter-civilizational relations; they are equally applicable to the study of nation-states. A pioneering study of American diplomatic history took as its leading assumption that 'the cultural setting is less a backdrop than a vital cog in the workings of foreign affairs'.[26] Indeed, it has long been accepted that of all nations the United States' approach to international relations was particularly informed by intangibles, whether that meant some notion of national character, a particular susceptibility to moralism and idealism or, in a more recent formulation, an ideology compounded of a quest for national greatness, racism, and a suspicion of revolutions not like its own.[27] A standard trope in discussion of American foreign policy has been the idealism/realism dichotomy in recognition of the combination of can-do pragmatism and missionary elements in American foreign policy-making.

These instances are enough to show that culture has been accepted as a factor in discussions of foreign policy and international relations. Addressing the question of the precise ways in which culture impacts on international relations is less straightforward. I propose to take three topics in which discussion of culture can be shown to make a vital difference: nationalism, terrorism carried out in the name of Islam, and the promotion of democracy by the United States. Each of these topics has a large literature and the aim here is illustrative rather than definitive. The claim is not that culture explains all the phenomena under consideration, but that a cultural perspective is indispensable to an understanding of them.

Culture and nationalism

The value of a multi-faceted approach is particularly strong in the case of the theme of nationalism. On the one hand, nationalism is associated with the establishment of the nation-state as the primary political unit of the world system, a process which is conventionally held to have taken root in the seventeenth century with the Peace of Westphalia (1648) and to have come to full fruition in the twentieth century with the collapse of empires and the proliferation of the nation-state model throughout the world. The concept of sovereignty, enshrined in international law, the Charter of the United Nations and other international organizations and agreements, is not absolute but in most instances is decisive. In the absence of a world government, nation-states are, if not supreme in their own territories, the primary sources of authority, though inevitably this varies according to the size and power of the state. Such authority as they grant to international organizations as the UN is conditional, however much moral authority and persuasion the UN can muster.

On the other hand, nationalism is associated with communities which may or may not be embodied in nation-states. There is a notion here of an organic community in which groups and individuals find meaning. The basis of nationalism in this model may be ethnic, linguistic, religious or a combination of these. While the aspiration to statehood has proved all but irresistible, there remain many instances where nationalist aspirations for a variety of reasons remain unsatisfied. Needless to say, the complexities of the relations between nation-states and ethno-religious and linguistic factors are legion. Perhaps the most useful historical generalization that can be offered is that nineteenth-century nations were characteristically formed by amalgamation – examples being Germany and Italy – and twentieth-century nations by a process of splitting away from larger units, typically empires and colonial systems.[28] The reality, however, was rarely so neat. Czechoslovakia and Yugoslavia are twentieth-century examples of states formed out of parts of old empires and thus represent a combination of splitting and amalgamation. Both are now of course defunct, having further split into ethno-religious parts. At any rate they provide evidence that nationalism based on various types of local identities is alive and well. Indeed, as globalization advances, it seems that the cultivation of local identities becomes ever more urgent.

There is no space here to explore the many definitional and empirical difficulties which have attended attempts to bring precision to the discussion of nationalism. It is sufficient to say that efforts to base nationalism on any one factor have generally fallen foul of the complex and hybrid forms which nationalism has assumed historically. One approach, however, that promises to meet such challenges is the view that at bottom nationalism is an idea. In the words of Liah Greenfeld, author of the most substantial historical study of nationalism in recent years,

> the only foundation of nationalism as such, the only condition, that is, without which no nationalism is possible, is an idea; nationalism is a particular perspective or a style of thought. The idea which lies at the core of nationalism is the idea of the 'nation'.[29]

If this sounds somewhat circular, then it must be stressed that everything depends on the historical detail with which Greenfeld fleshes out the idea of the nation, its origins, changing forms over time, and varying manifestations. The key insight is that nationalism is associated not merely or primarily with a set of institutions or a given territory nor with language or race or ethnicity but a conception of a particular type of community. That community has particular historical antecedents in the collapse of dynastic and feudal institutions, but takes root as an idea before it becomes an achieved fact. Another scholar, Benedict Anderson, has gone even further in this direction by describing the nation as an 'imagined community': 'it is imagined because the members of even the smallest nation will never know most of their fellow-members, meet them, or even hear of them, yet in the minds of each lives the image of their communion'. It was no coincidence that nationalism dawned with the 'dusk of religious thought' – the period of Enlightenment; the nation supplied a new secular frame of reference in place of the waning religious communities and dynastic realms. The claim is not that that 'the appearance of nationalism toward the end of the eighteenth century was "produced" by the erosion of religious certainties, or that this erosion does not itself require a complex explanation'. 'Nor', Anderson continues,

> am I suggesting that somehow historically nationalism 'supersedes' religion. What I am proposing is that nationalism has to be understood by aligning it, not with self-consciously held political ideologies, but with the large cultural systems that preceded it, out of which – as well as against which – it came into being.[30]

These interpretations offer powerful arguments for thinking of nationalism as a cultural as much as a political force. They also render suspect interpretations which seek to play up one element at the expense of the other or which seek to reduce one element to the other. How to define the relationship in any particular instance will depend on the precise context and the dynamics at work in any particular situation. In a general way, however, we can conceive of culture as a lens through which politics and power relations are viewed; it is thus neither simply a form of legitimation, which presupposes that culture is secondary or after the fact, nor is it wholly determinative of decisions. Culture, as expressed through nationalism, can set limits to the kinds of options available in line with nationally conceived values and modes of behaviour, and these are products of history and tradition. In an important sense nationalism expresses the collective sense of history of a community, though it is a history not of professional historians testing theories against the evidence but of publicly sanctioned ideology.

Culture and terrorism

On the theme of terrorism committed by radical Islamists against Western targets, we are typically confronted once again by two extremes of interpretation. At one end of the scale, notoriously President Bush explained the attacks of September 11 as a consequence of the terrorists' hatred of American freedoms and way of life, which is close to a purely cultural explanation of terrorism, divorced from consideration of particular political or historical contexts. At the other end of the scale is the argument that the attacks of September 11 and other similar acts are explicable in terms of particular grievances on the part of Islamists, such as the stationing of American troops on the holy ground of Saudi Arabia, Israeli and American policy towards the Palestinians, and American support for corrupt Middle Eastern leaders. Indeed these are the reasons given by Osama bin Laden, in what is generally taken to be the founding statement of al-Qaeda, for the declaration of a fatwa against all the enemies of Islam.[31] More generally, according to this view, anti-Americanism has resulted, not from generalized hatred for America or Americans, based on irreconcilable cultural differences, but from specific actions of the West since the collapse of the Ottoman empire in 1918 and the Second World War.[32] Each of these arguments has something to recommend it but is also open to criticism. A cultural explanation divorced from political context excludes considerations of agency in understanding events and relies too heavily on underlying conditions. It also enables the American leadership, for example, to ignore the possibility that America's own actions may have contributed to the causes of terrorism. However, an explanation based exclusively on proximate causes fails to account for the forms in which political conflicts are expressed and also excludes the possibility that cultural differences may contribute to the causes of political conflict and terrorist acts. An explanation of bin Laden's actions, for example, cannot rest with the stated aims he offered in public statements. A full analysis would need to take account of other ingredients of his hatred of America, including the sources of Islamist ideas in the writings of Sayyid Qutb, whose political hostility to America, based on his revulsion against American social life and values as well as the Truman administration's support for Zionism, 'matured into cultural and spiritual hostility as well' during a visit there of twenty-one months from 1949 to 1951.[33]

One of the difficulties in addressing these issues is that, as has been mentioned before in a different context, each of the extreme positions outlined above is influenced by self-serving motives. It is in the interest of political leaders such as George W. Bush to play up cultural factors and downplay politics, since it relieves them of the burden of asking whether American policies may have played a role in arousing the emotions which produced September 11. Those who ascribe causative power exclusively to politics or other aspects of 'hard power' may be seeking for the best reasons to downplay the role of cultural difference on the grounds that exaggeration of the cultural factor may exacerbate conflict and render practical solutions all but impossible. The challenge, however, is to find ways of integrating these elements in analysis.

Culture and democracy

The issue of democracy presents an interestingly different and in some respects opposed set of considerations. For reasons to be discussed later, in the sphere of democracy promotion, which has become a central goal of post-Cold War American foreign policy, the tendency of the right is to deny the significance of cultural factors on the grounds that democracy is a universal good which can and should be applied everywhere, while the liberal or leftist tendency is to insist on the importance of cultural and historical differences which might set limits to the idea of democracy promotion, or at the very least give pause for thought about how it can be reconciled with local cultural traditions and practices. For advocates of the universal applicability of democracy, democracy is a solvent of cultural difference. While democracy is a Western invention, the argument goes, it is patronizing and arrogant to assume that others cannot share it or are not ready for it or are better off with institutions growing out of their own pasts. The riposte to this position is that the arrogance lies with those who assume that the meaning of democracy is single and self-evident and who fail to acknowledge the extent to which our notion of democracy is a product of particular historical conditions and may be far from representing a universally conceived good. That is not to say that democracy is inapplicable to cultures which have no history of it, but it is to say that in democracy promotion it is wise to start with an understanding of the target culture rather than with an assumption that democracy is the key to unlock all political and cultural doors. At its worst democracy promotion may end up being a new form of Western imperialism.

There are many intermediate positions between these poles, but the nub of the difference is between the view that the essence of democracy is institutional or procedural – most obviously a multi-party electoral process – and the view that democracy is first and foremost a certain type of political culture. In the former case few obstacles in principle are conceived to the transfer of democracy to other cultures, while in the latter view institutional and procedural innovations can only succeed if they are attended by changes in cultural attitudes. Furthermore, from a pragmatic point of view, advocates of the latter position might point out, the importation of democratic electoral practices in a country which had no tradition of using them and/or in which sharp ethnic or religious splits existed, might at best simply reproduce such splits or at worst might bring to power a faction whose aim was to overthrow democracy. Democracy might thus be the means of overthrow of the system.

Historical evidence from societies in the throes of establishing democracy suggests that fears about the latter or comparable scenarios are not uncommon. The first decade and a half of the United States' political experience, from the first elections under the new Constitution in 1788 till 1800, when for the first time an alternative party won the presidential election, is a good example. The election of 1800 – the so-called 'revolution of 1800' – is so important because the election of the Republican Jefferson after three terms of Federalist rule of the presidency demonstrated that a change of party could take place without an overthrow of the system. Many Federalists had regarded the prospect of a Jeffersonian victory with horror because they believed him to be a dangerous radical who was bent on destroying all that the Federalists had built. In the event Jefferson did not undo the Federalist legacy, at least not to the extent of violating the Constitution, and the passage of power served to legitimize the framework of American government and politics. Anxieties about how well embedded are democratic norms have been repeated in many post-colonial and post-communist nations in the second half of the twentieth century and in some cases were justified, most commonly when post-independence leaders sought to hold on to their power and prevent the democratic process from following through, as was the case in Zimbabwe. Vladimir Putin's consolidation of presidential power in Russia, which has taken the form of suppression of dissent and a partial reversion to autocratic ways characteristic of both the czarist and communist periods, is a comparable case. An ironic confirmation of the truth that democracy is not to be identified wholly or exclusively with the electoral process came with the West's reaction to the suspension of elections in Algeria in 1991. With the prospect of victory by the Islamic FIS party, the military-backed government of Algeria cancelled the elections and moved to ban the FIS, a decision tacitly endorsed by the Bush administration in the United States despite the obvious violation of the democratic process. Endorsement of what was in essence a military coup was evidently preferable to the prospect of victory by an Islamic party, elements of which publicly stated that the democratic process was un-Islamic, indicating that for some in the FIS participation in the elections was a tactical move designed to assure power and thus the opportunity to establish an Islamic state.[34]

The conclusion to be drawn from these historical instances is surely that democracy cannot be considered only as a set of institutions and practices; least of all can it be identified simply with elections in isolation from other democratic norms such as acceptance of genuine multi-party politics and safeguards for civil and political rights. However, it is easy for advocates of democracy promotion to find themselves embroiled in contradictions on this issue. Pressure is frequently brought to bear on nations to introduce democracy, which in practice generally means multi-party elections. A recent case in point is the Egyptian elections of 7 September 2005, the first multi-party elections of Hosni Mubarak's presidency. While, however, some of the trappings of democracy were introduced, they were hedged around with qualifications and restrictions which together seriously limit the democratic character of the process. Among these were the hugely dominant media presence of Mubarak's own party, assured by his control of the media outlets; the non-participation of the largest Islamic grouping in the country (the Muslim Brotherhood); the employment of various irregular methods and abuses of procedure for voting; and the refusal to allow international monitoring of the election. Yet if Mubarak is to be condemned by the democracy promoters for failing to uphold democracy to the full, how is that position to be squared with the acknowledgement, evident in the Algerian case, that democracy can easily bring about the 'wrong' result, namely the election of Islamic parties?

It is often overlooked that Western democracies were 'liberal' societies long before they became democratic. Indeed, democracy was a late development in Europe. Not until after the First

World War was universal suffrage established in the UK, though democratic elements had long been present – regular elections, partial suffrage, and so on. Democracy may be associated with certain procedures but it is a great deal more than procedure. Even this may be to ascribe too much uniformity or universality to the concept of democracy. It may be more accurate to say that democracy will inevitably be inflected according to the culture in which it is embedded, even if there must be certain common features for it to be called democracy at all.

In short, returning to our starting point in this discussion of democracy, to reduce democracy to a set of institutions or procedures is to underestimate the degree to which it relies for its success on the presence of certain values and norms. However, to say this is not to deny its applicability outside the orbit of its origins. The Japanese case demonstrates the portability of democracy, even as it also illustrates adaptations of democracy to local cultural values. The question is how far democratic norms and values can be stretched before it becomes impossible to speak of democracy at all in certain contexts. Hence the crucial question which has been posed repeatedly in recent years: is Islam compatible with democracy? At one end of the scale, we can take certain Islamists at their word and give the answer No. As one Algerian Imam declared during the political crisis in 1991, 'Islam is light. Why do you fear it? It is in democracy that darkness lies.'[35] On the other hand, analysts point to Turkey as a Muslim country with a modern multi-party democracy. It is, however, in many ways an exceptional case, the product of a concerted programme of secularization and modernization initiated in the 1920s which has thus had close to three generations to become established. Even so, there is evidence of Islamic activism in Turkey, and the qualms of some Europeans about Turkish entry into the EU stem from doubts about whether its polity and culture is really compatible with the West. The sober conclusion of one notably liberal specialist in Islamic studies is that 'despite democratic tendencies in the Muslim world and among some Islamic activists, multiple and conflicting attitudes towards democracy continue to exist and leave the future in question'.[36] This was written in the 1990s, since when the theme of democracy in the Arab world has become more explicit and urgent. George W. Bush envisages a democratic transformation in the Arabic world, spearheaded by America's own interventions in Afghanistan and Iraq, whose fruits included elections in Afghanistan in December 2004 and in Iraq in January 2005, Palestinian elections following the death of Yasser Arafat, the popular uprising in early 2005 in Lebanon against the Syrian military occupation, the introduction of multi-party elections in Egypt, and even an element of accountability in Saudia Arabia.

Can these developments be collectively regarded as a wave of democracy sweeping the Middle East? Are they a vindication of the Bush administration's aspiration to revolutionize the Middle East by means of active intervention and democracy promotion, thereby also confirming the argument that democracy is a universal system which knows no cultural boundaries? The problem with the latter view is that it fails to take account of the specifics of these individual societies and in particular the ways in which the impulse toward democracy is channelled and often restricted by local needs and circumstances. How far, for example, were the moves by Egypt and Saudi Arabia token gestures to meet American demands for progress towards democracy and simultaneously to appease domestic pressure for change? On this score there is considerable scepticism inside and outside Egypt about how deep these measures are designed to go. The implementation of democracy in Iraq is more complex, since it involves establishing a political constitution and a voting system from scratch in a climate of military conflict and social divisions based on religious and regional differences. It remains to be seen how successful these efforts will be. What can be said is that this situation illustrates the degree to which the transfer of the theory and practice of democracy is dependent for its success on a variety of contextual conditions – social, cultural, economic, military. The danger inherent in the idea of democracy promotion is the assumption that the elements of consensus – at a minimum on procedural issues – needed to make a system work can be created by external action, a product perhaps of the notion that post-war Germany and Japan offer precedents for Afghanistan and Iraq. To follow through on these analogies is beyond the scope of this chapter. Suffice it to say that such comparisons fail to take account of some important differences between these cases: first, the experience of crushing defeat of Germany and Japan served comprehensively to delegitimize the defeated regimes; second, there existed relative ethnic and religious homogeneity in Germany and Japan, and above all a history of a stable sense of nationhood; third, though seriously damaged and depleted, these societies possessed trained workforces and knowledge of modern infrastructures. The task from the American point of view was thus state-building rather than nation-building. Even then, the forms which democracy took in these two nations in practice represented a compromise between the desires of the occupying powers and indigenous traditions. These factors either did not exist in Afghanistan and Iraq or not to the same degree. The likelihood of success in democracy promotion is thus heavily context- and culture-dependent. Furthermore, that element of dependence is such that it makes sense to ask in any situation where democracy promotion is contemplated, what democracy might *mean* in the case of any particular society. There is thus an intellectual task prior to any action plan which involves addressing directly that element of context dependence. It means in turn addressing the problem of culture in international relations.

Conclusions

The conclusion must be that efforts to paint culture out of the picture of international relations or, alternatively, to rely on culture as the main or sole explanation for conflict in international relations, are doomed to failure for practical and much as theoretical reasons. Nor should we assume that the cultural element will be present in equal measure all the time. Michael Mazaar may be justified in arguing that, while cultural conflict is a salient feature of current international relations, the influence of 'parochial divisive cultures' will decline. Those who have stressed the role of culture, he suggests, have recognized 'transitional instabilities brought about by the shift from the industrial to the information age – transitional instabilities that, if properly managed, will give way to a new era in which the impact of unique cultures in world affairs subsides'. Ultimately, he suggests, under the impact of globalization, convergence of world cultures, even if not homogenization, will take place under the aegis of the 'Western idea'.[37] Such a view may, however, be overly schematic and may also underestimate the degree to which globalization provokes particularist reactions and new forms of international conflict and disorder, of which the rise of global terrorism is one manifestation.[38] Either way, culture remains a vital ingredient in international relations and cries out for explanations which resist the sorts of self-serving political motives which have often characterized such discussions. Given the complexity of cultural phenomena and their links with other fields of human action and experience, it cannot be expected that definitive conclusions can easily be reached. This is not, however, a reason for failing to make the attempt.

3 No common ground?

Islam, anti-Americanism and
the United States

The great divide

In the wake of 9/11 there seem diminishing prospects for the development of understanding between the Muslim world and the West. Try as moderates on both sides have done to deny the existence of irreconcilable differences, far less a 'clash of civilizations', to a considerable extent extremist attitudes have dictated the way the relationship has developed. Events since 9/11 have provided continuous fuel for animosity and mistrust, from the invasion of Iraq, the terrorist attacks across the globe, involving the almost routine use of suicide bombings by jihadists, and the continuing and worsening conflict between Israel and the Palestinians. Even Muslims who reject terrorism out of hand have been influenced by the sight of the West attacking Muslim countries. At a day to day level, in Western societies with substantial Muslim populations, aggravations have surfaced over religious customs and behaviour, including the wearing of the full-face veil by women and the role of faith-based education, producing a general sense that Muslims and the host societies are becoming increasingly separate and at odds with each other. A survey by the Pew Global Attitudes Project published in the summer of 2006 concluded that, despite some variations in detail and occasional hopeful signs,

> most Muslims and Westerners are convinced that relations between them are generally bad these days. Many in the

West see Muslims as fanatical, violent and lacking in tolerance. Meanwhile, Muslims in the Middle East and Asia
generally see Westerners as selfish, immoral and greedy – as
well as violent and fanatical.[1]

Even attempts at reconciliation can be tainted by the climate of
fear and mistrust. Calls by Western leaders for ever more categorical public denunciations by Muslim leaders of 'Islamic terrorism' are frequently received as insulting to Muslim communities
since such demands imply that terrorism is a problem purely
internal to Islam rather than of the relationship between Islam
and the West. If ever one doubted that religion had the capacity
to arouse intense existential anger, then the following litany of
instances should surely confirm it: the murder of the Dutch
film-maker Theo Van Gogh in November 2004, the global
Muslim reaction in the early months of 2006 to the publication
of cartoons of the prophet Muhammad in Danish and other
newspapers, and the response later the same year to the Pope's
quotation of a fourteenth-century Christian emperor's judgement that Islam had produced only evil.

As far as many in the West, and particularly the United States,
are concerned, year zero of the 'great divide' between the West
and the Muslim world was 2001. Admittedly, this is a short-
sighted view of a complex story with deep roots, but it is in the
nature of crises such as 9/11 to impose an artificial simplicity
on perceptions of the course of events. Scholars had been talking
and writing about relations between the West and Islam for a
long time before then, though their audiences were relatively
small and specialized. There were plenty of high-profile precedents for the apparent Muslim hatred of the West, such as the
seizure of American hostages by Iranian revolutionaries in 1979,
though that was long ago and took place on another continent.
The Cold War was still on and the Soviet Union was the real
enemy. The Iranian fatwa against the novelist Salman Rushdie
was headline news for a while, though more so in Europe than
the United States. In a sense there was no excuse for the West to

be surprised at the eruption of the issue of Islam, but September 11 propelled it to the top of the list of global problems. The terrorist attacks on the United States opened a new era in more senses than one. They not only brought the issue of Islam to the fore but also the issue of American vulnerability to physical attack. Both raised the overwhelming question of why some people should hate the United States so virulently. It went beyond even the 'sneak' attack on Pearl Harbor. Pearl Harbor, it could be argued, was an act of war in the classical sense: a continuation of politics by other means. September 11 broke all the rules of war and of civilized behaviour. The attacks on the twin towers and the Pentagon conveyed nothing if not intense emotion on the part of the terrorists, yet were carried out with cold and ruthless efficiency. That was perhaps the most shocking feature – the combination of blind anger and controlled action directed at huge, vulnerable and symbolic targets. Indeed, this explosive combination may be precisely what is meant by the word 'hate'. Understanding the sources and the implications of such hatred is clearly of great importance, not merely for policy-makers but for ordinary citizens who have their own needs to make sense of these acts.

There is more than one way to seek such understanding. Numerous historical and political analyses of the events have been published since September 11. Virtually all commentary on public affairs since then has been informed by an awareness that this date constituted a great divide in contemporary experience. No attempt is made here to repeat the many and varied efforts to explain why the events of September 11 occurred. Nor do I wish simply to repeat the question of 'why do people hate America?'[2] This is certainly a legitimate question to ask but it tends to yield narrow answers which often amount to little more than a register of attitudes and prejudices which on their own are not very useful or interesting until they are placed within a larger framework. In fact the theme of anti-Americanism itself risks inviting simple-minded conclusions both about America and those whose views of America one is trying to comprehend. The interesting and important questions lying behind the question 'why do people hate America?' include the following: What sorts of interactions have given rise to such negative attitudes? To what extent are they representative? Are there counter-currents, complicating factors? In short, the entire relationship is involved, not just a particular set of attitudes. This explains the title of this investigation: not 'why do Muslims hate America?' but 'no common ground?', which invites us to examine the relations between America and Islam in terms which are much broader than placarded slogans. Ultimately the issue needs to be addressed precisely because of the temptation to assume that the attacks of September 11 are representative of relations between the United States and Islam.

Three further preliminary points must be made. The first has to do with the religious sources of political conflict. Anyone interested in current American foreign relations will have had to give some attention to Islam even if they are not specialists in US–Middle East relations. The question of whether or how the United States (and the West generally) and the Islamic world can come to terms with each other is a central dilemma in current international relations. One does not have to swallow Samuel Huntington's 'clash of civilizations' thesis whole to believe that cultural difference, and in particular religious belief, is an increasingly important factor in international relations. Since the Iranian Revolution of 1979, Islam has thrust itself on to the stage of world politics. In the words of one Western specialist on the Middle East: 'for the first time in modern history ... a revolution took place in which the dominant ideology, forms of organization, leading personnel and proclaimed goal were all religious in appearance and inspiration'.[3] Though it is important not to underestimate secular and materialist factors, to attempt to explain the Iranian Revolution exclusively in these terms is to touch the body but not the soul of the Revolution. Like it or not, Western secularized post-Enlightenment minds are forced now to grapple with motives and forces which many thought had been ironed out of international politics.

Perhaps the spectre of potent religious belief in the Iranian Revolution helps to account for the American response and subsequent relations with revolutionary Iran which, in the words of an American official, represented the 'most emotional foreign policy relationship to confront America since the Vietnam War'.[4] The claim is not, of course, that religion explains everything about the Iranian Revolution or America's response to it; only that it is a dimension that cannot be ignored. Moreover, it is a model with which, it can be argued, current models of international politics are not well equipped to deal.

Second, among the preliminary points, it should be clear that the present writer is a specialist in United States history and foreign policy, not Islamic or Middle Eastern studies. It is unavoidable, however, that Americanists should make the attempt to get outside the skin of America in an effort to understand the impact of America on other nations and cultures, just as scholars of Islam and the Middle East must make it their business to understand the United States. Americanists, moreover, are in a position to help explain the nature of the American reaction to Islamic militancy. If common ground is be found at the level of international politics between these nations and cultures, such efforts are more likely to succeed if they are supported by networks of relationships and understandings at other levels.

Finally, it might be asked of the present inquiry: 'how can you compare a country (the United States) with a religion (Islam)?' Without attempting a precision which may be impossible to achieve, it should be made clear that when referring to America (or the United States) I mostly mean the nation but on occasions 'the West', on the grounds that this is how Americans frequently identify themselves with reference to Islam. The same is true in reverse. Muslims mean by 'America' sometimes the country but sometimes a congerie of attitudes and values associated with 'the West'. By the same token, when I refer to 'Islam' I mean mostly the religion but sometimes individual states in the Middle East, on the grounds that Islam is at one and the same time a religion with claims to universality – including an aspiration to nationhood in the form of the Islamic Nation or 'Umma' – as well as an integral element of most states of the Middle East.[5]

The cooperation model

I propose to develop two models which represent broad approaches to America's relations with Islam. All the usual caveats about models apply. They constitute not rigid interpretive systems but short-hand ways of understanding a range of facts and possibilities in the relations between America and Islam. Neither model is commonly present in a pure form; they represent abstractions drawn from bodies of data, events and experiences and are useful in so far as they enable us to identify broad tendencies and patterns. The first model – the 'cooperation model' – is characterized by the following features:

- Acceptance that geopolitical boundaries (nation-states or groupings of states) and cultural boundaries do not and need not coincide. Nations, cultures, and civilizations are not hermetically sealed entities. They interact at a number of levels on an increasing scale. Global travel and communications, movement of populations whether for political or economic reasons, trade and finance, cultural interactions – indeed much of what is involved in globalization – all, according to this model, make for a world in which different nations and cultures have important reasons for seeking cooperation.
- A corollary of this is acceptance that 'multiculturalism' is not only a given condition of modernity but that it is a healthy condition which is to be prized. Diversity, pluralism, interaction bring benefits to all.
- Acceptance that differences of religious belief are no obstacle to fruitful relations between nations and, more specifically, that Islam's supposed incompatability with Christianity has been grossly exaggerated and is based on a partial and distorted understanding of Islam.

- A belief, following on from the last point, that there is no inherent incompatability, as some claim, between Islam and modernity or between Islam and democracy.
- Encompassing all these assumptions is the view that the real obstacles to cooperation are political rather than cultural and are thus susceptible to acts of choice rather than being set less malleable cultural values and institutions.

In illustration of this model we start with some details about America's own Muslim community in order to emphasize the point that America's relations with Islam are not only a matter of foreign relations. First, the United States contains a substantial and rising Muslim population. No official figures for religious affiliation exist and estimates vary widely, but the figure currently accepted by the US State Department is approximately 6 million. Some estimate that by 2010 the Muslim population will overtake the Jewish population by virtue both of immigration and natural increase.[6] Second, to say that American Muslims are a 'group' is at best a half-truth. American Muslims come from many different national and ethnic origins and some – such as African-American Muslims – are Muslims predominantly by conversion (or are the children of converts). Furthermore, only about 23 per cent of American Muslims are from the Middle East. Nor, despite popular impressions, are all Arab-Americans Muslims; indeed of the estimated 3–3.5 million Arab-Americans a large proportion are Christian.[7] In short, making generalizations about 'American Muslims' is a hazardous enterprise. What can be said is that crises such as the one provoked by September 11 tend to focus a level of attention on group identifiers which in other circumstances would be of markedly less significance. American Muslims have perforce become more of a group because of September 11, not because of any change generated among American Muslims themselves but because of events outside the Muslim community.

At one level American Muslims are simply one other social group identified by religion and in part ethnic origin in a society whose lifeblood has been assimilation of incomers from a variety of different societies and cultures. The experience of German-Americans in the First World War, of Japanese–Americans in the Second World War and of Catholics at a number of points in America's history demonstrate the vulnerability to prejudice to which ethnic and religious groups can be subject. However, systematic prejudice is neither necessarily consistent nor permanent. Assimilation is a complex process which takes different forms among different groups; there are powerful motives for identification with the host culture just as the host culture has reasons for promoting the assimilation or Americanization of immigrant groups. Specific instances of prejudice do not of themselves invalidate the notion of a cooperation model. The evidence suggests that in general American Muslims have been treated like other immigrant groups in America, and indeed have thrived economically and socially as compared with some other groups. American Muslims earn more than the median American income and have higher than average educational attainment. In both these respects they compare favourably with Muslims in Europe.[8] There exists, therefore, a basis in American society for positive relations with Islam.

One example of the pressures for assimilation and reconciliation at work is the opening in Jackson, Mississipi, on 15 April 2001, of the first museum in the United States devoted to Islam. The inspiration for the museum came when an exhibition entitled 'The Majesty of Spain' was due to come to the city. When it was discovered by leaders of the Muslim community (numbering about 1,000) that the exhibition was to cover only the Christian era and would largely ignore the 700 years (AD 711–1492) of Muslim presence in Spain, they were able to persuade the exhibition's organizers to include exhibits covering the Islamic era. This move received support from leaders of the Jewish and Catholic communities in the city. 'We are particularly pleased', said the director of the Museum of the Southern Jewish Experience, 'at the great efforts made by your project to educate the public about cross-cultural exchange and to foster tolerance and understanding between people of different religious, racial and ethnic backgrounds.' Subsequently a separate International Museum of Muslim Cultures was established and among the first visitors was Bill Clinton.[9]

Needless to say, September 11 placed a huge strain on relations between Muslim and non-Muslim Americans. Public figures went out of their way to spread a message of tolerance. The claim that the war on terrorism was not a war on Islam became an almost daily refrain after a few early wrong notes such as calling the war on terror a 'crusade' and labelling the military action against the Taliban 'Operation Infinite Justice'. In his first major speech to Congress after September 11, President Bush declared that 'I want to speak tonight directly to Muslims throughout the world. We respect your faith. It's practiced freely by many millions of Americans, and by millions more in countries that America counts as friends. Its teachings are good and peaceful, and those who commit evil in the name of Allah blaspheme the name of Allah.'[10] President Bush's wife, Laura Bush, invited Muslim leaders to breakfast at the White House. National Security Adviser Condoleezza Rice said to a meeting of Muslim Women Lawyers for Human Rights that 'Islam is a great faith that inspires people to lead lives based on honesty, justice, and compassion, and reinforces the values of democracy and human rights'.[11] Significantly, these sentiments were roundly condemned by members of the Christian right, one of whom called Islam 'very evil and wicked, violent and not of the same God'. Another described Muhammad as a terrorist. Bush made a point of distancing himself and his administration from these views.[12]

For their part American Muslim leaders moved quickly to condemn the terrorist attacks and to declare sympathy with the victims, among whom, of course, there were a number of Muslims. The Council on American-Islamic Affairs issued over forty pages of statements on the internet from numerous American Muslim organizations and from Muslim organizations around the world. The following, from Arsalan Tariq Iftikhar, Midwest Communications Director of the Council on American

Affairs, is representative, conveying as it does a hint of despera-
tion as well as affirmations of loyalty and a sense of belonging:

> We are no less American than we were on September 10. I
> was born in the United States. I took my first steps on this
> soil. I have been a ball boy for the Chicago Bulls. I have been
> to four U2 concerts. I am a second-year law student spe-
> cializing in international human rights. I and my 7 million
> Muslim brothers and sisters are contributing members of
> American society. Two members of President Bush's cabinet
> are of Arab descent. It was a Muslim who was the architect
> of the Sears Tower. Islam is the fastest growing religion in
> America. We are doctors, lawyers, engineers, mechanics,
> teachers, and store owners. We are your neighbours.[13]

The last statement contains a telling appeal to the consciences of
American Christians, but part of the force of the statement lies
in the reminder of the size of the Muslim minority in the
United States. In so far as there is pressure towards cooperation
between American Muslims and the rest of the population it has
a basis in inescapable demographic and social realities. Those
pressures are likely to grow, furthermore, in the light of
increased Muslim immigration into the United States. In 2005,
the *New York Times* reported, 'more people from Muslim countries became legal permanent United States residents – nearly
96,000 – than in any year in the previous two decades'. After
September 11, 2001, there was a sharp decrease in numbers but
from 2004 the flow resumed and quickened. This included
many who disagree with American policies towards the Middle
East. 'One needs to distinguish between the government and the
people', said one immigrant.[14] In short, there are powerful
historic trends, such as migration of peoples for economic reasons, which ensure that America will continue to be in the
business of practical cooperation with Muslims.

Looking at this issue from the side of the Muslims of the
Middle East and elsewhere, we can discern features which

complicate some of the usual stereotypes and which indicate the potential for cooperation between America and Islam. As far as September 11 is concerned, not only did the governments of most Muslim countries condemn the terrorist attacks (Iraq was a significant exception) but most prominent Muslim clerics and spiritual leaders rejected bin Laden's invocation of the Koran to justify the terrorist attacks. This includes figures such as the Hizbollah leader Sheik Muhammad Hussain Fadlallah, who had a long history of supporting terrorist acts on behalf of other causes.[15] In short, many Muslim leaders abroad were as keen to distance themselves from the terrorism of September 11 as were Muslim leaders in the United States.

Underlying this point is the larger issue of the diversity of the world of Islam. It is perhaps understandable but unfortunate that the West should become so suddenly acquainted with Islam as a result of singular acts of extremism. Indeed, since 1979 Islam has been news in the West virtually only to the extent that it has been associated with dramatic events and extreme forms of action. The association has tended to stick, the inevitable conclusion being that Islam is an extreme form of religion which poses a distinct threat to Western interests and values. Evidence to the contrary – including the historical record of peaceful as well as bellicose interaction between Islam and Christianity, extensive Western borrowings from Islamic culture, and so on – tends to get sidelined. This is but one instance of a common phenomenon – the capacity of news to obscure ordinary experience and to render deeper currents invisible and hence of no account. The effort must be made to look at these deeper levels.

We can begin with the popular misconception that Islam as a whole is constitutionally resistant to modernity. The case of Iran since the Revolution of 1979 may seem to be a poor one to take as an example, since the conventional wisdom has it that Iran was captured by Islamic fundamentalists in its Shi'ite form and turned into a theocracy. The reality is more complicated.[16] The Ayatollah Khomeini did indeed institute effective rule by the

Mullahs but even he, as one commentator has put it, came to believe by the end of his life that 'government must be emancipated from the constraining laws of traditional religion'. Indeed, in the Shia tradition the separation of church and state is an article of faith on the grounds that the world of politics is inevitably corrupting.[17] Following Khomeini's death, and particularly after the election in 1997 of Sayeed Muhammad Khatami as president by a massive majority against the candidate favoured by conservative clerics, there was a reexamination of Iran's relations with America and also of the role of religion in politics. Greater press freedom was introduced than existed in any of Iran's Arab neighbours and there was a move in the direction of greater democracy. Khatami called for a 'dialogue of civilizations' in which he envisaged change in both Iran and the West. Nor is it insignificant that after 9/11 large crowds filled the streets in Tehran and held candle-lit vigils for the victims of the terrorist attacks. In addition, Iran gave support to the United States in the early stages of its military action in Afghanistan following 9/11. It seems clear that an opportunity was lost by the American administration after 9/11 to achieve closer relations with Iran.[18]

Needless to say, relations between the United States and Iran soon took a downward turn. President Bush's inclusion, in his 2002 State of the Union Address, of Iran in the 'axis of evil' precluded any improvement of relations. It was a severe blow to Iranian reformers and seriously undercut their credibility with conservatives inside Iran. The Iranian parliamentary elections of February 2004 which swept conservatives back into power (helped, it must be noted, by a ban dictated by the religious leadership on most reform candidates from standing), followed the next year by the election of Mahmoud Ahmadinejad to the presidency, soured relations with the United States and the West as a whole. The new president not only issued inflammatory statements about Israel but seemed generally determined to be confrontational, not least on the question of Iran's nuclear programme. Next to Iraq, the issue of Iran's nuclear programme became the most troubling Middle Eastern issue for the United States. By the middle of 2006 relations between Iran and the United States were at a new low. The sobering conclusion of one experienced observer was that 'all in all, a major crisis is in the making'.[19]

However, those who look beyond the current government's policies discern other forces at work in Iran which have the capacity to produce different relations with the outside world. The Iranian middle class which, one commentator writes, 'is increasingly urbanized, wired and globally connected', seeks democratic reforms and given the right conditions – which would include an easing of American economic sanctions against Iran – could be a powerful force for change in Iran.[20] Moreover, despite the current dominance of the religious leadership over the political system, secularism is growing in Iran and is likely in the long term to exert a powerful influence on Iranian society. The tendency for those in the West to think of Iran exclusively in terms of the revolution of a generation ago has had a stultifying effect on perceptions of Iran. There has been 'a marked failure', says the author of a recent study, 'to distinguish between the state and the nation, and to recognize social changes and the political dynamic'.[21] While the conservatives will insist on the retention of political power, writes another commentator, 'they are likely to compromise on social and economic reform'.[22] These are, of course, provisional judgements which are conditional upon events which cannot be foreseen. However, they are a reminder that Iranian society is more diverse and more complex than the images generally presented in the West would suggest. Inexorable demographic and social changes are likely to moderate the capacities of the religious leadership to dictate the future. Besides, Iran's leading intellectual, Abdolkarim Soroush, a professor at Tehran University, suggests that every Iranian has three identities: Shia, Persian and Western.[23] Evidently it cannot be said that cultures are hermetically sealed entities; nor are they immune to change.

By the same token, Islamic specialists never fail to emphasize the diversity in Islam as a whole. While our headlines are dominated by the murderous activities of extreme Islamists, for whom 'there is only one Islam, that of the age of the Prophet', the reality is of complex traditions and a variety of practices and beliefs.[24] Even the Islamic revivalism of recent decades which calls for a re-Islamicization of the Muslim world on the basis of a return to the 'straight path' of early Islam – so often seen as merely a desire to revive the medieval world – bears the imprint of modernity in the methods by which it is spread, the organizational means used, and many of the teachings themselves. Furthermore, while revivalism has affected the whole Muslim world and dominates the news, more moderate reform-minded voices, whose approaches are as deeply rooted in Islamic traditions as those of the revivalists, continue to think and write and argue for dialogue with the West.[25] By the same token, though much is heard of 'fundamentalist' readings of the Koran, there exists also the tradition of 'independent reasoning' or 'personal interpretation' (*ijtihad*) in interpreting the Koran and other holy writings, suggesting that Islamic law must be progressively reinterpreted according to changing circumstances. In addition, while the term 'jihad' is routinely interpreted according to its most aggressive meaning, i.e. holy war against the enemies of Islam, the term has had other, more temperate, inflections in Islamic history. According to the Sufi tradition and some modern Islamic writers, the 'greater jihad' is the personal or spiritual struggle to become a better person, to overcome the evil within oneself, to become nearer to God.[26] While it is true that the militant and military form of jihad is the one most commonly invoked publicly by militant Islamists, the other meaning is nevertheless available in the Islamic tradition.

Looking beyond issues of doctrine to wider questions of the relations between Islam and 'modernity', it is clear that there is no simple contrast between a West which embraces modernity and an Islamic world which rejects it. As James Piscatori has pointed out, though there is deep ambivalence among many Muslims on the question of globalization, not all Muslims see it as an unequivocal evil. Nor indeed is it possible for the Muslim world to insulate itself from global trends, and many Muslim leaders see positive benefits from modern technology, foreign investment and global communications. Furthermore, Piscatori observes, the relationship between Islam and the West in this globalizing world is not all a one-way street. A 'demographic Islamization of the western world' is taking place 'owing to the large and permanently settled Muslim minorities now living in Europe, North America, and Australia'.[27]

Similar sorts of arguments can be put forward on the question of Islam and democracy. While there are voices to be heard both within Islam and the West that Islam and democracy are inherently incompatible, there is some evidence of a desire in the Islamic world for greater popular participation in politics, even if it is argued that democracy in Islamic nations should be adapted to Islamic conditions. Concepts exist in the Islamic tradition, scholars have pointed out, which are counterparts to Western ideas of popular participation in decision-making, consent, and consultation, which open out the possibility of the 'Islamicization' of democracy. 'Democracy', concludes John Esposito, 'has become an integral part of modern Islamic political thought and practice', though 'questions as to the specific nature and degree of popular participation remain unanswered'.[28] Besides these developments at the level of ideas, certain social changes are creating demands for greater participation, among them the 'fragmentation of authority' in the Muslim world and the emergence of a number of political groups focusing on human rights and women's rights.[29] None of these trends indicate that Muslim countries are about to adopt Western forms of democracy wholesale or overnight. The experience of Turkey, which of all Muslim countries has gone furthest in the direction of secularism and democracy, suggests that there are deep-seated difficulties in reconciling democracy and Islam. Nor would a form of democracy imposed by the West be likely to succeed. Nevertheless, the evidence suggests that, irrespective of any promptings from outside, considerable pressures exist inside the Islamic world for the opening up of political participation on terms which meet the needs of Muslim societies.

In all these respects we can discern areas of potential common ground, or at the very least scope for conciliation and compromise. For their part, Americans could point out that they have intervened in several instances since the end of the Cold War in defence of Muslim populations – in Kuwait, Bosnia, and Kosovo. Furthermore, of all nations, it would seem logical to think, the United States would be most open to the cooperation model since its population is an amalgam of the world's peoples. Multiculturalism is a given condition of the United States; pluralism is the basic principle of its political system and values, however difficult it may have been to live up to all that these words imply. From that point of view there are few nations and cultures in the world which do not have reason to look to the United States for sympathetic treatment and understanding. Indeed, the sorts of analyses which have been offered above of the diversity and moderating influences within Muslim societies can be applied equally to the United States. The Bush administration represents only one face of America and a particularly strident one. If 'liberal' America is silent or unlistened to in present circumstances this is not to say that it does not exist. A glance at the other model of relations between America and Islam, however, will indicate why after 9/11 especially the reality has so often been of confrontation with the Muslim world.

The confrontation model

The easiest way to sketch this model is to invoke Samuel Huntington's 'clash of civilizations' thesis, since its fundamental premise is the high likelihood of conflict between civilizations and cultures in the post-Cold War world.[30] Since he is especially concerned with Islam, his writings serve this present project well. His thesis is that 'in the post-cold war world the most important distinctions among peoples are not ideological, political, or economic. They are cultural'. In short, the rivalry of the superpowers is replaced by the clash of civilizations. ... In this new world the most persuasive, important, and dangerous conflicts will not be between social classes, rich and poor, or other economically defined groups but between peoples belonging to different cultural entities. And the most dangerous cultural conflicts are along the fault lines of civilizations.[31]

The deepest – and from the West's point of view most troubling – fault line, according to Huntington, lies between the West and Islam, though it is by no means of recent origin. Islam, Huntington concludes, has always had 'bloody borders'. Even more troubling, he adds, is that 'the underlying problem for the West is not Islamic fundamentalism. It is Islam, a different civilization whose people are convinced of the superiority of their culture and are obsessed with the inferiority of their power.' By the same token, for Islam

the problem is not the CIA or the Department of Defense. It is the West, a different civilization whose people are convinced of the universality of their culture and believe that their superior, if declining, power imposes on them the obligation to extend that culture throughout the world.[32]

Huntington's emphasis on the radically distinct natures of different civilizations rests on a concern with defence of the values of the West. The threat comes equally from advocates of multiculturalism at home (i.e. in the United States) and of universalism abroad. 'Both', Huntington argues, 'deny the uniqueness of Western culture.' A multicultural world, he says, is 'unavoidable because global empire is impossible', but 'a multicultural America is impossible because a non-Western America is not American'. In short, 'the preservation of the United States and the West requires the renewal of Western identity'.[33] In Huntington's world, civilizations are, or should be, like billiard balls with hard, shiny, impermeable surfaces which might make contact but do not establish real connections. In this respect, as in the concern with the West's decline, Huntington's model is Oswald Spengler's *Decline of the West* rather than Toynbee's *Study of History* which is centrally concerned with the connections between civilizations.

Huntington evidently assumes a close identity between the geopolitical and the cultural, and he assumes that cultural homogeneity, or something close to it, is the desired condition. Cultural diversity will tend to be productive of conflict and it is precisely because this is inevitable at the international level that it is important to insist on maximum possible consensus at home, since it is a necessary defence against external danger. In short, Huntington's model rules out the first two principles which I suggested were characteristic of the cooperation model: first, acceptance that geopolitical and cultural boundaries do not and need not coincide and, second, acceptance of multiculturalism within societies. Among the further features of the conflict model are the following:

- The view that religion is the defining difference between nations and cultures.
- The view that there is a basic incompatability between Islam and modernity and between Islam and democracy. Specifically, the apparent absence of separation between church and state – the feature of Western history which is generally taken to have been a central condition of 'the rise of the West' – coupled with the extent to which religion governs all aspects of individual and social behaviour, its enveloping and even 'totalitarian' quality, differentiate Islam radically from Western civilization. Furthermore, Islam is said to be an aggressive, proselityzing religion, spread originally by force and still prone to such methods. As for Islamic democracy, not only do the required socio-economic conditions not exist, but the theology and traditional practices of Islam effectively forbid it.
- Encompassing all these conditions and assumptions is the view that cultural differences present fundamental obstacles to cooperation. Culture goes deeper than politics.

Thus the conflict model – or at least the Western expression of it. It is not hard to find counterpart views in the Islamic world. Indeed, a summary by Islamic specialist John L. Esposito of the guiding assumptions of the Islamic revivalist organization the Muslim Brotherhood (founded in 1928 by Hasan al-Banna) displays their explicit grounding in anti-Westernism. Beginning with the view that 'Islam is a total, all-encompassing way of life that guides each person', the list includes insistence on the adequacy of Shariah law as a basis for Islamic society quite independent of Western models, the harnessing of science and technology but once again 'within an Islam context', and the pursuit of 'jihad' with the aim of bringing about 'a successful Islamization of society and the world'. Encompassing all these imperatives is the conviction that 'departure from Islam and reliance on the West are the causes for Muslim decline'.[34] In the hands of the next generation of Islamists, in particular the Muslim Brotherhood's hugely influential leader Sayyid Qutb, such sentiments were forged into a militant instrument of revolutionary change which put anti-Western jihad at the centre of the desired Islamic Revolution. Qutb's ideas in turn found expression in the utterances and actions of such figures as Ayatollah Khomeini and Osama bin Laden.[35]

There is no intention here to suggest a simple equivalence between the ideas of Huntington and those of the Islamists cited above, only a broad parallelism. Nor, it should be observed, are the Western and Islamic confrontation models simple inversions of each other. They disagree fundamentally about the facts. Huntington fears decline of the West in the face of Islamic resurgence while many Islamists are preoccupied with the disastrous long-term decay of Islam in the face of the rise of the West, whose impact, particularly that of the United States, is held to have been insidiously destructive of Islam.[36] However, if these visions of conflict are not entirely inversions of each other, they are systematically opposed. It is not hard to find evidence in recent events to confirm the validity of these views of the world.

We could start, as we did with evidence for the cooperation model, with the experience of American Muslims at home in the aftermath of September 11: the widespread suspicion of individuals who were thought from their appearance to be Muslims (including Sikhs whose turbans were taken to be Muslim headwear),[37] the instinctive fear of Muslim-looking passengers on airlines, the arrest of Muslims on suspicion of terrorism often on the flimsiest basis, demands on Muslim leaders to go ever further in condemning the attacks of September 11, and more generally the readiness to assume the worst of Muslims and suspect them of instigating all major accidents, disasters and crimes (such as the anthrax scare and the crash of flight 587 on Long Island in November 2001). Nor, of course, were such suspicions current only after September 11, as the initial reaction to the Oklahoma bombing demonstrated. Encompassing all these instances is the association implied in the term 'Islamic terrorism' between the religion of Islam and political extremism.

To these examples of what might be called street-level prejudice might be added the United States government's insensitivity to the overtones of certain types of speech, such as the naming of the action against the Taliban government in Afghanistan as 'Operation Infinite Justice' (later changed to 'Enduring Freedom'), raising deep theological and historical objections among Muslims. While this gaffe was soon corrected, as the war against terror developed there appeared to be little difference between street-level prejudice and government attitudes. Many Muslims in America and elsewhere were not convinced that the government's claim to be fighting terrorism rather than Islam was anything more than rhetoric. The language of many public statements by the Bush administration, heavily freighted as they were with religious associations, confirmed the views of some Muslims that, despite the claims, this was indeed a war of religion, a clash of civilizations. If anything, according to some, the tenor of the war against terror became more militant, more indiscriminate, and more threatening to Muslims in general as it gathered momentum with the toppling of the Taliban government in Afghanistan.[38] At home the passage of the Patriot Act gave the government sweeping new powers to detain suspected terrorists for extended periods and placed Arab and Muslim immigrants under unprecedented scrutiny, while at Guantanamo Bay rights and liberties under the US Constitution and the Geneva Convention on the treatment of prisoners of war were suspended.

More complicated than these instances of what many Muslims could only regard as deep-seated prejudice against their community and faith was the evidence that many Muslims were deeply sceptical of American claims about who was responsible for the terrorist attacks of September 11. 'America's efforts to enlist street-level support among Arabs and Muslims in the fight against terrorism', reported the *Christian Science Monitor* in November 2001, 'is running into a brick wall', the chief reason being that many among the elites and public opinion in the Islamic world believed the attacks were carried out by the Israeli intelligence service Mossad. '"The level of conspiracy theories just makes you want to scream," said a Western diplomat based in Amman, who had just been lectured by a senior Jordanian official about the Mossad's "obvious" role.' Among the many competing conspiracy theories around the globe – including the view that the attacks were carried out by Japanese extremists in revenge for Hiroshima – this was undoubtedly the most damaging since it threatened the American goal of obtaining global support for the war on terror where it mattered vitally.[39] Most damaging of all was the evidence it provided of a pre-existing deep-seated distrust of the United States in the Arab and Islamic world.

In short, the evidence for the Muslim version of the confrontation model was of much longer standing than the events of September 11. We have seen in the American version of the confrontation model – Huntington's 'clash of civilizations' – that the model relies on a reading of history and not just contemporary events. Similarly behind the immediate consequences of the terrorist attacks of September 11, as far as many Muslims were concerned, lay centuries of Western aggression against Islam. If the paradigm for the Western assault on Islam was supplied by the crusades of the middle ages, its modern manifestations were to be found in the abolition of the caliphate in 1924 and the founding of Israel in 1948. The first destroyed the unity of the 'Umma' or community of Islam. The second represented the renewal of the direct Western assault on Islam in that it involved the enforced displacement of Arab inhabitants by a state which was regarded as an entering wedge of Western imperialism, even if much of its new population after 1948 was of Arab and African origin.[40] America's presence in the Middle East since the Second World War, including its support for the state of Israel, showed, according to this version of history, that the United States was at best indifferent to Islam and at worst openly hostile to it, and even determined to destroy it. On this reading of history, the United States, in conjunction with the state of Israel, was heir to the crusaders. Osama bin Laden routinely denounced the 'Zionist-crusaders war on Islam' in the recorded statements he issued on a regular and strategically timed basis.[41]

No doubt few Muslims subscribe to the most extreme versions of the confrontation model. Indeed, the sorts of historical leap implied in this model fly in the face of much evidence that anti-Americanism in the Arab and Muslim world is of relatively recent origin. 'Anti-Americanism', suggests historian Ussama Makdisi, 'is ... not civilizationally rooted, even if it is at times expressed in civilizational terms.' The truth is that hostility to America in the Arab and Muslim world is based 'not on *long-standing hatred* of "American" values, but on more *recent anger* at American policies in the region, especially toward Israel' (emphasis in original).[42] Israel was not the only issue, however. The most obvious new element in the relationship between the United States and the Middle East during the twentieth century was the discovery and exploitation of oil, which brought them directly into contact but on unequal terms. Middle Eastern nations 'owned' the oil since it lay under their land but only the United States and other Western powers had the knowledge and the resources to exploit it. Much more was involved, though, than disparity in wealth. The possession of such a resource did not lead swiftly or automatically to the modernization of many of the countries which possessed it: notably Saudi Arabia, Kuwait, and the Emirates. What it did do was to tie the United States and other Western countries very closely to the Middle East as a whole, and not just to those states with oil, while sharply exposing historical and cultural differences between them. For at least two decades after the Second World War the language of anti-imperialism in the Middle East was predominantly that of secular nationalism and socialism – ideas born in the West – though Islam also played a part. When Arab nationalism failed – the catastrophe of the 1967 war against Israel being the chief cause – radicals turned to Islam for inspiration. In short, it is hard to separate the 'civilizational' elements in the US relationship with the Middle East from America's material interest in oil and its effect on the peoples and governments of the region. The one is not reducible to the other.

The tendency to express hostility to the United States in 'civilizational terms', whatever its actual sources, has been a key ingredient of American relations with the world of Islam in the last three decades or so, given the rise of what has variously been called 'Islamic fundamentalism', 'Islamic revivalism', 'Islamism' or 'political Islam'.[43] This is not the place to explore this phenomenon in detail. Suffice it to say that the conjunction of the politicization of Islam and American interventionism in the Middle East since the Second World War have made for an explosive mixture. Nor are the two phenomena unrelated. Islamic fundamentalism has often been fuelled directly by hostility to the United States, as is shown by the case of the Iranian Revolution which was defined explicitly in opposition to the 'Great Satan'. Given the legacy of American intervention in 1953 to restore the Shah to power and the decades of American support for the Shah, the connection was not hard to make. However, Islamic fundamentalism had internal roots too in the failures of many Arab and Muslim states, following decolonization, to generate economic growth and political stability, above all in the *relative* failure of growth as compared with the West and the ability through travel and communications to make such comparisons. Furthermore, exposure to Western values provoked ambivalent responses, ranging from the extreme rejectionism of Sayyid Qutb and Osama bin Laden to a more or less welcoming embrace of things American. On occasions, it has often been pointed out, the two apparently contradictory responses are to be found in one and the same person. 'Anti-Americanism' need not be and has not always been a simple all-or-nothing response, and in this respect it mirrors the broader response to modernization and globalization. Anti-Americanism, from this point of view, in the Muslim world as elsewhere, is often a convenient form in which various sources of anger and frustration can find expression. Among the sources of such anger in the Muslim world is the absence of means to express opposition to national governments, and in such contexts anti-Americanism is a licensed form of protest, an outlet for anger which in other circumstances – i.e. if the political system permitted it – might be directed at the protesters' own governments. Needless to say, however, in many instances the opposition is against both governments – America and the protester's own – the charge against America being that it sustains in power undemocratic regimes in the service of its own imperial interests.

The enveloping sense, if one is to judge from the most extreme statements of Islamic militants, is of humiliation, resentment, and anger, a crushing sense not so much of poverty or deprivation as of powerlessness, combined with an equally powerful conviction of the rectitude and indeed sanctity of the cause. Among some this has resulted in a resort to terrorism, which is a means of exploiting what advantages may remain to the relatively powerless – secrecy, a sufficiency of funds and of silent supporters, and a willingness to sacrifice all – against America's 'weaknesses': the openness of its society and institutions and its low tolerance of the loss of life of its citizens. This may well be described as anti-Americanism but it is a good deal more than a matter of attitudes or opinion. It results from a basic condition of the relationship. It is a case of 'Islam embattled' just as, from its own perspective, America too is embattled when confronted by the actions of Islamic militants. In such circumstances a relationship which is not tainted by coercion is hard to conceive.

From the point of view of the confrontation model, the extremes cannot be dismissed as of no account since as often as not it is they which effectively dictate the nature and the pace of the political agenda. In the American as in the Muslim world there are powerful forces making for a confrontational frame of mind, among members of the Bush administration whose belief systems contain a powerful religious component.[44] Moreover, while the cooperation model makes much of the fact that America is composed of many nationalities and that this is potentially a source of tolerance and sensitivity to difference, it can be said in reply that this very diversity has placed a huge premium on a unifying ideology – the ideology of Americanism. Its power has waxed and waned according to domestic and international conditions and has been most powerful when these conditions have reinforced each other. At present both arenas exert powerful pressures for consensus. The Bush administration's agenda of national assertiveness, in conjunction with a deep-rooted traditional 'Americanism' and combined with the shattering blow of September 11, has made for a potent synthesis of cultural assertion and political power.[45]

Conclusion

What, then, can we conclude about the applicability of these models to US–Islamic relations? How much scope for progress is there? It would be a piece of self-deception to say that the cooperation model is the dominant one in the world at large, but it is worth pointing out that it does describe the aspirations of some individuals on all sides if not the actuality in the world at large. How far these aspirations can be made real is a matter of vital concern.

We would do well to begin an assessment of the possibilities for positive change by acknowledging the scale of potential

obstacles to it. Chief among them is the list of major international crises and unfinished business: Afghanistan, Iraq, and the
Palestinian–Israeli conflict. Not only are these huge issues in
themselves but they are touchstones for the wider relationship
between Islam and the United States (and more broadly, the
West) and for the possibility of progress towards political stability in the Middle East generally. Integrally linked to these issues
but extending far beyond their geographical bounds is the wave
of terrorist activity from Casablanca to Bali, Riyadh, Istanbul,
Madrid, London and beyond mounted by al-Qaeda-related
organizations. To the extent that these atrocities serve to sustain
and even intensify the emotions generated by the terrorist
attacks of September 11, then the chances for achieving a sea-
change in American relations with Islam are seemingly perpe-
tually postponed. No number of assertions by the American
administration that the war against terror is not a war against
Islam can entirely remove the suspicion of ordinary Americans,
born of the knowledge that these acts of terror are undertaken
in the name of Islam, that at some level Islam *is* to blame,
however perverted a notion of Islam it is which is used by the
terrorists to justify their actions.[46] Nor can America's assertions
entirely reassure Muslims at home and abroad that the American
government means what it says since its actions appear to belie
them: the war against terror seems inexorably to impact on
Islamic societies. Indeed the aim of al-Qaeda's terrorism appears
precisely to provoke the deepest possible chasm between America and Islam – to produce in effect a 'clash of civilizations'.

Furthermore, these conflicts are fed by underlying conditions –
economic, political, social, and military – whose combined effect
is to point up the relative weakness of the Islamic countries of
the Middle East *vis-à-vis* the West and to fuel distrust and discord.
As far as economic conditions are concerned, the disparity in
level between the West and the Arab countries of the Middle
East is sufficiently large as to constitute a substantial barrier to
accommodation and mutual respect. Coupled with the fact of
relative economic weakness is the conviction that America

wishes to maintain this state of affairs; witness its generous support for Israel and differential support for Arab nations depending on their usefulness to the United States. In short, according to this view, United States relations with the Middle East mirror the larger global imbalance between those who control and benefit from globalization and those who are controlled by it. Militarily the combined forces of the Arab nations have been unable to defeat an Israel which has a small population but is heavily backed by the United States and has access to modern weaponry. Iraq has been subject twice to overwhelming US military force. Politically, the nations of the Middle East have been divided even when there appeared to be unequivocal reasons for unity. Western support for authoritarian regimes in the Middle East reinforces the belief that the West wants the Middle East to remain weak and divided and subject to Western hegemony. The sense of embattlement is profound and among the most disenchanted groups and individuals the most extreme forms of resistance have been adopted.

Given the above conditions and presuppositions, the scope for suspicion and disenchantment is huge. Moreover, the cultural differences involved are real and cannot be wished away. Nevertheless, if cultural differences are real, they are rarely total. As Bikhu Parekh has written:

> Contrary to the current rhetoric, there can be no clash between cultures or civilizations. Cultures do not speak or fight; rather, people speak and fight from within and about their cultures. Cultures, further, are not homogeneous wholes and contain different strands and currents of thought. Cultures or civilizations therefore do not clash, only their particular strands and interpretations do. There is no inherent clash between Islam and the West.[47]

It is one thing to utter such hopeful and noble sentiments, but quite another to conceive of ways of making them real. Arguably the United States starts with two advantages which, if exploited to the full, could yield positive results. The first is the presence of a substantial Muslim population of its own which has made a clear contribution to American society and possesses a proven ability to thrive in the United States. It may be that in the years since 9/11 some of this credit has been squandered by government in the discriminatory way in which the war on terror has been fought at home, but the interests on both sides in maintaining trust are surely so strong as to make this the highest of priorities. Regarding the Muslim community in America as a resource rather than a liability in the war on terror might also have an impact on the way Islam is regarded abroad. The second advantage lies in America's own historic experience of absorbing the most diverse of populations, faiths, and cultures. As has already been pointed out, this has sometimes been a conflict-ridden process and there are groups and interests in American society which have stood against immigration and cultural diversity in the past and can be relied upon to do so in the future. The following chapter on 'Americanism' shows how deep this strain goes. However, opponents of change have ultimately never succeeded in stopping, far less reversing, these historic processes and American society has gained hugely from the endless renewal of its human resources. In living up to its best traditions, the United States may ensure that the worst will not happen.

There may also be much to be gained by thinking anew about the relations between culture and politics. Cultural differences need not necessarily be a source of conflict, though they may become so if people are encouraged to believe that they are. The problem with Huntington's theory is not his argument that culture has become more salient in the post-Cold War world but in the relationship he posits between culture and politics. Arguably he has the relationship the wrong way round. The case can be made that it is not the conflict of cultures which gives rise to political conflict and war but political conflict, and especially the collapse of political authority, which provokes cultural conflict. Indeed, this case has been made convincingly by Michael Ignatieff in relation to the wars resulting from the collapse of Yugoslavia.[48] To the extent that there is a relationship between ethnic and religious hatred and an absence of effective political institutions, then concentrated attention to political solutions and structures may in the long run provide resolutions of cultural conflict. It would be folly, for example, to postpone action on a settlement of the Palestinian–Israeli conflict until a condition of perfect trust existed between the two communities. There is a possible analogy here with race relations. It is often said that changes in attitudes cannot be legislated for. However, the evidence from the history of civil rights in the United States and elsewhere in the last forty years suggests that, while legislation does not remove prejudice and fear at a stroke, over time, and in conjunction with the active fostering of new attitudes among young people, it has an educative effect on public opinion. Furthermore, the consequences of doing nothing – i.e. waiting for attitudes to change of themselves – may be catastrophic in so far as it leads people to assume that the expression of prejudice is publicly acceptable. By the same token, active pursuit by the United States of political solutions in the Middle East which focus on the achievement of frameworks of stability may yield over time changes in attitudes which will render cultural difference a positive rather than a negative factor. Nothing is more damaging to the American image in the Middle East than the suspicion that it does not really care about resolving the central conflict between Israel and the Palestinians.

Such aims at the moment may appear utopian, but it is no more than to suggest that the need is for the development of habits of cooperation in American relations with the Islamic world of the sort which have long been present, for example, in American relations with Europe. Relations there rely on numerous mediating institutions and contacts at a variety of levels. Western relations with Islamic countries are sporadic and are not institutionalized to the same degree. Admittedly, American relations with Europe in the post-Second World War period rested on a commonality of interest arising out of the specific circumstances of the Cold War; the habits of cooperation, which included contacts at all levels of government and society, did not grow of themselves. Recognizing precisely where the commonality of interest between the United States and the Islamic world lies will be more challenging, not because it does not exist but because the political and cultural dimensions of the relationship are more complicated than is the case with Europe. The challenge is to develop simultaneously concerted efforts to reach solutions at inter-governmental level and wider networks of contacts and channels of communication to provide a rich soil – common ground – in which such governmental relations can grow. Only in this way can the extremists be isolated in their extremism and cultural determinism give way to the politics of choice.

4 Americanism

A short history

Does anti-Americanism really exist?

In discussions of anti-Americanism certain arguments regularly recur. Criticism of American policies, it is affirmed, must be distinguished from the broader and often irrational sentiment of anti-Americanism. It is necessary to make the distinction, we are told, not only because opposition to America takes many forms and has many different motivations but because, when closely analysed, even the most extreme negative reactions to the United States turn out to have identifiable sources in particular situations of power relations. Taken to its logical conclusion, such arguments result in the view that, for all the hatred directed towards the United States by specific nations or groups on specific grounds, anti-Americanism as such, i.e. a generalized opposition to American life and culture, does not exist. 'There is no such thing as anti-Americanism in the Middle East', declared a member of an audience following a lecture on anti-Americanism given by the present author, 'only specific objections to the record of American policies in the Middle East since 1945.'

Another comment frequently made about anti-Americanism is that such sentiments reveal more about those voicing them than about America. 'Ultimately,' writes a Canadian resident in the United States after 9/11, 'Canadian anti-Americanism says more about Canada than it does about the United States.' Similarly in the French case, notes the author of an essay entitled 'Does Anti-Americanism Exist?', 'it would be impossible to understand French anti-Americanism/pro-Americanism ... without realising that it is part and parcel of an internal French debate that is more or less unrelated to American realities'.[1] On this view, America is the pretext or the occasion for emotions and attitudes which have their sources in the situation of the subject. The case for the existence of a clearly defined sentiment called anti-Americanism loses further credibility.

A further reason for being sceptical about the nature and sources of anti-Americanism is that it assumes that there is a high degree of unity in American society and culture; indeed that there is an identifiable essence of America which can be associated with the term 'Americanism'. Such essentialism, it is claimed, belies the diverse and conflict-ridden character of American society. 'Once you have an appreciation of the conflicting ideologies and cultures within America', writes Brendon O'Connor, 'summing up the essence of America with a pat definition or examples of Americanism seems impossible.'[2] From this standpoint, postulation of something called 'Americanism' smacks of dated studies of the 'American character' in the 1940s and 1950s which assumed the primacy of unifying and consensual factors in American culture and history. 'Consensus history' of this sort comes with so much baggage, not least as far as liberal-minded scholars are concerned its association with politically and intellectually conservative approaches to the study of the United States, that it must be rejected on these grounds alone. The revisionist scholarship of the 1960s and the subsequent proliferation of scholarship across a range of fields presented a kaleidoscopic rather than a unified picture of the United States, putting paid, so it is said, to any naïve consensus theories by demonstrating the deep tensions and fissures beneath the carapace of conformity in the 1950s.[3] Such studies had implications for the study of the United States in general, not merely for the 1950s. If there has been a theme in study of the United States since the 1960s it has emphasized the *e pluribus* rather than the *unum* in the American motto.

In these and other ways it is possible systematically to deconstruct the notion of anti-Americanism. No one disputes that the United States has been the target of much opposition from around the world in recent history, but what is in doubt is whether such opposition adds up to an integrated concept. The difficulty alone of establishing a definition of anti-Americanism – a problem discussed *ad nauseam* in the literature – demonstrates the problem of knowing what is being talked about or indeed whether there is anything to talk about. And yet one is reluctant to abandon the notion entirely if only because the term's currency suggests that there is something to be discussed. It seems prudent to try another tack, to approach the subject indirectly. Given the prevalence of the term it is curious how seldom the spotlight has been turned on the nominal target of anti-Americanism: namely, 'Americanism'. One searches in vain in most histories of American ideas or of American nationalism or even of anti-Americanism for anything more than passing references to 'Americanism'. And yet Americanism does have a history.[4] From the second half of the nineteenth century onwards, it is regularly invoked, discussed, and disputed. Furthermore, since 9/11 there has been a resurgence in usage of the term, with websites devoted to furthering values associated with Americanism. The purpose of this inquiry is to explore this history with a view to contributing to our understanding of anti-Americanism in the present. While the emphasis here is on Americanism rather than the nature of the reactions to it, the broad conclusion is that the emotions and ideas we term anti-American contain a large cultural component. Without denying that anti-Americanism often takes the form of opposition to particular policies or that its roots frequently lie in the motives of those who stand opposed to the United States rather than in America itself, the claim here is that such attitudes are mixed with, or intensified by, the projection of Americanism which we can define as the cultural form in which American nationalism expresses itself. Of course, Americanism is also the source of much positive feeling on the part of non-Americans, but it should come as no surprise that a nation as large, diverse and successful in so many fields as the United States should arouse such contradictory feelings and opinions.

Americanism and Americanisms

We can dispose of certain usages of 'Americanism' fairly quickly since they have specialized meanings and restricted ranges of reference. An 'Americanism', noted the critic and historian of the American language H. L. Mencken, is a 'word taken into the English language which has not gained acceptance in English or retains an element of foreignness'.[5] Specific as this use of the term is, it is nevertheless important to note that it reflects the growing influence of American culture which is associated with the process of 'Americanization' in the latter decades of the nineteenth century and the early years of the twentieth. Indeed, the first full-length study of this theme was published as early as 1901 by the British journalist W. T. Stead.[6] If language is one vital component of culture, then religion is another. 'Americanism' in religion was the name given by the Roman Catholic church around the turn of the twentieth century to what was regarded as the American Catholic bishops' heretical embrace of extreme forms of modern principles such as the separation of church and state, free speech, liberalism in ethics, and in general a predisposition to stake out their own positions on these and other issues rather than relying on the authority of the church. Passing reference should also be given to the view of Julius Streicher, the Nazi ideologue, that 'Americanism' was to be equated with 'the Jewish spirit'.[7] Specialized as these usages are, they demonstrate both a growing influence of the United States beyond its shores and the projection of an identifiable national identity.

Americanism as cultural identity

Americanism, as has been suggested, was a facet of the growth of American nationalism. Nowhere was the question of Americanness more deeply involved than in the field of culture. In the words of literary historian Richard Ruland 'the self-conscious effort to develop a native aesthetic sensibility'[8] was an endless focus of discussion and debate among writers, critics and artists from the outset. However, it appears that this effort became associated with an 'ism' only after the Civil War. Civil War veteran, unitarian minister and writer Thomas Wentworth Higginson wrote in an article published in *Atlantic Monthly* in 1870 that

> the voyager from Europe who lands on our shores perceives a difference in the sky above his head; the height seems loftier, the zenith more remote, the horizon-wall more steep; the moon appears to hang in middle air, beneath a dome that arches far beyond it.

Here, he went on,

> one wishes to be convinced that the intellectual man inhales a deeper breath, and walks a bolder tread; that philosopher and artist are here more buoyant, more fresh, more fertile; that the human race has here escaped at one bound from the despondency of ages, as from their wrongs.

Furthermore,

> the true and healthy Americanism is to be found, let us believe, in this attitude of hope; an attitude not necessarily connected with culture nor with the absence of culture but with the consciousness of a new impulse given to all human progress.

It seemed 'unspeakably important', he concluded, 'that all persons among us, and especially the student and the writer should be pervaded with Americanism ... [which] includes the faith that national-self-government is not a chimera but that, with whatever inconsistencies and drawbacks, we are steadily establishing it here'.[9]

With Higginson we are not yet in the realms of ideology or of militant nationalism but rather of aspiration and hope. His writings on this subject are in the 'optative mood', as Emerson described that sense of endless possibility experienced by the writers and artists of the mid-nineteenth century. American nationhood was still in the making. If it is hard to define exactly what is meant by 'Americanism' at this stage, it is evidently a quality which emerged in the encounter with a physical and social environment which was unlike anything in the Old World. Higginson's reflections on the cultural effects of the American environment stood in a tradition going back at least to Crêvecoeur in his *Letters from an American Farmer* (1782).[10] Indeed it could be argued that the urge to define, assert and celebrate the American difference from Europe was the leading pre-occupation of the major American writers of the nineteenth century. More ambivalent in approach was Henry James, whose exile from America did not, however, mean total repudiation of 'Americanism'. It remained a source of fascination throughout his life and in a sense constituted the chief subject of his work. In his remarkable account of a visit made to America in 1904–5, published as *The American Scene* (1907), James meditated on the grandeur of Washington, DC and wondered what effect the elaborate design of the city would have on the consciousness of Americans and whether it would indeed, as seemed intended, 'prepare thereby the American voter, on the spot and in the pride of possession, quite a new civic consciousness'. In the absence of any conclusive evidence, James observed that:

> There is always, in America, yet another lively source of interest involved in the execution of such designs, and closely involved just in proportion as the high intention, the formal majesty of the thing seems assured. It comes back to what we constantly feel, throughout the country, to what the American scene everywhere depends on for half its appeal or its effect; to the fact that the social conditions, the

material, pressing or pervasive, make the particular experiment or 'demonstration', whatever it may pretend to, practically a new and incalculable thing. This general Americanism is often the one tag of character attaching to the case after every other appears to have abandoned it. The thing is happening, or will have to happen, in the American way – that American way which is more different from all other native ways, taking country with country, than any of these latter are different from each other; and the question is of how, each time, the American way will see it through.[11]

Tangled up in James' elaborate prose is as categorical assertion of 'American exceptionalism' as one can find in this period, though it is hardly an unambiguous celebration of it. Its importance for the present theme is that it identifies certain qualities as distinctively American, even if their precise character is 'incalculable'. It is apparently enough that it is 'new'. America will express itself, and has no choice but to do so in its own way.

Responses to this aspect of American culture have been as varied and often ambiguous as the American expressions of it. Europeans have frequently celebrated America's opportunities and aspirations, as in Goethe's line: 'America, you have it better than our continent ... you have no ruined castles.'[12] But just as often Europeans have been irritated or worse at inflated claims by some Americans for their culture and institutions – both when America was an upstart nation during the nineteenth century and when it took over Europe's role in the twentieth, at which point irritation frequently turned to resentment when American claims for its culture were combined with the power effectively to project it.

Old-fashioned Americanism

Later on others would adopt this seeming determinism of the American way and give it a more militant and threatening political and ideological cast. Meanwhile, though, there were other shades of meaning to 'Americanism' in the post-Civil War decades which were more consonant with the cultural forms of Higginson and James, but which also indicate political applications. In James Russell Lowell's biography of Abraham Lincoln the president emerges as the epitome of the republican idea in his modesty, simplicity, and 'unconsciousness of self':

> Mr Lincoln has never studied Quintilian but he has, in the earnest simplicity and unaffected Americanism of his own character, one art of oratory worth all the rest. He forgets himself so entirely in his object as to give his 'I' the sympathetic and persuasive 'we' with the great body of his countrymen. Homely, dispassionate, showing all the rough-edged processes of his thought as it goes along, yet arriving at his conclusions with an honest kind of every-day logic, he is so evidently our representative man, that, when he speaks, it seems as if the people were listening to their own thinking aloud.[13]

Similar qualities were celebrated in America before Lincoln and also long after him. Benjamin Franklin's doubtless more studied cultivation of simplicity famously endeared him to the courts of Europe as to Americans. In a very different era, when Henry Wallace referred in his speech accepting the nomination as presidential candidate for the Progressive Party in 1948 to 'the old-fashioned Americanism that was built for us by Jefferson, Jackson, Lincoln, Theodore Roosevelt, and Woodrow Wilson', he had the same homely, essentially pre-industrial values associated with heartland America in mind. This notion of Americanism, which has perhaps the same relationship to reality as a Christmas card to Christmas, draws on images of an idealized past and also certain qualities taken to be of perennial value to America's well-being as a society. Such values are embodied in individuals, but in their representative character they image the process whereby individualism becomes a social value.

Americanism as individualism

There are several steps on the way from this picture of a harmonious relationship between individualism as a private value and a public ethic to a more embattled and ideological conception of Americanism as individualism which emerges in the late nineteenth century. On this theme, as on many others, Tocqueville remains an essential guide. Individualism was a central theme of his *Democracy in America* and he used the term in the awareness that it was a new coinage. 'Individualism', he wrote, 'is a recent expression arising from a new idea. Our fathers knew only selfishness.' The novel element in individualism, which distinguished it from selfishness, was that its effects were felt not just in personal behaviour but throughout society:

> individualism disposes each citizen to isolate himself from the mass and to withdraw to one side with his family and friends, so that after having thus created a little society for his own use, he willingly abandons society at large to itself.[14]

Individualism, he suggested, was associated with the growing conditions of equality and the advent of the democratic idea which had progressed further and faster in America than anywhere else. Tocqueville recognized that even in America individualism was mixed with other values which mitigated its worst effects,[15] but there was no disguising its centrality in American society. Tocqueville's insight has proved of lasting significance and interest to generations of observers of the United States.

Any number of examples could be offered to show how deep individualism goes in American culture, but the concern here is specifically to illustrate its connections with the theme of Americanism. One starting point could be Grover Cleveland's presidential inaugural address of 1893 in the perhaps unlikely context of a discussion of the tariff issue. It is hard now to comprehend the degree to which the tariff issue dominated national party politics through the nineteenth century and through the first three decades of the twentieth. The tariff aroused emotions which extended far beyond the economics of the issue; the debate linked with fundamental questions of the role of government and ultimately with moral values. Cleveland's party, the Democrats, were historically in favour of low tariffs which were taken to be of benefit to farmers and the working man, but Cleveland's rhetoric shows very clearly his belief that a great deal more was at stake. The adoption of 'protection for protection's sake', he declared, was 'the bane of republican institutions and the constant peril of our government by the people. It degrades to the purposes of wily craft the plan of rule our fathers established and ... perverts the patriotic sentiments of our countrymen'. And why was the protective tariff so evil? Because it introduced 'paternalism', undermined 'self-reliance', and puts 'in its place dependence upon governmental favouritism'. In short, 'it stifles the spirit of true Americanism and stupefies every ennobling trait of American citizenship'. The lesson for the American people must be that 'while the people should patriotically and cheerfully support their Government, its functions do not include the support of the people'.[16] Once again an effort of imagination is required to grasp the reality that for many Americans, and particularly those in power and/or possessing wealth, the function of government was simply, as the late nineteenth-century sociologist William Graham Sumner is reported to have said, 'to protect property and the honor of women'. This admittedly extreme argument by the high priest of atomistic individualism did not, of course, go unchallenged but Cleveland's statement is close enough to it to suggest that it spoke to the views of many Americans. The early nineteenth-century argument for 'internal improvements' notwithstanding, it is a largely twentieth-century notion that government should be a supplier of goods and services and an active intervener in the economy and society rather than merely a protector of rights and guarantor of external security (an essential function not listed in Sumner's formulation). Needless to say, such anti-statist views often co-existed with a predisposition on the part of business leaders to accept any government largesse which might be available. The private companies which built America's transcontinental railroads sought and gained enormous grants from government. Theoretical consistency could not necessarily be expected in this field or any other. The key point is that American 'individualism' was in principle suspicious of government, and in the nineteenth-century context for a significant proportion of Americans Americanism and individualism were different names for the same thing. Among the most influential ideologists of individualism was Andrew Carnegie who, in his Darwinian proclamation of the 'Gospel of Wealth' (1899) spoke of the 'intense individualism' which was the basis of American and indeed of Western society. More than a generation later President Herbert Hoover extolled the virtues of 'rugged individualism' in defiance of the growing resort to 'collectivist' ideas as the depression took root in the United States.

The advent in the early twentieth century of very different attitudes towards the role of government, stimulated by war and depression, did not lead to the disappearance of the equation between Americanism and individualism, as the example of Hoover demonstrates. It only led to become more extreme and more shrill expressions of it. As progressives and liberals pushed for governmental intervention in the economy and social affairs to regulate the growing power of corporations and to provide safety nets for the poor and unemployed, the advocates of Americanism as individualism mounted a rearguard action which resonated strongly with many Americans who felt that Franklin Roosevelt's New Deal and comparable innovations were against the American way. The beginning of the Cold War intensified the emotions surrounding this issue because the United States was now faced with an enemy whose values were diametrically opposed to those of the United States. In 1946, the year of Winston Churchill's 'Iron Curtain' speech which symbolized the end of any expectation that the wartime alliance with the Soviet Union could be salvaged, the novelist and political writer Ayn Rand published her *Textbook of Americanism*. In truth her ideas were the product, not merely of the outbreak of the Cold War but of her own personal experience of flight from the revolutionary Russia in 1917 and her subsequent dedication to combating communism and Soviet power by any means she could. 'The basic issue in the world today', she wrote, 'is between two principles: Individualism and Collectivism.' According to individualism, 'the power of society is limited by the inalienable individual rights of man. Society may only make such laws as do not violate these rights.' Meanwhile, collectivism says that 'the power of society is unlimited. Society may make any laws it wishes, and force them upon anyone in any manner it wishes.' The United States was self-evidently an embodiment of the principle of individualism and the United States Constitution was the guarantor of that principle. The 'proper function of government' was 'to protect the individual rights of man; this means to protect man against brute force'. Rand took to its logical conclusion the view that there is no such thing as society in her assertion that 'there are no crimes against "society"; all crimes are committed against specific men, against individuals'.[17]

Ayn Rand was briefly an influential figure in the anti-communist cause of the 1940s and 1950s by virtue of her novels – notably *The Fountainhead* which was turned into a film starring Gary Cooper – and her very public stand against communism. In 1947 she appeared as a friendly witness before the House Committee on Un-American Activities.[18] We shall return to the issue of anti-communism under another heading, but for the moment it is important to note the elements of continuity between Ayn Rand's notion of Americanism as individualism and that of figures such as Grover Cleveland, with the singular difference that Ayn Rand's tone is noticeably more militant and combative, as befits the ideological climate of the Cold War. To the militant American individualist, much of the political evolution in America from Franklin Roosevelt's New

Deal onwards has constituted a violation of American individualism and indeed of Americanism. Yet however valid individualism remains as a cultural value, as a basis for a political ethic it
has been firmly marginalized. The intense anti-statism associated
with figures such as Ayn Rand has become a minority and an
embattled position, even if it continues to resonate because of
the depths of its roots in American society and history. To the
extent that it has continued to resonate with Americans it has
also been regarded with bewilderment by many Europeans for
whom such expressions of individualism are deeply anachronistic and out of keeping with the strong statist tradition in
Europe.

Americanism and Americanization

Nothing gets closer to the heart of nationhood than ideas about
who should be admitted as members of the nation and on what
terms. In the well-worn cliché, America is a nation of immigrants. At times of high immigration, such as has been the case
since the 1960s, intense public debate takes place about the
impact on society of large numbers of new citizens, in addition
to the issues posed by illegal immigration. The debate has been
particularly heated in recent years because the main sources of
recent immigration (as a result of changes in immigration law
in the 1960s) have been Asia, Latin America and the Caribbean
rather than the 'old stock' countries of Europe and Canada. The
result has been anxiety that immigration on this scale and of
this type will challenge the values as well as the ethnic compo-
sition of American society. Samuel Huntington's *Who Are We?*
(2004) is the most discussed of these polemics, but the issue
became of huge national significance in the spring of 2006 as
Congress moved to legislate on illegal immigration. What is
significant about this debate, so far as a discussion of Americanism is concerned, is that while the primary focus is on
immigration it also exposes a divide in elite attitudes between
broadly conservative and liberal positions, the conservatives

presenting themselves as the true Americans, defending inherited values and traditions, and liberals being portrayed as un-American to the extent that they endorse policies which are regarded as compromising American identity.

A comparable debate took place between the 1880s and the early 1920s, at which point immigration restriction legislation was passed which severely limited the numbers of incomers and also defined the national origins of permitted immigrants in ways which stemmed the tide of 'new' immigrants. The fear was not only that many of these immigrants adhered to religious faiths – predominantly Catholicism and Judaism – which challenged the dominance of Protestant Christianity, but that they were from countries such as Russia, Poland and Italy which had no experience of democratic politics or liberal society. Many were of peasant origin. Such people could be easily manipulated by unscrupulous political bosses. There were doubts about whether they could assimilate – become true Americans.

It was in this context that the call came to be heard for the assertion of 'true Americanism' or '100 per cent Americanism' in a bid to reaffirm the traditional terms and values of American citizenship. Such calls were not against all immigration but rather for its regulation in the service of Americanism. Among the most prominent advocates of this stance was Theodore Roosevelt, who in 1894 published a call to patriotic arms entitled 'True Americanism'. Significantly, Roosevelt's target was not only immigrants but 'Europeanized' intellectuals whose allegiance to Americanism was as open to doubt as that of certain immigrants. The debate in America, then as now, divided the elite. 'Americanism', he said, 'is a question of spirit, conviction, and purpose, not of creed or birthplace.' But what precisely was 'Americanism'? In the first place it meant an allegiance to the nation rather than a section or local area – an important priority in a nation which was not only large in extent but had experienced a civil war in the not too distant past. America must think nationally and act nationally, its writers 'write as Americans'. Second, Americans must embrace patriotism and eschew cosmopolitanism.

Americanism was a positive choice; passive citizenship would not do. 'One may fall very short of treason', Roosevelt declared,

> and yet be an undesirable citizen in the community. The man who becomes Europeanized, who loses his power of doing good work on this side of the water, and who loses his love for his native land, is not a traitor; but he is a silly and undesirable citizen.

Nor was Roosevelt in any doubt that America was the best of countries. This advocate of 'the strenuous life' had nothing but contempt for those Americans who hankered after European culture. Such individuals were 'weaklings who seek to be other than Americans'. Should they choose to live in Europe (was he thinking of Henry James?), 'he becomes a second-rate European, because he is over-civilized, over-sensitive, over-refined, and has lost the hardihood and manly courage by which alone he can conquer in the keen struggle of our national life'. The third aspect of Americanism meant thorough assimilation of newcomers into the national life, a deliberate cutting off of themselves from the language, customs and way of life of the old country. In short, the immigrant must become 'thoroughly Americanized'.[19] Woodrow Wilson urged the same result, if with less strenuous breast-beating, when he told a group of newly naturalized citizens in Philadelphia in 1915, that

> a man who thinks of himself as belonging to particular national group in America has not yet become an American, and the man who goes among you to trade upon your nationality is no worthy son to live under the stars and stripes.[20]

As American participation in the First World War loomed, Theodore Roosevelt's temperature rose further. To fail to embrace 'thorough-going Americanism' was to be 'un-American'. Nor, once again, was this simply a matter for immigrants: 'we must make Americanism and Americanization mean the same thing to the native born and to the foreign born; to the men and to the women; to the rich and to the poor; to the employer and to the wage-worker'.[21] Americanism was the ultimate solvent of all differences.

It should not be thought that this form of Americanism went uncontested. Henry James, who doubtless felt himself personally attacked in Roosevelt's comments on the Europeanized American, noted that Roosevelt 'appears to propose ... to tighten the screws of the national consciousness as they have never been tightened before', and this at a time when the connections between nations were becoming ever closer and more ramified by virtue of the global expansion of transport and communications. James refused to rise to Roosevelt's bait, kept his tone level and contented himself with noting the 'puerility of his simplifications'.[22] In a very different key was the approach taken by essayist and political radical Randolph Bourne to the sort of argument presented by Roosevelt. His writings are of particular value to the historian of Americanism since Bourne was not content merely with a critique of the model proposed by the likes of Roosevelt but proposed an alternative model of citizenship which is of continuing relevance. His starting point was the failure of the melting pot theory – a point which he shared with the advocates of immigration restriction, if for very different reasons. The outbreak of the war in Europe in 1914 had starkly revealed the existence of 'diverse nationalistic feelings among our great alien population' which in turn had provoked 'hardhearted Brahmins' to righteous indignation at the 'spectre of the immigrant refusing to be melted' along with insistence on forcible assimilation 'to that Anglo-Saxon tradition which they unquestioningly label "American"'. The conclusion should be, not to admit the failure of Americanization but 'rather to urge us to investigation of what Americanism might rightly mean'. In Bourne's view it meant in the first instance acknowledging that America was 'a unique sociological fabric'. Exceptionalism was evidently not a preserve of militant nationalists. America's unique feature lay in the absence of a 'native "American" culture'. There was no distinctively American culture, but 'rather a federation of cultures'. Furthermore, to accept this fact about America was at last to look to the future rather than the past. So long as Americanism was thought of in terms of the melting pot,

> our American cultural tradition lay in the past. It was something to which Americans were to be moulded. In the light of our changing ideal of Americanism, we must perpetuate the paradox that our American cultural tradition lies in the future. It will be what we all together make out of this incomparable opportunity of attacking the future with a new key.

In defiance of the Rooseveltian injunction to spurn cosmopolitanism, Bourne embraced the 'cosmopolitan ideal'.[23]

Bourne's acceptance of the possibility of dual allegiance to the old country and the new, coupled with his advocacy of 'dual citizenship', was highly provocative in the climate of the times, which was one of a military 'preparedness' campaign in which a premium was placed on national unity. In a sense Bourne's article was an anti-war manifesto even before American entry into the First World War, which came a year after the essay was published. The story of Bourne's stance against the war, his death in the flu epidemic of 1918, and the posthumous publication of his coruscating manuscript 'The State' made him the stuff of legend for the radical left. As far as the theme of Americanism is concerned, Bourne's significance lies in the fact that he demonstrated an alternative pluralistic reading of the American project which has nevertheless always had to run the gauntlet of the less complicated and apparently more plausible idea of unitary nationalism.

However, Bourne's stance was and has remained a minority position, not merely because of the inflammatory potential of the immigration issue but because war, and hence pressure for loyalty to the nation, has featured so large in the twentieth and twenty-first centuries. The First World War posed a particular challenge to the United States, both because America had large sections of population from belligerents on both sides, and because participation meant the abandonment of the hallowed principle of non-entanglement in European affairs. Indeed, Wilson had sought for two years to avoid entering the war in part in order not to provoke splits in the nation, and he fought the election of 1916 on the slogan 'He kept us out of the war.' However, once the decision was made to embark on a mission to 'make the world safe for democracy', Wilson believed it possible to avoid the development of 'war-mindedness' and announced with great optimism that America's participation would be on a more detached and benign basis then of the other belligerents because America's was not for gain. It was not to be. Wilson and his government became caught up in the emotions of war, not least because of the existence of consider-able domestic opposition which challenged the government to make its case vigorously. The government resorted not only to Espionage and Sedition Acts to silence the most radical voices but also to modern techniques of advertising and propaganda to sell the message of the war to the people. Former journalist George Creel, made head of a Committee for Public Informa-tion, was charged with this task, which he took up with relish, employing the concept of 'Americanism' as his most important tool. The title of his account of this campaign was *How We Advertised America: The First Telling of the Amazing Story of the Committee on Public Information That Carried the Gospel of Americanism to Every Corner of the Globe* (1920). The fight for Americanism became indissolubly linked with the war effort.

After the First World War it is rare to find 'Americanism' used in anything other than a highly charged way, embodying asso-ciations with militant nationalism, the drive for unity in the nation and conformity to a limited and uncomplicated set of ideals. There were occasional challenges, as we shall see, but they were sporadic and generally ineffective. More characteristic of the post-First World War period was the appropriation of the term by the Ku Klux Klan.[24] Originally founded during the post-Civil War period of Reconstruction, the Klan's goal was to resist the efforts by the North to impose its will on the defeated South. Using tactics of intimidation and terror, the Klan waged a guerrilla war against the Reconstruction governments, whose members in some instances now included former slaves, with the aim of reasserting white supremacy in the South. The organization faded by the early 1870s as the North grew weary of Reconstruction, but it was revived in 1915, coinciding with the screening of D. W. Griffith's film *Birth of a Nation* which gave a rendering of Reconstruction which was sympathetic to the Southern position. By the early 1920s it had accumulated around a million members and held significant political power in half a dozen states in the North as well as the South. The Klan's target now was wider than it had been in its first incarnation. Its self-styled responsibility was to 'speak for the great mass of Americans of the old pioneer stock'. Under the banner of 'Americanism' the Klan's Imperial Wizard, Hiram Evans, sought to defend and promote the interests of the 'Nordic race, the race which, with all its faults, has given the world almost the whole of modern civilization'. Behind his message was the sense of marginalization, which was at once moral, economic, political and social, of 'Nordic Americans' over the last generation – in effect the period of industrialization and urbanization in America. The Nordic American, said Evans, 'is a stranger in large parts of the land his father gave him', a consequence of a falling birth-rate among old stock Americans, economic disasters caused by immigrant taking over American jobs, 'moral breakdown' including the violation of the 'sacredness of the Sabbath', and the assumption of political control by urban 'bosses' commanding the votes of 'every kind of inhabitants except the Americans'. The First World War, Evans concluded, had revealed the true cause of the troubles of the old stock Americans, which was the disloyalty of numerous incomers or aliens whose passage to the United States apparently did not alter their national allegiance.

Like Randolph Bourne, Hiram Evans regarded the melting pot theory as having failed, but he drew the opposite conclusion: namely, that the fault lay with those who apparently refused to melt rather than with the society which demanded that they do so. The Jews were singled out as being among those who 'most determinedly refuse to melt' but the charge extended somewhat indiscriminately to Catholics and to the swathes of recently arrived 'aliens' in cities. Between 1900 and 1914 close to a million immigrants arrived in the US, bringing the proportion of foreign-born in the United States to a new high. African-Americans were also targets, and to that extent the Klan of 1915 was a holdover from the post-Civil War decade.[25]

However, the animus of the new Klan was also directed at what it regarded as the moral decay of the nation, which could be summed up in the word 'liberalism'. This meant a departure from the moral and religious values which lay at the heart of American civilization. Liberalism denied the reality of the difference between right and wrong and it undermined religion by casting doubt on the literal meaning of the Bible. The real authors of decline, Evans was convinced, were a certain section of the ruling elite who had presided over the betrayal of 'Americanism'.[26] The immigrants and ethnics who refused to melt were merely pawns in the game. The Klan's fight was thus a revolt of the 'plain people' against what Evans termed 'intellectually mongrelised liberals',[27] and to that extent was only one episode in the long series of culture wars in the United States which have pitted the American heartland – as much sociological as a geographical conception – against the sophisticated intellectualized urban elites. Long before the era of Senator McCarthy, liberalism was presented as a polar opposite to Americanism. Liberalism was simply un-American. 'Liberalism', Evans thundered, 'is today charged in the mind of most Americans with nothing less than national, racial and spiritual reason.'[28]

The Americanism of the KKK was backward-looking and inward-looking. While some of the sources of the Klan's anxieties lay in the conditions in Europe which led people to emigrate to the United States, the Klan was scarcely interested in these remote causes. It was the local effect of immigration in the United States which preoccupied the Klan. It was backward-looking in that it sought the revival of a clearer, simpler America in which the small man was king. The Klan was acutely aware of its image as a collection of 'hicks', 'rubes', and 'drivers of second-hand Fords', and recognized that its lack of public relations skills was a serious handicap. But it wore its garb of simplicity with pride and rested its case on the conviction that its cause was right and was based on ancient values going back to the dawn of civilization. However, because its Americanism excluded so many categories of Americans, because its methods were so often vicious and illegal, and because elements of its leadership were revealed to be corrupt, it was unable to present itself as anything other than a pressure group for a discontented minority, however significant its message might prove to be in the short term. As a vehicle for the promotion of Americanism the KKK's success was limited, even if as a white supremacist organization it continued to exist in the South.

The KKK can hardly be taken as representative of American attitudes, but it did express anxieties which have surfaced on a number of occasions in the past and continue to have echoes in present debates about American national identity. From outside America, this strain of Americanism as Americanization looks deeply troubling, given the historical experience in twentieth-century Europe of demands to submerge one's identity into that of the nation. While it is true that the phenomenon of large-scale immigration from developing nations is shared by all developed countries, meaning that issues of assimilation are universal, in no other country does the debate about immigration seem to attach so firmly to the question of national identity. The explicitness of the American national creed strikes many outside observers as potentially threatening not only to incomers to America but also, in its sweeping universalism, to the life of other cultures and nations. In a globalizing world,

America's ideas about its own identity have implications far beyond America's shores.

Americanism as political ideology: anti-communism and beyond

The twentieth century presented new challenges to the advocates of Americanism, and these grew largely from the United States' growing international involvement. The First World War was a turning point. While the history textbooks still often speak of a 'retreat to isolationism' in the interwar period, following the Senate's failure to approve the Treaty of Versailles and the consequent American absence from the League of Nations, in actuality the First World War initiated new connections between America and the world across the spectrum of economic, cultural, and even political relations. The United States' new status as an international creditor created complex economic ties with European nations; its largest companies established branches in several European countries, including such new multinationals as Ford and Proctor and Gamble. American music and American films swept Europe. The United States was a key player in efforts to control naval armaments in the 1920s. None of this amounted to the assumption by the United States of an international political role consonant with its economic power – it is important not to replace the fiction of isolationism with the fiction of total involvement – but the First World War did initiate a sea-change in American perceptions of the outside world and the outside world's perception of America.

One of the many new organizations established in the wake of World War I, reflecting America's new relationship with the world beyond its shores, was the American Legion. Founded in Paris in 1919 by officers of the American Expeditionary Force, its goal was, in the words of the preamble to the Legion's constitution:

> To uphold and defend the Constitution of the United States of America; to maintain law and order; to foster and perpetuate

a one hundred percent Americanism; to preserve the memories and incidents of our association in the Great Wars; to inculcate a sense of individual obligation to the community, state and nation; to combat the autocracy of both the classes and the masses; to make right the master of might; to promote peace and goodwill on earth; to safeguard and transmit to Posterity the principles of justice, freedom and democracy, to consecrate and sanctify our comradeship by our devotion to mutual helpfulness.[29]

The Legion was a civilian organization, though membership was limited to members of the armed forces, including the Coast Guard. No ranks existed in the organization and no military titles were to be used. It was also 'absolutely non-political', though politicians over the years have often found it in their interest to accept invitations to address the organization. Besides, the term 'non-political' meant only that the Legion would not engage in partisan political activity, not that it would avoid political questions in its work. Indeed the Legion took a lead in the drive, which began in the 1930s, against 'un-American activity' and was an active promoter of Americanism from the outset, as its constitution promised. This continues today.

In a general way it is clear what the Legion was for since it was spelled out in the preamble to the constitution quoted above. Its message was sharper edged, however, when it came to defining what it was against, as is evident in its 1937 publication *Isms: A Review of Alien Isms, Revolutionary Communism and Their Active Sympathizers in the United States*. From the start the Legion was sensitized to the dangers of communism. The year the Legion was founded (1919) was also the year in which the third Communist International was established, with the goal of promoting communism globally. *Isms* was produced by a sub-group of the Legion called the National Americanism Commission, and the report took the form of a detailed history of 'un-American activity' in the United States from the foundation of the Communist Party of the USA (CPUSA), through recognition of the Soviet Union by the United States in 1933 (a move initiated by the incoming President Franklin Roosevelt and which the Legion deplored) to details of Soviet subversion in the United States and its use of front organizations such as labour and pacifist groups, and data on communist propaganda outlets such as bookshops, newspapers, and magazines. It was the sort of material which would become familiar in the anti-communist drive after World War II. Indeed, the forerunner of the post-war House Committee on Un-American Activities (HCUA), the Dies Committee, was set up in 1938, in part at the prompting of the American Legion. The book ends with a short section on Nazism, reprinted from a Congressional committee, though it is clear that for the Legion (as for the Dies Committee) communism presented by far the deepest challenge to the United States. Communism was godless, it was destructive of private property, it sought to destroy representative democracy and ultimately to establish the dictatorship of the proletariat by means of world revolution.[30]

The agenda of the HCUA and of Senator McCarthy after the Second World War was essentially that of the American Legion, which had pushed hard for such a committee to be established and supported its message at every opportunity. Despite this element of consistency, the important change in the post-war decade was that anti-communism now had a national platform and was able to exert considerable pressure on the Truman administration. The external fact of the outbreak of Cold War was the obvious trigger for change. Its effect was to render suspect all political opinion left of a not very precisely defined centre, the litmus test being the attitude to communism itself. Open support for communism was clearly beyond the pale, as was fellow-travelling (that is, endorsement short of actually joining the Party). Equally suspect, however, were views which tended to show an understanding of the Soviet position, one example being that of Secretary of Agriculture Henry Wallace, who was forced to resign after making a speech in which he conceded that the Soviets had a right to a sphere of influence in

Eastern Europe to match that of the United States in Latin America. His crime was that of assuming a moral equivalence between the United States and the Soviet Union. Those who called themselves liberals were thus forced to redefine their liberalism in such a way as to meet the anti-communist test. An example here is Arthur Schlesinger Jr's re-casting of liberalism as 'the vital center' which sought explicitly to avoid any confusion between liberalism and sympathy – however mild – for communism or Marxism.[31]

Historians dispute about how far Truman was himself responsible for fomenting the anti-communist crusade. Was the cornerstone of his foreign policy – the so-called Truman Doctrine of support for free peoples everywhere against the threat of communism – an overreaction which helped to heighten tension with the Soviet Union and raise the temperature at home? Was his Loyalty Programme of 1947, which required government employees to undergo stringent checks on their political opinions, a clever move to head off more drastic legislation by a hostile Congress, or did it play into the hands of vigilante-like apostles of Americanism? Conceivably both propositions were true.[32] Certainly Truman and his administration, along with actors, writers, union leaders and others, came under virulent attack for being 'soft on communism' and via Congressional investigations in many cases were forced to make an account of their stance towards communism. In this climate, as journalist Gary Wills has written, 'it was not enough to be American in citizenship or residence – one must be American in one's thoughts. There was such a thing as Americanism. And lacking right thinking could make an American citizen un-American.'[33] Wills' comments were those of a historian and critic bewailing the excesses of the times. For those such as J. Edgar Hoover, who had cut his teeth as an anti-communist in the post-World War I 'Red Scare', Americanism was the solution, not the problem. In testimony before the HCUA in 1947 he asked: 'What can we do? And what should be our course of action?' The best antidote to communism, he answered, was 'vigorous, intelligent old-fashioned Americanism with external vigilance'.[34] There is some irony in his employment of the phrase 'old-fashioned Americanism', given, as we have seen, Henry Wallace's use of the same term in the election of 1948 when he stood as a Progressive, the party he formed which was well to the left of the Democrats and was even endorsed by the CPUSA. Evidently 'old-fashioned Americanism' meant very different things to different people.

The Cold War had the effect of cementing the association of Americanism with a militant national ideology. It went so deep and was so hard to shift because it was a response to a real external threat which challenged not only American power but also American values. The Soviet system was not only different but systematically opposed to the values of the United States since Marxism-Leninism was founded in direct contradistinction to the capitalist West. But this notion of Americanism took such a hold also because it was congruent with earlier notions: with Americanism as an exceptionalist culture, Americanism as individualism, and Americanism as Americanization. As suggested earlier, an element of continuity in values is of the essence in American history.

As a focus for anti-Americanism, the projection of American political ideology did not begin or end with the Cold War. Indeed, the war on terror since 9/11 brought American ideological militancy once again to the fore in the form of the neo-conservative-influenced agenda of George W. Bush. Americanism has appeared resurgent in Bush's America, as we shall see later. America is mobilized again, and when America mobilizes, Americanism provides essential fuel both for the national mission and for the negative reaction to it from outside. To put it bluntly, such occasions remind others of how different America is and of how much power it has to project that difference.

Alternative Americanism

For all that has been said in the foregoing pages, it is evident that Americanism as it has been characterized here was not the only or even at all times the dominant idea in the United States. And yet even those opposed to the versions of militant Americanism described above felt a need to address Americanism in their own terms. We have already seen that Henry James and Randolph Bourne in their very different ways set direct challenges to the narrow and oppressive Americanism expressed by Theodore Roosevelt. Bourne's was a case for a pluralistic and liberal Americanism which accepted diversity and mixed loyalties on the part of the American citizens. A different version of an argument for mixed loyalties was mounted by the CPUSA in its bid in the late 1930s to appropriate the label for its own purposes. 'Communism', said Willam Z. Foster, 'is twentieth century Americanism.' The immediate occasion for the CPUSA's partial accommodation to non-socialist 'progressive' parties was the need to establish a common front against the rise of fascism. Many in the party accused the leadership of selling out, but it has been pointed out that the CPUSA's Americanism was seized on enthusiastically by young second-generation immigrants in the Party, many of them Jewish, who saw in the CPUSA a possible vehicle for their assimilation to American life. 'As Communists', writes Maurice Isserman, 'they were part of an organization in which (in numbers admittedly unrepresentative of the country as a whole) they could meet and work with Connecticut Yankees, Georgia and Harlem blacks, Northwestern Finns, and Midwestern Poles.' The party served as 'a bridge between the Russian origins and socialist beliefs of their parents and the "progressive" borderlands of New Deal America'.[35] Needless to say, such a move cut little ice with the establishment guardians of 'true Americanism'. It was regarded as a subversive ploy and doubtless also as a perversion of the word Americanism. The CPUSA's bid for Americanism was launched at the time the American Legion was compiling its report on 'alien isms'. Nevertheless, it is of some significance that two such opposite-leaning groups should have appealed to the same symbol. In principle, Americanism is a consensual ideology; yet everything depends on how it is defined and who manages to dictate the definition.

Complications of another sort are introduced by the example of gangster Al Capone, who did for organized crime what the CPUSA attempted to do for communism – to align it with the American way. In an interview held in 1929 with British journalist Claud Cockburn, Capone protested his loyalty to 'the American system'. 'Listen', said Capone,

> don't you get the idea I'm one of those goddam radicals. Don't get the idea I'm knocking the American system. ... My rackets are run on strictly American lines and they're going to stay that way. ... This American system of ours, call it Americanism, call it Capitalism, call it what you like, gives to each and every one of us a great opportunity if only we seize it with both hands and make the most of it.[36]

It is possible that Capone's protestations would receive more credence among the guardians of Americanism in the United States than would the claims of the CPUSA, since Capone's individualism and ethic of opportunity sat more comfortably with the commonly accepted meaning of Americanism.

Further perspectives on Americanism can be gained from a range of scholarly works which appeared in the decade after the Second World War. Max Lerner, Louis Hartz, and the British author and Labour Party politician Harold Laski published comprehensive studies of American culture and history of the sort which few have attempted since then except in the form of multi-authored encyclopaedic compilations. Each of these studies constituted in its own way a critique of Americanism, written in a period in which a strident and ideological form of Americanism was current. In his interpretation of American democracy which is notable for its balanced view of the United States, Laski wrote that Americanism was flawed to the extent that it became a

> beatification of things as they are, which is a denial of one of the central principles of American history, the right of

Americans to change the substance of their social institutions and the directions they may seek in their voyage
through life.

In Laski's analysis Americanism was an analytical term describing the complex of values which constituted American 'civilization', but it always had the potential to be simplified and
reduced to a rigid formula.[37] Max Lerner, in a comparably
compendious volume entitled *America as a Civilization* (1957),
offered the perhaps predictable liberal critique of Americanism
that it was a device used by politicians for enforcing ideological
conformity and discriminating against ethnic minorities.[38]
Louis Hartz's influential *The Liberal Tradition in America* (1955)
explored the arresting thesis that the defining characteristic of
the American political tradition was an irrational devotion to
the rational liberal philosophy of John Locke. In Hartz's analysis,
'Lockean liberalism' and 'Americanism' were the same thing
and they brought with them 'the danger of unanimity' and (in
Tocqueville's phrase) 'the tyranny of opinion'. The 'compulsive
power' of liberalism was so great that it 'posed a threat to liberty itself'.[39] Hartz's thesis provoked much debate on the
grounds that it apparently took to an extreme the consensus
theory of American history, but for present purposes the
important point is that Hartz was deeply out of sympathy with
the consensus.

And yet, for all the critiques one can find of Americanism, for
all the counter-currents and alternatives on offer at various
points in America's past, these were not generally the loudest or
most effective voices when it came to debates about the core
values of the United States. Carl Schurz, a German émigré from
the revolutions of 1848 who became influential in the liberal
reform movement of the late nineteenth century in America,
aimed to rescue Americanism from the hyper-patriotism of figures such as Theodore Roosevelt when, in a lecture given in
1896, he sought to distance Americanism from jingoism and
militarism. America, he said, should not

swagger among the nations of the world, with a chip on its shoulder, shaking its fist in everybody's face. ... It should be so invariably just and fair, so trustworthy, so good-tempered, so conciliatory, that other nations would instinctively turn to it as their mutual friend and natural adjuster of their differences, thus making it the greatest preserver of the world's peace.

Is not this, he concluded, 'good Americanism' to set against the recent 'loose speech about "Americanism"'.[40] However, it is the Roosevelts rather that the Schurzes who have been heard down the years in America, and it is the militant voices which have generally been projected abroad and become associated in the minds of non-Americans with 'Americanism'. During the 1920s the philosopher John Dewey suggested that 'Americanism as a form of culture did not exist, before the war, for Europeans. Now it does exist and as a menace.' Moreover, he noted with some alarm, 'no world-conquest, whether that of Rome or Christendom, compares with that of "Americanism" in extent or effectiveness'.[41]

The association Dewey made between war and the projection of Americanism surely helps to account for its salience in the twentieth century. It is clear also that an elective affinity exists between Americanism and conservatism.[42] It has always been easier for those on the right to substantiate their claims to be representative of American values. There is always the sense that liberal and leftist ideas have their sources outside America and that the allegiance of those who hold such ideas is compromised thereby, however hard those on the left have asserted that they too are real Americans. These conclusions hold true today. The presidency of George W. Bush is living proof of the continuity of Americanism. Americanism is news in a way it has not been since the early years of the Cold War. Among the many websites which have sprung up since the new millennium is 'Common Sense Americanism', whose list of contributors reads like an honour role of post-Second World War American conservative intellectuals and journalists, including William F. Buckley, Robert Novak, William Safire, Phyllis Schlafly, George Will, Jack Kemp, Charles Krauthammer, and Rush Limbaugh.[43] The organization is devoted to 'rediscovering our foundations' and aims to restore faith in and promote knowledge of the US Constitution and an array of values which are conceived to underpin the 'unique and successful experience we call Americanism'. These values include, among others, 'faith in a greater power', 'a rooted concept of morality', and 'the role of truth'. To this site must be added the activities of the American Legion, the Americanism Education League and associations such as the Freemasons which continue to promote the value of Americanism.[44]

Perhaps it is not surprising that in a climate of mobilization for a war on terror, challenges should have arisen to the concept of Americanism purveyed by such organizations and implicitly by the Bush administration itself. Under the headline 'The War on Americanism', one dissenter declared: 'forget the war on terrorism. The president is now engaged in a full-blown war on Americanism.' If, he said, Americanism 'includes such essentials as freedom, responsibility, justice, humanity, respect and fairness ... then George Bush is indeed at war with Americanism' – witness Abu Ghraib, Guantanamo Bay, numerous violations of international law, violations of civil rights at home, equivocation on global warming, and so on. 'However counterintuitive', this critic concluded,

> it is hard to reach but one conclusion about a president who has bankrupted America morally, fiscally and militarily, who has alienated the world and deeply divided his own country, and who has trampled roughshod over our most sacred liberties, as if he were some sort of self-appointed king.[45]

This voice can be added to those of earlier dissenters from conservative Americanism, but as in the cases already discussed it is a small voice of protest against a dominant tradition. For the

most part Americanism was and remains a conservative preserve. The values listed by 'Common Sense Americanism' as
being fundamental to Americanism are among those most fer-
vently invoked by the Bush administration. The first of these
principles, 'faith in a greater power', is integral to the politics of
George W. Bush and many in his administration, as is the
emphasis on the founding values and their continuity in American history. 'I will bring the values of our history to the care of
our times', declared President Bush in his first inaugural
address.[46] Of no less significance is a factor which is harder to
be precise about but which is nevertheless essential to Bush and
to the advocates of Americanism: namely, an unembarrassed
sense of national pride which goes beyond simple patriotism or
indeed the 'old fashioned Americanism' of the nineteenth century, but extends to the conviction that America stands for
something much larger than the nation, that America is indeed
an 'ism'. It is surely plausible to conclude that part of what we
term anti-Americanism attaches to this potent element in
America's culture.

As we have seen, Americanism has a long history and has
accumulated a variety of mutually reinforcing associations along
the way. At the same time it has resisted attempts by liberals and
others to soften its edges or to inject complications or counter-
propositions into the concept. The issue for non-Americans
must be how to keep in mind that the complex of abstractions
called 'Americanism' does not represent the whole of America,
try as its advocates might to suggest that it does. As far as
American advocates of Americanism are concerned, one must
assume that there will continue to be a competition for the right
to define the content of the term. For the foreseeable future it
appears that the Right will maintain its ascendancy. Its hold
looks simply too powerful to be easily dislodged. American
progressives and liberals might reflect on whether it is wise to
seek the mantle of 'Americanism' for themselves, since the
associations of the term are so strongly with a tradition of
thought which is inimical to liberalism.[47] Moreover, it must be

asked whether it is wise to seek to define the nation's values in terms of a one-word slogan, not merely because it is so reductive and resistant to complexity but because in its very goal of inclusiveness it is bound to exclude many people and ideas. This does not mean abandoning the justified and necessary attempt to reinstate liberalism and progressivism in the American mainstream, but it does mean challenging the notion that American ideals can usefully be described in terms of 'Americanism'. 'Americanism' may be the problem, not the solution.

5 What's the big idea?

Models of global order in the post-Cold War world

Globalization and structural change

Fundamental structural change is a relative rarity in international politics. Wars have tended to mark the boundaries of particular systems, though not every war produces systemic change. The Peace of Westphalia at the end of the Thirty Years War is conventionally held to be the beginning of the modern nation-state system, since in that settlement were enshrined the ideas of national sovereignty and balance of power, as well as the beginnings of international law, which have been guiding principles of international politics since the seventeenth century – or at least until the late twentieth century.[1] Among scholars and observers of international affairs there is widespread agreement that the closing years of the twentieth century saw another of those great divides, even if the transition to a new system or a 'new world order' is not yet complete. At the centre of such discussions is the waning significance of the nation-state as the basic unit and organizing principle of the international system. The argument is not that the nation-state is disappearing but that, in the telling words of one analysis, it is being 'hollowed out'.[2] According to this view, globalization and its attendant processes have undermined the nation-state both from above and below. Internally many states are splitting into pieces on the basis of ethnic, religious, and/or linguistic differences; externally, numerous inter- or multinational organizations, especially large companies, have garnered powers larger than those of many nation-states, and even governments of large states are subject to forces, especially trade and financial fluctuations, which severely restrict their independence. Numerous non-governmental organizations (NGOs) in a wide variety of fields play important roles which involve routinely working across national borders. 'Interdependence' is frequently described as the operating principle of international politics. Even the term *international* politics is often held to be a misnomer, 'world politics' being considered more apt.[3]

Deciding exactly how significant recent changes are in the light of long-term processes is difficult, if not at this stage impossible. It is easy, for example to overstate the degree of continuity in the nation-state system between the seventeenth and twentieth centuries; the 'system', in so far as it can be described as such, accommodated numerous radical changes, not least the French Revolution, the Napoleonic wars, and the world wars of the twentieth century. The changes we observe now in international politics may simply be comparable shifts within a basically continuous system based as ever on the nation-state. After all, there is good evidence that the national principle is thriving as never before. In 1945 the world contained approximately 50 nation-states, while by 2006 the number was over 190. It would be paradoxical indeed if we should identify this multiplication with the death of the nation-state. On the other hand, can we really describe the United States and, say, Nauru as belonging to the same political species? Admittedly, these are extremes (the population of Nauru is 12,000) but there is sufficient variation in size, power and influence among the world's nations to throw some doubt on the notion that one model of the nation-state can encompass the variety of existing states. There are, of course, rejoinders to this claim and no doubt counter-rejoinders. There is evidently no sure way of measuring the long-term significance of the processes associated with globalization. What can be said is that traditional, or Westphalian, ideas of the nation-state have come under severe challenge.

Such notions have been reinforced by the global changes associated with the end of the Cold War. Globalization has been under way for decades but the end of the Cold War brought it to a new stage. Indeed, it could be argued that the end of the Cold War was in part a *result* of globalization and the failure of the Soviet bloc economies to respond to its challenges, not least the revolution in information technology. As some theorists would have it, the end of the Cold War brought globalization to fruition on the basis of global capitalism and the all but universal acceptance of the idea of democracy. Even those who do not accept the strong or triumphalist version of this argument – most obvious in Francis Fukuyama's theory of the 'end of history' – recognize that the removal of the communist challenge hastened the development of new levels of transnational activity, especially in the economic field.

Viewed from this perspective, the collapse of the Berlin Wall was of greater significance for the world political system than were the terrorist attacks of September 11, 2001. Devastating as these attacks were, they did not produce structural change, which is to say a fundamental change in the relationship between the units of the international system. Indeed, the attacks could be said to have been in part a consequence of the structural change brought about by the end of the Cold War. During the Cold War, mutual deterrence and the associated policies of containment served to check the behaviour not only of the superpowers but of insurgent groups whose activities might have influenced relations between the superpowers. International terrorism, while certainly not a new phenomenon, thrived on the new elements of instability in world politics attendant on the end of the Cold War.[4]

Given that these events and processes are so close to us, there is no sure way of fully gauging their scale or significance. One possible measure of change, however, is the degree of consciousness of change as manifested in public discussion. What is indisputable at the beginning of the twenty-first century is the multiplicity of *models* of global politics available. Big ideas are in vogue. The period since the end of the Cold War has been immensely fertile in models of the global political system. It seems generally accepted that what happened in 1989–91 was not just the collapse of communism or even of antagonism between two opposing systems of ideology and government, but something more abstract – the end of a particular conception of world order. That the ideas on offer were so varied and in many cases contradictory suggests that there were deep-lying processes at work. Furthermore, the centrality of the United States in many of these models, if in some cases only by implication, indicates something important about both the United States and the global political system: namely, their integral character. The United States is often a factor in many situations where it is not apparently directly involved. Even a non-decision on the part of the United States can have as much impact as a decision by many another power. Hence the routine use of the term 'hegemony' to describe the United States, even by those who have no particular ideological or theoretical axe to grind.[5]

In what follows I propose to examine a range of American 'big ideas' about the shape of the post-Cold War world and America's place in it with three ends in view. First, as has been indicated, the proliferation of models of world politics and their variety is itself suggestive of upheaval. Characteristically, attempts to understand the contemporary world on a grand scale, especially those associated with theories of historical development, achieve the widest audiences at times of crisis or fundamental change.[6] More particularly, in such circumstances debate focuses on the very terms of analysis, throwing basic assumptions about international order into question. An examination of the range of ideas about global order offers clues to the nature and scale of changes in the material world.

Second, it is surely no accident that the bulk of the influential big ideas about world politics should have originated in the United States and in one way or another seek to understand and justify particular conceptions of the United States's place in the international order – and this includes the writing of those such as

Noam Chomsky who are most critical of the United States.[7] Evidently the success of a big idea depends not merely on its content but also on its provenance. To put it another way, America's hegemony operates in the theoretical as well as the practical realm. Third, I wish to suggest that, varied as the models of world politics are, they have in common that they miss, or perhaps take for granted, an important dimension of the global reality: namely, the distinctive character and salience of American nationalism. I will suggest that the connections between American nationalism and globalizing tendencies in the world system provide important clues to the workings of the system and help to explain the continuous contestation of American power.

In order to lay foundations for discussion, two further preliminaries are necessary. First, it is important to distinguish this inquiry from debate about whether US foreign policy has a grand design and more particularly whether the United States found itself 'bereft of strategy' with the end of the Cold War.[8] This question is certainly related to the issue of conceptions of global order but is not identical with it. While the difficulty of creating a grand strategy for the United States in the 1990s was connected to the apparent indeterminacy of the international order, it also had other domestic sources. The concern in this inquiry is not with American policy as such but with the intellectual problem posed by the end of the Cold War. I focus on answers to the question, 'what kind of global system do we live in?', not 'what kind of policies does America need in the post-Cold War world?' Where policy-makers contributed to debate about the shape of the international system – George Bush's New World Order is one example – these are discussed alongside those of foreign-policy intellectuals and commentators. Where appropriate I shall indicate points where big ideas are reflected in government policies and where government policies have stimulated the production of big ideas.

Second, it is worth asking why big ideas are necessary and what functions they perform. In the first place they are designed to make sense of often complex and confusing situations which may have little obvious structure and few obvious ordering principles; in that they sense they have an *explanatory* function. Second, they operate as general plans of action which indicate how best to achieve desired goals. Such schemes are therefore dynamic and have a *strategic* function. Big ideas do not of themselves constitute strategies but are preconditions for them. Third, they serve as *justificatory* mechanisms for possible courses of action. Even if particular courses of action or policies are not envisaged by the authors, conclusions about such actions can be drawn by readers and policy-makers. Above all, in their justificatory role such schemes of thought help to relate ideas of international order to key national values. In short, big ideas set many of the key terms of public discourse about foreign policy and international affairs. Finally, big ideas can be highly revealing in ways their authors are not always aware of, in that they betray unspoken assumptions, prejudices and preconceptions. We can thus use them as windows on the times, clues to tensions and conflicts which are generally unstated.

In order to keep the following analysis within bounds it will be useful to establish some criteria for comparing the schemes. I shall discuss them according to the following four categories:

1 assumptions about the basic unit of global politics (nation-state, civilization, etc.)
2 assumptions about the basic driving force in world politics (national interest, force, economic processes, culture, etc.)
3 judgements about the direction of global change (towards order, disorder, integration, disintegration, etc.)
4 assessments of the role of the United States in global politics (the position it adopts towards other powers, whether the United States' role is fundamentally benign, etc.).

Needless to say, it will not be possible to offer comprehensive analyses of the many schemes under review here. The aim rather is to provide a schematic overview in order to provide means of comparison.

The 'New World Order'

Among the most visible and earliest attempts to re-envisage the post-Cold War system was President George Bush's 'New World Order', announced in a series of speeches between January and March 1991 during the war in the Persian Gulf in response to Iraq's invasion of Kuwait. The war against Iraq, he declared in his 1991 State of the Union Address, was about more than Iraq; it was about 'a big idea, a new world order where diverse nations are drawn together in common cause to achieve universal aspirations of mankind: peace, security, freedom, and the rule of law'.[9] The Wilsonian echoes in this statement are clear, yet Bush's adherence to Wilsonianism or 'liberal internationalism' was less complete than the rhetoric would suggest. Wilson was prepared to sacrifice all to his goal of embedding the League of Nations in the Treaty of Versailles, and in the end he lost virtually all he had striven for. Bush's commitments were more equivocal, more conditional. While there is no reason to doubt that, other things being equal, he would have preferred internationalist solutions across the board, had they been achievable, it is also clear that these would not be pursued at the cost of compromising American national interests. Taking full advantage of the unusual climate of amity, most obviously with respect to the Soviet Union, which followed the collapse of communism, Bush seized the opportunity to declare a vision for the whole world which was at once universalist and American. In the coalition against Saddam Hussein, which included the Soviet Union and many Arab countries – unthinkable during the Cold War – all the traditional polarities of American foreign policy seemed neatly resolved: idealism and realism, internationalism and nationalism, moral consistency and the pursuit of national interest. The sequel, however, demonstrated that neither the Bush administration nor any other in the post-Cold War period would elevate internationalism consistently above nationalism. While the rhetoric of the New World Order continued until the end of Bush's administration, once the immediate goal of removing Iraqi troops from Kuwait had been achieved, the ring went out of the phrase when it became apparent that the element of consensus which had secured this immediate goal would not be forthcoming for more complicated or more controversial ventures. Among these were the establishment of the no-fly zones in Iraq and the crises in Bosnia and Somalia. This is not to say that the 'New World Order' was merely a political ploy, though it was undoubtedly that, but rather to acknowledge that the structure of the international system was insufficiently developed to sustain such a vision. The New World Order, in short, was testimony in part to a kind of euphoria consequent upon the shifting of the tectonic plates of international politics; as in the aftermaths of all wars, the times encouraged a certain expansiveness even arbitrariness of vision. Visions of world government and perpetual peace are never so prevalent as at the ends of wars, and the end of the Cold War was no exception. Indeed, one important interpretation of the post-Cold War order argues that it is best understood as a kind of peace settlement.[10] In Bush's case there was the added incongruity of such a grandiose vision coming from a man who, as he admitted, 'lacked the vision thing'.

In terms of our criteria for analysing the various schemes, it is clear that for Bush the primary unit of international politics remained the nation-state but in an internationalizing context in which there was the possibility of an enhanced role for international organizations such as the UN. Second, the driving force of international politics took the largely traditional form of conflict between national interests which in principle could be moderated by the promotion of cooperation through international organizations. Third, the tendency of the system, in principle at least, was towards greater harmony which, finally, would depend greatly on the United States as an enabling and guiding hand. There was nothing novel about Bush's vision; it was a compound of several elements, each of which could be traced to the American past. In any case, revolutions are not to be expected from sitting presidents. This did not stop his vision from being attacked. Each aspect of it could be and was questioned, largely because in practice there was a good deal less consistency than his principles would seem to suggest, and because the actions and policies associated with the New World Order seemed designed to serve American national interests rather than the global collective good. Concerns, for example, were expressed inside the United States about whether American leadership would be forthcoming.[11] Doubts, and even deep cynicism, were voiced from abroad about the Bush administration's commitment to internationalism, a widespread conclusion being that the New World Order was little more than a vehicle for American national interests.[12] Nevertheless, Bush's vision reflected one set of potentialities within the system, and to that extent it remained a model with considerable appeal since it embodied global, cooperative principles, whatever its manifestations in practice.

From 'The End of History?' to 'The Clash of Civilizations?'

Francis Fukuyama's vision pre-dated that of Bush. His most important contribution, 'The End of History?', was published in the spring of 1989, before the Cold War can be said definitively to have ended, indeed at a time when the Bush administration was still highly sceptical about the Gorbachev revolution in the Soviet Union.[13] As late as May 1989, Secretary of Defense Dick Cheney expressed the view that Gorbachev's *perestroika* was likely to fail and that he was likely to be replaced by a hardliner.[14] If nothing else, Fukuyama can be credited with a certain amount of foresight at a time when few were prepared to commit themselves to judgements about the direction of the Soviet Union and the Cold War itself. Fukuyama's 'The End of History?' has frequently been characterized as a triumphalist hymn to the Western liberal democracy which relies on an idiosyncratic and faulty notion of history. His definition of 'history' as the conflict of great ideologies, compared with which mere 'events' are outside history and apparently of little account, was widely greeted by academics with derision or incomprehension, though among a wider public it achieved considerable success. Viewed more dispassionately, Fukuyama's work appears firmly in the mould of post-Cold War models which expressed an essentially American vision of the world disguised as an internationalist theory.

Applying our criteria to Francis Fukuyama's 'The End of History?' (appearing first in article form in 1989 and then as a book in 1992) one finds that he is not specific about the basic constituents of world politics, since the currency he deals in is ideas rather than institutions. His central notion of the 'triumph of the West' offers a broad notion of geography but he goes on quickly to add 'and of the Western idea', indicating that his is a theory less of world politics than of world ideologies. This also indicates that for Fukuyama the driving force in world politics is in the realm of consciousness, and also that his judgement about the direction of change is broadly positive (despite his professed 'sadness' about the consequences of the end of history). By implication the United States is a positive force, though he has very little to say about the United States itself, save for some pages on the Civil War. 'United States' does not appear in the index of *The End of History and the Last Man*.

In many ways this was a curious candidate for a bestseller since it scarcely touched base with political realities; yet it was considerably more influential than more pragmatic and apparently grounded arguments. Why should this have been so? In part it is to be explained by the centrality of the idea of liberal democracy. Though in Fukuyama's scheme the United States does not claim direct responsibility for bringing about the end of history, the association of liberal democracy with 'the West' and the association of the United States with both is enough to make clear the assumption about American leadership in these transformations. Furthermore, the very generality of the thesis enables people with many and often different ends in view to appropriate Fukuyama's ideas for their own purposes. Fukuyama was a signatory of the 'Statement of Principles' of the 'Project for a New American Century' which can be taken as a credo of the right in America; it was couched in direct opposition to the policies of the Clinton administration. However, the Clinton administration's idea of 'democratic enlargement' differed, if anything, only in tone from the belief of the right that the triumph of democracy was a necessary and desirable goal of American policy. Clinton's national security adviser, Anthony Lake, criticized the idea of 'the end of history' in a key policy paper of 1993 but embraced the idea of the 'enlargement' of democracy.[15] Clinton's policies were broadly consonant with the Fukuyama thesis. In short, Fukuyama's analysis helped to set the American agenda for the 1990s and beyond of spreading democracy.

Samuel Huntington's 'The Clash of Civilizations?' (1993) matched Fukuyama's 'The End of History?' in its currency in intellectual circles and was also followed up by the publication of a full-length book some years later.[16] His thesis that cultural conflict between 'civilizations' was replacing conflict over economics and ideology between nations as the prime motor of global politics had the merit, like Fukuyama's, that it was easily reducible to a few simple propositions, however complex the exposition. Again like Fukuyama, Huntington introduced new terminology and concepts – or rather reintroduced old ones in a new context – which addressed the widespread awareness of the fundamental character of the changes brought about by the end of the Cold War. Once again, it turns out that what is presented as an internationalist theory is largely a projection of anxieties about the survival of American national interests and goals in a dangerous world.

In Huntington's scheme the unit of international politics is the 'civilization', the driving force behind global politics is cultural conflict rather than economics, national interest or ideology, and Huntington's judgement is that conflict is likely to increase. Huntington focuses rather more than Fukuyama on the United States, albeit the United States is still generally subsumed under 'the West'. On a number of occasions Huntington notes

America's special role in Western civilization as a crusader for democracy. 'The central problem in the relations between the West and the rest', he writes, 'is the discordance between the West's – particularly America's – efforts to promote a universal Western culture and its declining ability to do so'. Again: 'The West, and especially the United States, which has always been a missionary nation, believe that the non-Western peoples should commit themselves to the Western values of democracy'. And again: 'the collapse of the Soviet Union generated in the West, particularly in the United States, the belief that a global democratic revolution was underway'.[17] The United States features in Huntington's analysis as carrying a special interest in and responsibility for the values associated with 'the West'. It is for this reason that Huntington pays special attention to 'challenges' to the United States' capacity to continue with this exemplary function, the main challenge being immigration and the attendant idea of 'multiculturalism' which be believes threatens America's national identity by questioning the identification of America with Western civilization and undermining the unity of the United States. The centrality of this theme for Huntington is indicated by the fact that he has since devoted a new book to this question – *Who Are We?* (2004).[18]

Neither Fukuyama nor Huntington conform to 'realist' notions of international relations, though Huntington is closer to this approach in his vision of the international arena as one of chronic conflict. In a sense his 'civilizations' play the role which nation-states play in realist analyses of international relations. However, to the extent that the thrust of his analysis is towards cultural conflict between entities called civilizations which are considerably larger than nations and more shadowy in structure and organization, Huntington leaves a question mark over the implications his analysis might have for policy, particularly American policy. Indeed, the nation-state is almost wholly absent in his analysis, despite the pro forma statement at the beginning that 'nation states will remain the most powerful actors in world affairs'.[19] And yet, Huntington's analysis provided both an explanation for emerging forms of global disorder and a rationale for national opposition to its most extreme and apparently dangerous forms. Huntington offered no policy recommendations but made clear the nature of the enemy in today's disordered world: the cultures of 'Islam' and 'Confucianism'. Given the salience of conflict in the Middle East, the growing level of 'Islamic terrorism' in the 1990s and then the terrorist attacks of September 11, it is not surprising that most attention should have focused on this feature of Huntington's analysis. His suggestion that Islam had 'bloody borders' was especially provocative. That his idea of civilizational conflict had penetrated deep into the popular psyche was apparent in the lengths to which George W. Bush and members of his administration went – without, it has to be said, convincing critics of their sincerity – explicitly to deny that the war on terror involved a clash of civilizations.[20] The links Huntington made between global disorder and American domestic disorder indicated that American identity as a nation was at stake in the era of the clash of civilizations. The national perspective was implicit in his scheme; it was merely that the emphasis had switched from politics to culture.

Realist ideas and the national interest

We look now at a pair of analyses which are very different from those of Huntington and Fukuyama. What they have in common is a 'realist' bias in that both see nation-states as the primary units of global politics. The first is Charles Krauthammer, whose article 'The Unipolar Moment' entered the vocabulary of many who may never have read his article.[21] His was another example of a memorable phrase which conveys a great deal more than the bare information contained in it. His thesis was that the global system was now oriented round a single pole – the United States – and that this nation provided the necessary ordering principle for the whole system. Indeed, it was an opportunity to be seized by the United States because the United States was the only nation capable of establishing and enforcing order. The gap in power between America and the others was so large as to be unique in modern history. He believed, therefore – bearing in mind our criteria for comparing these analyses – that the nation-state was the essential constituent of world politics, that national interest was the main driving force, that order was possible and that the United States was in a position to provide it. This was a vision which was easier to operationalize than those of Huntington and Fukuyama; it was also susceptible to critiques on various grounds, the main ones being arrogance and excessive optimism. It did, however, make sense to many American observers of that snapshot of a moment following the collapse of the Soviet Union, the Gulf War against Iraq, and the heady sense that past policies had been vindicated. Moreover, it was hard to argue with the fact of American primacy, whatever judgements might be made of it. Krauthammer updated his ideas more than a decade on, insisting that the essentials of his vision had received further confirmation by events. Indeed, he declares that after September 11, 'the unipolar moment has become the unipolar era'. Significantly, Krauthammer insists that the realism he is arguing for is to be clearly distinguished from the selfish pursuit by America of its own narrow self-interest. Given its preponderant power, he writes, America should be prepared 'to self-consciously and confidently deploy American power in pursuit of ... *global* ends' (emphasis added).[22] Nevertheless, Krauthammer's version's version of realism is strikingly narrow, based as it is on traditional realist notions of power and global order. There is little acknowledgement of the changes which are associated with globalization. Indeed, to the extent that he considers alternative outlooks to the one he proposes he does so in terms of an outdated polarity between 'liberal internationalism' and 'realism', as if these were the only options available. While acknowledging the power of the American nation in the current context, his scheme does not offer a means of understanding either American nationalism or its global context.

John Mearsheimer's article 'Back to the Future: Sources of Instability After the Cold War' presented a very different vision of the global future.[23] His theme was what he believed to be the inevitable onset of instability, especially in Europe, in the absence of the old balances and restraints supplied by the Cold War – above all nuclear deterrence, which gave the bipolar system its characteristic stability. Mearsheimer's is a classically realist, indeed Hobbesian, vision in which international politics is conceived of as a war of each against all. The demise of bipolarity could produce only multipolarity, and the pursuit of self-interest in a multi-polar system could only produce instability. Fear was the driver of international politics. It was for this reason that Mearsheimer hatched the seemingly absurd idea that managed nuclear proliferation was the best way to re-create a climate of healthy anxiety about the motives of other nations and hence produce stability. In a separate analysis of the prospects for the newly independent Ukraine and its neighbouring powers, Mearsheimer applied the general thesis to a particular case. Using our criteria, for Mearsheimer the constituents of world politics were nation-states, national interest was the driving force, instability was the ever present threat and most likely future, and the United States, in so far as it could be a force for order, could best secure it by managing the process of balancing up the potential antagonists. Mearsheimer is more determinedly anachronistic than Krauthammer in his insistence on the overriding significance of military power to the virtual exclusion of all other considerations. The limits of realism are nowhere more vividly demonstrated; testimony perhaps to the struggle of theorists to catch up with the reality of changes in global politics. The tendency is to describe the new in terms of the old; in this case to project Cold War nuclear deterrence onto a very different post-Cold War screen.

These were not the only realist models on offer but they were the most striking. Others saw the resurgence of less dangerous forms of multipolarity engendered by the rise of balancing powers, most notably Japan and the European Union, though there was a recognition that the EU did not yet act like a sovereign state. (It is worth recalling that the late 1980s and early 1990s was a time of anxiety in America about being overtaken by Japan. One of a succession of such analyses was entitled *The Coming War with Japan*.[24]) Behind such visions were traditional ideas of the balance of power, though the precedents were by no means all favourable. The descent of the Balkans in the 1990s into a succession of wars stimulated recollections of the way the First World War began. Moreover, Yugoslavia was a good example of a new and disturbing phenomenon – the disintegration of a nation-state, bringing in its train the threat of the spread of more general instability. Realist theories struggled to make sense of such cases because the precondition for the realist approach – the presence of legitimate governments presiding over sovereign states within clear borders – seemed not to exist.

It was some such sort of recognition no doubt which led the Clinton administration to adopt, if only as a loose framework, a model of global politics which its author, Madeleine Albright, called 'the four food groups'. It was, she said, her 'way of explaining the world in the absence of Cold War divisions'. The first group 'consisted of those who were full members of the international system' and they had governments, institutions, and legal systems which functioned in ways which secured material well-being, domestic stability, and protection of rights. The second group contained those nations, predominantly of the former communist bloc, which were making the transition to democracy and were essentially in the business of nation-building. The third group 'comprise countries with weak or nonexistent governments, often held back by poverty or mired in conflict', and the fourth 'was represented by governments that, for one reason or another, were hostile to the rules of the international system and sought to subvert or circumvent them'. These were, in the common parlance of the time (though Albright does not herself use the term), 'rogue states', of which Iraq and North Korea were prime examples. American policy towards the groups were 'to forge the strongest possible ties with the first', 'help the second group succeed', 'aid those in the third group who were most willing to help themselves', and 'strive to protect ourselves by reforming, isolating, or defeating those in the fourth group'.[25]

It is perhaps characteristic of the practitioner to develop a model which serves directly in the formulation of policy. What is notable about this scheme is its openness to the untidiness of reality. While prescriptive in its own way, in the sense that there are clear judgements being made about the members of the various groups, it does acknowledge that the nation-state is a complex institution which takes a variety of forms. Being realistic here involves a sacrifice of the theoretical rigour of 'realism'. This scheme also remains open to the possibility that there are wider processes at work in the international system to which some nations are more subject than others. Among the most important of these are economic. Some nations and some governments have a good measure of control, even if not total, over the vital factors affecting their economic well-being; others are the playthings of the market and the more powerful players in it. For strong countries interdependence can be a positive; for the weak it is often a negative. Albright's model allows for such conclusions to be drawn, and in doing so it allows space for discussion of globalization and its uneven effects. If we apply our criteria, then we can say that for Albright the basic units of world politics remain nation-states but there are some qualifications and discriminations being made; nation-states are diverse in character and are affected differentially by global processes. The driving force behind global politics in this model is only in part national interest; there are cross-cutting pressures. As a practitioner with a reputation to defend, one would expect Albright to see the direction of world politics in a broadly positive light, not least because (moving to the last of our criteria) so much depends on the stance taken by the United States. America's influence, on Albright's reading, is predominantly benign; America's motives and policies rise above self-interest to encompass the well-being of the larger international community.

Ideas of globalization and American empire

The unspoken term in the above scheme is globalization, and indeed this is the next model of global politics which we need to examine. The most common form of the argument says that the number and scale of transactions across the globe, whether in trade, finance, business operations (including manufacturing), information of all types and by all means, is now such as to have generated a qualititative change in the overall character of global relations. Marshall McLuhan's 'global village' is now a reality; national boundaries mean less and less, rendering the distinction between domestic and foreign policy of declining significance. Nation-states still exert a measure of influence; they are still the primary location for the bulk of the institutions which govern our day-to-day lives. However, they have diminished control over many of the activities inside their borders and are beholden to numerous transnational organizations and processes which scorn national borders.[26]

There are many interpretations of this process, from fervent welcome for the extension of market capitalism to all corners of the globe to deep fears about its effects on those who for one reason or another are unable to participate as full members of global society, or who see global society and do not want to be members of it. Anxieties about the excessive power of multinational companies, the homogenization of cultures, the marginalization of minorities, and many other features of what one sociologist has called 'the runaway world' abound. Some speak of 'uneven globalization', others of irreconcilable conflict between 'jihad' (using the word as a short-hand for various types of religious and political fundamentalism) and 'McWorld'.[27]

What is clear in the many and diverse writings on this subject is that the units of international politics are much more difficult to specify because they are associated with processes and transnational bodies rather than with nation-states, identifiable cultures, or regional groupings. We seem to be in a condition in which the traditional levers of power have no control. The internet symbolizes the radical diffusion of power which is characteristic of globalization. There are some active agents but they are shifting and only loosely subject to controls. If the constituents of global politics are not clear, the chief driving force is perhaps more so – economic processes, the market. Judgements about direction are extremely diverse, as are ideas about the United States' role. For some the whole process seems to be driven by the United States – Americanization writ large – but in from another point of view it is only incidentally a matter of government policy or national interest, more an outgrowth of the dynamism of the American economy and its culture. Even here qualifications have to be made, since globalization has not been in the past and is not now a uniquely American process but has drivers in many other parts of the globe.[28]

Given the indeterminate nature of these processes it is not surprising to find some analysts developing more or less complex syntheses which seek to integrate the great variety of phenomena discussed above, and others besides. John Gaddis, a leading historian of the Cold War who has also written a great deal about international affairs since then, sees an emerging competition between forces of integration and disintegration. He offers the arresting thought that broadly speaking the desire for satisfaction of intangible desires, such as freedom, tends to produce fragmentation in world politics while the satisfaction of material needs tends to produce integration. His preferred solution is for strategies which will seek to balance the forces of integration and disintegration, and to this end he offers the US Constitution as a model: 'for what is our own Constitution if not the most elegant political text ever composed on how to balance the forces of integration against those of disintegration?'[29] It is a neat solution, if overly abstract and schematic. Is it the case, for example, that attempts to satisfy material needs necessarily tend to produce integration? There are surely many situations in which pursuit of economic advantage will generate conflict. Moreover, this analysis reveals the immense difficulty of linking national interests – his article begins with a discussion of these – with abstract processes; it is as if two different vocabularies of international relations are in collision with each other. It is thus not easy to analyse Gaddis' argument according to the criteria set out above. His unit of analysis shifts according to the subject under discussion; the world may be moving towards order or disorder, integration or disintegration; his vision is neither pessimistic nor optimistic but carefully hedges bets; finally, as far as America's place in this world is concerned, discussion is restricted to the suggestion that the United States must continue to adhere to its traditional goal of seeking a balance of power.

It may be that the indeterminacy of Gaddis' analysis is unavoidable because of the nature of the reality being analysed. However, Joseph Nye offers a different take on similar sorts of issues. After considering the merits of several schemes – multipolarity, three economic blocs, unipolar hegemony, and multilevel interdependence – he concludes that 'the world order after the Cold War is *sui generis* ... power is becoming more multidimensional, structures more complex and states themselves more permeable'. Nye offers a developmental model which links the past with the future and a conception of national interest with globalization, unilateralism with multilateralism. In short, in terms of our criteria, Nye retains the nation-state as the primary unit of analysis while acknowledging the significance of new transnational institutions; he sees a complex of forces driving international relations forward, including traditional notions of national interest and globalization; he is cautiously optimistic about the direction of global change, concluding that 'in short, the new world order has begun'; his conception of the United States' role rests on the judgement that 'in realist terms the United States will remain the world's largest power well into the next century'. For this reason the United States cannot 'leave the task of world order to the United Nations', though it must seek multilateral solutions wherever appropriate. In sum the

United States must steer a 'middle course between bearing too much and too little of the international burden'.[30]

The final category of analysis to be considered here is the vogue for the idea of American empire, a concept which has been used to characterize not only American foreign policy but also the international order. The starting point for such analyses is the statement, which has assumed the status of a cliché, that 'the United States dominates the world as no state has'.[31] This is not a new theme but in the past has generally taken the form of critiques from the left, most notably in the writings of William Appleman Williams.[32] Such critiques still feature in the recent debate. Indeed Andrew Bacevich's *American Empire* (2002) is in some respects an updated version of Williams' argument. However, there is a new edge to the debate in that the term 'empire' has been adopted, indeed embraced, by some analysts on the right. No longer arguing defensively that America is a nation with anti-imperial origins and in its growth as a republic anything but an empire, some conservatives point to the need for a *pax americana* to secure global order. 'Empires have unfairly got a bad name', writes Deepak Lal, which is 'particularly unfortunate, as the world needs an American pax to provide both global peace and security'.[33] British historian Niall Ferguson echoes these conclusions and adds the comment that America is in 'imperial denial', to the detriment of the global order.[34] In the debate as a whole, there is no longer a sense that the word 'empire' is being employed as a metaphor or a debating tool but rather as a scientific, descriptive term. America really *is* an empire – not just *like* an empire.[35]

Such views are much disputed on the grounds that a large element of distortion is required to fit the United States into the mould of empires such as those of Greece, Rome, and Britain. James Chace, a firm (though critical) advocate of the view that America is now an empire, asks

who would now deny that America is an imperial power? The American response to the attack on the World Trade

Center and the Pentagon was swift and merciless. Thousands of troops swept down upon Afghanistan in an effort to capture or kill the terrorists and their protectors.[36]

However, in the aftermath of September 11 and in the many other examples of American interventions in the past forty years there are visible limits, not merely to American power itself but on the willingness to deploy that power and these are in part self-imposed. From Vietnam through the many interventions in the following years the United States held back from the use of all-out military force. Indeed, the insistence of Lyndon Johnson on fighting a limited war in Vietnam is commonly given by those on the political right as a reason for America's failure to win the war. Constraints on American action are supplied by domestic opinion, by America's native ideology of anti-imperialism and anti-colonialism, by global opinion, by anxiety about triggering war with another major power, and by accepted norms of international behaviour – indeed by the total context in which American power is deployed. America may possess the material might necessary to be an empire but, as Martin Walker writes, 'the United States does not rule, and its shrinks from mastery'.[37] In fact arguably it was more clearly an imperial power during the Cold War when its hold over allies and clients was firmer because of the need to meet the challenge of the common enemy of communism. Furthermore, as one specialist in ancient empires notes, 'Athenians, Romans, Ottomans, and the British wanted land, colonies, treasure, and grabbed all they could get when they could. The United States hasn't annexed anyone's soil since the Spanish-American War.'[38] There is, needless to say, the rejoinder to this argument that, whatever the case after 1898, the territorial growth of the United States during the nineteenth century was a story of classic imperialist land-grabbing.[39]

There is no easy resolution to this debate. At worst it becomes an empty exercise in definitional gymnastics; at best it has stimulated an important reflections about the nature of American power and its role in the global system. There surely is, however, a qualitative difference between the exertion of Greek, Roman or British imperial power in an age of dynastic states and an American hegemony in an age of democratic norms and institutions. The difference is in the form and level of political control as well as in the mind-set and ideology. To make the United States qualify as an empire we have, as Ikenberry points out, to loosen the definition of 'empire' from meaning direct political control to 'a hierarchical system of political relationships in which the most powerful state exercises decisive influence'.[40] We can call America a 'liberal empire' if we want to; but we still need the qualifier to make America fit into the frame of empire.

The United States as a Westphalian state in a post-Westphalian world

Where do we go from here? Let us return to our criteria for understanding models of world order and set these against the salient events and processes of the post-Cold War period. What, then, can we take as the basic unit of international politics? In a theoretical sense and for many practical purposes nation-states remain the primary constituents of the world political system, if only because national governments are the responsible bodies to which most of the world's peoples are directly subject and to which they owe primary allegiance. Citizenship, which is at once political, legal, social and psychological, defines the relationship of individuals to governments. In most cases, furthermore, the governments of nation-states remain the chief vehicles for the representation of the interests of citizens at levels beyond that of the nation-state. For all the qualifications that can be made, and will be made below, to this mundane truth of international relations, there is no escaping its force.

Nevertheless, such a conclusion is misleading to the extent that it assumes that nation-states are the only constituents of consequence in the global political system. In international relations theory, 'pluralists' or 'neoliberal institutionalists' have for several decades noted the growing significance of non-state actors and transnational processes in global politics. 'We can imagine a world', wrote two of pluralism's leading proponents in the late 1970s, 'in which actors other than states participate directly in world politics, in which a clear hierarchy of issues does not exist, and in which force is an ineffective instrument of policy.'[41] The growing intensity of globalization has surely confirmed the essential insight of the pluralists regarding the growing power and significance of non-state actors, whether multinational companies, bodies such as the IMF, or non-governmental organizations and international 'regimes'. More-over, there is growing recognition that the variety of types of nation-state undermines the notion that they are all essentially comparable with each other. Nation-states may all seek to max-imize their power and effectiveness as international actors, but they do so in many different ways and with widely differing results. Albright's 'four feeding groups' and the adoption of terminology such as 'failed states' and 'rogue states' indicates that it is practitioners as much as theorists who find it useful to make distinctions among nation-states. Robert Cooper, a British author who plays both roles, has introduced a tripartite distinc-tion between 'pre-modern states' which are the product of post-imperial chaos and lack the attributes of genuine sovereignty and monopoly control of force within their borders; 'modern states' which pursue the classical realist goals of self-interest and tend to rely ultimately on the use of force as the guarantor of their security; and 'post-modern states' which operate in a cooperative environment where the boundary between internal and external affairs has broken down and groupings of states mutually agree to 'interfere' in each others' affairs.[42] In effect, Cooper is talking about the coexistence of three state *systems* which promote and require different types of state behaviour. In the category of pre-modern states Cooper places Somalia, Afghanistan, and Liberia. The United States, he suggests, is a characteristically modern state and the European Union a good example of the post-modern. In short, in trying to establish the basic unit of world politics it is apparent that the nation-state is an important but not exclusive constituent and also that the nation-state itself takes diverse forms.

Part of the usefulness of Cooper's model lies in his acknowledgement of the reality that there is no single world system of politics but rather the coexistence of several. It is evident also – moving to the second of our criteria for discussing ideas of world order – that the driving forces in world politics remain highly variegated. Contrary to the expectations of the pluralist theorists, the use of force has not been rendered 'ineffective' nor has it been displaced by the advent of new transnational actors and processes. Nevertheless, it could certainly be argued that force has changed its form in a number of ways in the last three decades. Terrorism and other forms of irregular fighting have become major weapons of insurgent groups, necessitating the development on the part of 'modern' nations such as the United States of new techniques of counter-terrorism and more flexible military methods, including the development of rapidly deployable mobile forces and increasing accuracy in airpower through the introduction of new technologies – everything that is implied by the phrase 'the revolution in military affairs' (RMA) which became current in the 1990s.[43] The conclusion must be that the driving forces in world politics are multiple and complex; there can be no single driver such as cultural conflict or the working out of an idea of liberal democracy or the economic processes associated with globalization.

For this reason, looking at the third criterion for judging ideas of global order, there can be no certainty about the direction of change in the global system. Tendencies towards order and disorder, integration and disintegration, as Gaddis, Nye and others have observed, vie with each other. However, what can be said is that the global system does not exhibit either extreme orderliness or extreme disorderliness; the absence of global government does not mean that there is an absence of governance. Theorists posit that order is in part a property of the particular distribution of power in the system, whether it be some form of multipolarity, bipolarity, unipolarity, or even, according to one analyst, 'apolarity'.[44] Different systems display varied patterns of balancing, according both to the structure of the overall system and the character of the units in the system. What can we say about the structure and balancing mechanisms of the current global system? Here we link consideration of the tendency of the system with our fourth criterion for assessing ideas of global order – the role of the United States. A possibility worth pursuing is that the United States can be seen as a link to all the other criteria: i.e. the units of the system, the driving force, and the tendency of the system.

We can start with the observation that the United States is both the largest and strongest nation-state in the system and also the chief agent of globalization which is purportedly leading to the demise of the nation-state. In a hybrid system in which the historic units of the system – nation-states – are being modified by processes of globalization, the United States plays a complex and often contradictory role. As the prime agent of globalization through the size of its economy and its global reach, the United States has a stake in numerous multilateral organizations and in the universalization of certain rules and procedures, above all in the economic field. In this field it has been an advocate of breaking down barriers between nations in order to facilitate flows of goods, capital and information. In a globalizing world, furthermore, there are numerous other fields – environmental, legal, military and so on – in which there is pressure for internationally agreed protocols. There are limits, however, to how far the United States is prepared to go in the direction of cooperative multilateralism, and these limits are defined in part by its historic nationalism. It is not simply the disparity in size and influence between the United States and other nations, but that America's national traditions disincline it to enter arrangements which might unduly compromise its sovereignty.

For all the attention given to the foreign policy of the United States, this feature of the United States history and current policy has been underestimated. Even where the domestic sources of American nationalism have been explored, its implications for the structure of international politics have not been adequately assessed.[45] Putting it perhaps over-schematically, America presents the paradox of a Westphalian state par excellence in a system which in important respects is post-Westphalian. The United States' origins and growth have inclined it to become the epitome of the Westphalian nation-state. There is no scope here for a full discussion of American nationalism, far less its long and complex history.[46] What can be said, as far as America's relations with the outside world are concerned, is that American nationalism historically is a compound of a missionary ideology of Americanism and dynamic economic growth and expansionism.[47] At the heart of this history and also its current significance lies the theme of independence. The intensity of the American devotion to this principle is generally illustrated by reference to the Declaration of Independence, but in some respects more telling is an arresting phrase in the text of the Treaty of Alliance with France (1778). Here at the heart of a document in which the United States tied itself to another power, carrying the risk of compromising its new-won sovereignty, lay the assertion that 'the essential and direct End of the present defensive alliance is to maintain effectually the liberty, Sovereignty, and independance absolute and unlimited of the said united states [*sic*]'.[48] America's will to independence – independence *absolute* – is visible not only in its separate declarations but also in the manner in which it enters into arrangements with others. The Treaty with France is the signal example. It is echoed in Woodrow Wilson's entry into the First World War as an 'associated' not an 'allied' power. It takes different forms in the period of American global power because now the United States is the director and leader of the treaties and coalitions it enters. It has greater freedom of choice, has the power to set the terms and conditions under which it participates, and to a degree can dictate terms to others. The 'coalitions' formed for the wars in Afghanistan and Iraq illustrate the possibilities but also the limits of these powers: the United States could ensure that the coalitions fought these wars on American terms but could not, in the case of Iraq, dictate who would become members of the coalitions. The determining factor in all cases was the maintenance of America's room to move, its 'independence'. As President Bush affirmed in the approach to the Iraq war, 'we will not seek a permission slip for our own security'. In short, independence is among the prime values in American foreign policy.

Moreover, the context in which this is now taking place is radically different from the setting in which the Westphalian system was established. American nationalism has always been a factor in American foreign policy, though its intensity has waxed and waned in response to perceived external threats. It has historically been compatible, as we have seen, with multi-lateralism. It continues to be a factor as the international system undergoes fundamental changes in the direction of inter-dependence, globalization, and efforts to institutionalize coop-eration in a range of fields from economics, trade, environmental protection, justice, aid and many others. As has been observed by Menzies Campbell, British Liberal Democratic party spokes-man on foreign affairs (and later leader of the party), 'for America, NATO and the other alliances are a matter of choice; for Europe and the UK, multilateralism remains a necessity'. 'We should be under no illusion', he added, 'as to the force of American pragmatism and the determined pursuit of its national interest.'[49]

Conclusion

These points have a bearing on the issue of American unilateralism in the policies of the Bush administration. In the light of the framework developed here, discussion of American unilateralism has been conducted on far too narrow a basis. What is at issue is not only a policy choice or a party programme or even a pre-sidential philosophy but a political culture with deep historical roots. George W. Bush has exploited to the full the potentialities of both the American tradition and the international context in which he found himself. Amidst the shock of September 11 the United States was able to draw on a deep vein of historical tradition which linked the moral and the national with the security challenge. The times offer scope for the United States to command greater sovereignty than other nations, to be less beholden to other nations and international institutions, more able to maintain freedom of action – in a word, more *independent*. The word connects present policies and behaviour with a core idea which is as old as the nation itself. Whatever the reigning orthodoxy or slogan, at whatever time in its history, whether it be non-entanglement, isolationism, manifest destiny, making the world safe for democracy, or ensuring the survival of liberty, the notion of independence has never been far from the surface.

Of course, all nations cultivate nationalism and also independence to one degree or other. The difference is that America's nationalism generally has greater consequences. America's peculiar privilege is old-fashioned nationalism at a time when most other nations cannot afford it or reserve it for football matches and the Olympic Games. For all its role as the arch-globalizer, for all its commitment to what a nineteenth-century advocate of manifest destiny called the 'expansive future', the United States at the beginning of the third millennium is also committed to a future based on its own past.[50] And there are few nations with a longer or more continuous past. This indeed is one of the key ingredients of American nationalism. This is nowhere more visible than in George W. Bush's second inaugural address, though the point could be substantiated with reference to such speeches by virtually any American president. 'From the day of our Founding', he declared,

> we have proclaimed that every man and woman on this earth has rights, and dignity, and matchless value, because they bear the image of the Maker of Heaven and earth. Across the generations we have proclaimed the imperative

of self-government, because no one is fit to be a master, and no one deserves to be a slave. Advancing these ideals is the mission that created our Nation. It is the honorable achievement of our fathers. Now it is the urgent requirement of our nation's security, and the calling of our time.[51]

The encounter between an intensified American nationalism and a world moving in the direction of interdependence is ripe for conflict and dissension. This is so in part because the aspirations of American nationalism, particularly as expressed by the administration of George W. Bush, are so extensive. Indeed they are couched as universals. The biggest and most potent idea among the many big ideas which have been spawned since the end of the Cold War is the idea of the American nation and its peculiar destiny. Americans need to understand this as well as others. They will then understand why American power is so fiercely contested.

6 The emperor's clothes

The failure of the neoconservative mission

September 11 did more than change the face of American domestic and foreign relations; it ensured that the two would be inextricably linked. The terrorist attacks removed any illusion that America's domestic well-being could be considered in isolation from its international position. This was by no means an unprecedented state of affairs. In fact it was a case of re-learning an old lesson in a new context. Combating international communism, especially in the early phases of the Cold War, had forced a comparable awareness of the interdependence of the foreign and the domestic. Countless domestic measures, from Truman's unsuccessful national health plan of 1948, to the building of the interstate highway system and federal aid to education in the 1950s, were justified in part on the basis of the need to meet the Soviet challenge. The whole McCarthyite episode demonstrated the tight link between foreign and domestic security in a world polarized between competing systems and values. Indeed war itself – and the Cold War must be considered as such in its psychological dimensions – has always been a powerful solvent of the boundary between domestic and foreign affairs. However, the Cold War was history. Relations between the domestic and the foreign were always subject to renegotiation and reinterpretation according to new circumstances. International terrorism of the sort pursued by al-Qaeda against the United States forged a peculiarly close connection between the domestic and the foreign since it represented foreign groups operating inside the

United States on a mission of destruction, not, as in the Cold War case, merely of ideological subversion. The political messages most likely to meet the sense of crisis would be those which most successfully responded to the dual challenge. In this context, one of the neoconservative movement's strengths was its crusading sense of urgency about the external threat, which brought with it a psychology of domestic mobilization. Neoconservatism was geared up for war; it thrived on a sense of embattlement; it craved a mission.

That mission was seriously compromised in the aftermath of the war in Iraq, as the hoped-for stability and order failed to materialize. As the insurgency continued and counter-measures made little obvious impact, by early 2006 talk of civil war in Iraq surfaced and the original rationale for the war came under serious question. A succession of post-mortems, among them a memoir by Paul Bremer, appointed in April 2003 as head of the Coalition Provisional Authority, told a story of confusion, absence of planning, and seriously counter-productive policies.[1] A clear index of the impact of these revelations at home in the United States was the number of high-profile defections from the neoconservative camp, particularly from early 2006 following the bombing of a Shia shrine in Iraq. This event, and the violence and disorder following it, caused some erstwhile supporters of the war to reconsider the rationale behind it. Even when the conclusion was that the problems lay with the execution of the policy towards Iraq and not with the mission itself, an acknowledgement of failure to achieve American objectives was made by such prominent supporters of the Bush administration as Richard Perle and William Buckley Jr.[2] These voices became louder in the wake of the Congressional elections of November 2006. However, some important defections had taken place earlier, as we shall see, questioning not only the performance of the mission but the mission itself.

These developments raise large questions not only about the neoconservative agenda but also about conservatism generally in America. In what follows, the initial focus is on the cracks in the neoconservative ideology opened up by the course of the war in

Iraq. What happens to a missionary ideology when the mission fails or becomes compromised by events? What do these events reveal about the relations between neoconservatism and traditional conservatism, and what does the failure of the neoconservative mission reveal about the original vision and the means by which it was projected? But the interest of these developments goes beyond the facts of the particular case. In the trajectory of neoconservatism lies an illustration of the life cycle of a political ideology. The emphasis in this chapter is on the rhetorical strategies used to promote a particular political ideology, the aim being first to show how a position previously considered to be marginal or even extreme was able successfully to present itself as lying at the core of national values; and second, to indicate ways in which that position of centrality can become vulnerable once conditions change. The premise employed here is that political rhetoric can be a powerful tool of political legitimation; equally political language can become hollowed out, not merely through overuse and repetition, but through growing disjunctions between language and the realities to which it purports to relate. The declining effectiveness of the rhetorical strategies employed by the Bush administration was part and parcel of the erosion of confidence in the policies.

Neoconservatism

A necessary preliminary to this discussion is consideration of the nature of neoconservatism itself. Not only is the character and history of neoconservatism the subject of much scholarly and political debate, there is disagreement about the extent to which the Bush foreign policy agenda can be described as neoconservative. On the first point, neoconservatism has never been a rigid ideology, more a tendency or a 'persuasion' which emerged in the late 1960s and 1970s among intellectuals disillusioned with liberalism and the politics of the left. As described by one of neoconservatism's founding figures, Irving Kristol, neoconservatism drew on a wide range of conservative ideas from such figures as Milton Friedman, Friedrich Hayek, Russell Kirk and Leo Strauss, but added a new 'ideological self-consciousness and self-assurance' which derived from its roots in the ideological battles of the left.[3] Significantly, as Kristol pointed out in an essay written twenty years later, though for certain purposes, especially running of the economy, neo-conservatives favoured limited government solutions, in some spheres, such as moral and social policy, neoconservatives were likely to favour certain 'liberal' or big government solutions rather than the anti-statism of America's libertarian conservative tradition. Government regulation of education, church–state relations and pornography, for example, were deemed 'proper candidates for the government's attention'.[4] It was these moral concerns which helped to forge the alliance in the 1970s and after between neoconservatism and the Christian right, an issue to be taken up later in this chapter.

In foreign policy, neoconservatives cut their teeth on what they regarded as the disastrous policy of détente in the early 1970s.[5] The failure to challenge Soviet power, indeed the open compromise with it, was held to be an abrogation not only of America's national interest but of the values America stood for. Latterly, neoconservatism in foreign policy, which is undoubtedly the area in which neoconservative values have been most contentious, has advocated the open embrace by America of the implications of its overwhelming military superiority. 'With power', notes Kristol, 'come responsibilities, whether sought or not, whether welcome or not.' Such a 'uniquely powerful' nation as the United States cannot rely on international institutions and it must 'have the ability to distinguish friends from enemies'. Traditional conservatives in the Republican Party, he added, 'have difficulty coming to terms with this new reality in foreign affairs'. By a happy chance, Kristol concludes, 'our current President and his administration turn out to be quite at home in this new environment'.[6]

Kristol's reading of the later phases of neoconservativism's history skates over some complexities associated with generational change. Not all the first generation acclimatized themselves to the new situation of the post-Cold War world. Some were left high and dry by the departure of communism. In the absence of the Soviet threat, was there still a necessity for a global definition of America's national interests and an interventionist foreign policy? No, said some of the old guard, who saw in the end of the Cold War an opportunity for America to concentrate its energies at home. Yes, said the younger generation coming of age intellectually in the late 1980s and 1990s, who saw in the 'unipolar moment' a chance and a duty for America to place its imprint on world order. The battle was won by the new generation, and their priorities of interventionism and global democracy promotion became the basis of the neoconservative foreign policy agenda.[7] Such figures as Kristol remained, however, to demonstrate important elements of continuity with the founders of neoconservatism.

Such a brief sketch leaves out many variations of emphasis and even differences among neoconservatives, not least over religion, all of which is to point up the fact that neoconservatism was not a movement but a tendency. However, during the 1990s it did become increasingly institutionalized via think tanks, journals, and such organizations as the Project for a New American Century (PNAC), of which more later. Furthermore, it became more policy-oriented and took stances on a range of public issues in direct opposition to the Clinton administration. There is warrant, therefore, for speaking of an identifiable neoconservative ideology despite the complexities of its origins and the wide variations of emphasis among some of its adherents. Above all, foreign policy was the field on which neoconservatism spoke most clearly with one voice, and it was in this sphere that the subject of neoconservative influence on the Bush administration was most widely debated. Not least of the reasons for this was the entry into important government positions in the George W. Bush administration of such neoconservative figures as Paul Wolfowitz, Deputy Secretary of Defense, John Bolton, Under Secretary of State for Arms Control (and later Ambassador to the United

Nations), Richard Perle in the unofficial yet powerful advisory Defense Policy Board, and many others in lesser positions.

There are those who dismiss the notion that Bush's foreign policy can be described as neoconservative. A minority of his advisers, so one influential account has it, 'were what the press often referred to as neoconservatives' but most were rather 'assertive nationalists deeply sceptical of nation-building, especially when it involved the US military, and scornful that American power could create what others were able to build for themselves'.[8] This view discounts the high degree of consonance between the Bush administration's policies after September 11 and the pronouncements of the PNAC in 1997–98. The impact of September 11 was to empower the implementation of this agenda, which is not, however, to endorse conspiracy theories implying complicity by the Bush administration in 9/11 itself. As has been observed by the authors of a major study of American conservatism entitled *The Right Nation*, the ease with which the Bush administration embraced the neoconservative agenda was a result, not of a neoconservative coup against a weak president – few serious commentators accept such a view – but of the fact that the Bush agenda 'struck a mighty chord with the rest of the Right Nation. A neoconservative foreign policy soon became a conservative one.'[9] In short, neoconservatism drew strength from the degree to which it overlapped, indeed drew on, traditional American conservatism even as it added a new ideological dimension and refocused conservatism's energy on military power and unilateral action in foreign policy.

Cracks in the neoconservative edifice

Systems, natural and man-made, reveal most about themselves when they begin to fail or break down, and neoconservatism is no exception. That neoconservatism is in crisis is apparent not merely in the continuing difficulty of pacifying Iraq but in the level of opposition to neoconservative policies and values among many American conservatives, some of whom at one time shared neoconservative values. A prominent example is Francis Fukuyama. As a signatory of the founding Statement of Principles of the Project for a New American Century (1997) and also of its open letter to President Clinton (1998) calling for the removal of Saddam Hussein from power as 'the main aim of American foreign policy', Fukuyama placed himself in the company of prominent radical conservatives, many of whom went on to serve in the Bush administration. Quibble as one might about the precise definition of neoconservatism, Fukuyama placed himself in that family of conservatives who sought to rebuild America, in the words of the PNAC's founding statement, on the basis of 'military strength and moral clarity'. Indeed, we can take these two priorities as core notions of neoconservatism so far as it relates to foreign policy, specifying as they do both ends and means of a revised American conservatism which placed emphasis on a global mission on behalf of American democratic values – 'Wilson in boots', in the words of one commentator.[10] More specifically, Fukuyama also subscribed to the PNAC insistence on the removal of Saddam Hussein from power as part of a larger strategy for dealing with the coming threat from the Middle East which may be 'more serious than any we have known since the end of the Cold War'.[11] All the more significant, then, that Fukuyama should have emerged as one of the sharpest critics of the Bush administration in the run-up to the war in Iraq and that he should have maintained and even deepened that stance thereafter. In the 2004 election he backed Kerry rather than Bush.

Fukuyama's opposition to the war in Iraq was based on detailed studies he had been asked to carry out by the Bush administration itself. He was part of a team which in March 2003 delivered a report to the US Defense Department which recommended prioritizing a 'hearts and minds' campaign in the Islamic world over military action and pointed to the danger of creating a 'world in which the United States and its policies remain the chief focus of global concern'.[12] The following year

Fukuyama took issue with prominent neoconservative journalist Charles Krauthammer, who had adopted the label 'democratic realism' to describe his own stance. In respectful but unmistakably stern terms, Fukuyama lambasted the neoconservatives' apparent refusal to acknowledge certain obvious realities in the aftermath of the intervention in Iraq:

> the failure to find weapons of mass destruction in Iraq, the virulent and steadily mounting anti-Americanism throughout the Middle East, the growing insurgency in Iraq, the fact that no strong democratic leadership had emerged there, the failure to leverage the war to make progress on the Israeli–Palestine front, and the fact that America's fellow democratic allies had by and large failed to fall in line and legitimate American actions ex post.

Krauthammer and his fellow neoconservatives indulged in 'excessive idealism' and 'failed to appreciate America's own current legitimacy deficit', and had abandoned any notion of prudence and subtlety in foreign relations.[13]

This comprehensive indictment was given a further twist the following year when Fukuyama posed an even more fundamental question. 'To what extent', he asked in a general review of US policy since 2001, 'has that policy flowed from the wellspring of American politics and culture, and to what extent has it flowed from the particularities of this president and this administration?' The question is potentially subversive of the rationale behind administration policy since Bush, in common with all presidents and indeed all national leaders, has sought to associate his policies with the heart of American history and culture, and thereby to enhance its legitimacy and popular appeal. By extension those who oppose administration policies can be charged with, at best, being out of touch with heartland America and, at worst, betrayers of America's deepest and best values – which is to say un- or anti-American. However, Fukuyama wants to reject the idea that Bush's policy choices, in particular the war in Iraq, flow inevitably from America's historic roots and foreign-policy traditions. On the contrary, Fukuyama argues, a number of options were open to Bush, any one of which would have been 'in keeping with American foreign policy traditions'. It could have

> chosen to create a true alliance of democracies to fight the illiberal currents coming out of the Middle East. It could also have tightened economic sanctions and secured the return of arms inspectors to Iraq without going to war. It could have made a go at a new international regime to battle proliferation.

In the event, Bush made different choices which, rather than flowing from America's core values, were dictated by the values of neoconservatives. Bush's policies were in fact the result of 'happenstance' – the coincidence of the president's need to find a justification for invading Iraq, given the question mark over the existence of weapons of mass destruction, and the neoconservatives' desire to hitch their wagon to a policy of democratic transformation of the Middle East.[14] The failure to find weapons of mass destruction increased Bush's reliance on the theme of transforming the Middle East, and it is worth noting that leading neoconservative Paul Wolfowitz (Deputy Secretary of Defense in Bush's first term and then President of the World Bank) implied in an interview given in May 2003 that weapons of mass destruction was never the chief justification for war. It featured as the publicly favoured reason because it was the one issue which everyone in the bureaucracy could agree on.[15]

If Fukuyama's stance towards the neoconservative goals he had once favoured were ever in doubt, these doubts were removed in the early months of 2006 when he affirmed both that 'the neo-conservative moment appears to have passed' and that 'neo-conservatism has evolved into something I can no longer support'. Neoconservatism was based on certain illusions about American power and the way it was regarded both in the rest of the world and at home. The Bush administration failed to comprehend that the world did not accept the idea that America was uniquely virtuous and therefore that its 'benevolent hegemony' would be acceptable to all; it failed also to demonstrate competence in formulating policy in Iraq and carrying it out. Moreover, it made faulty assumptions about what the American people would be prepared to support. 'Americans', he wrote, 'are not, at heart, an imperial people.' In the circumstance, the United States needs to 'reconceptualize its foreign policy' which means demilitarizing the war on terror, seeking multilateral means of promoting US interests, and injecting more 'realism' into its idea of democracy promotion.[16]

Fukuyama's defection from the neoconservative camp was, however, only one instance of the pressure under which the war in Iraq placed neoconservatism. The evidence suggests that events in Iraq provoked a general crisis in American conservatism. By the summer of 2004 talk was heard of the 'end of the neoconservative moment'.[17] Traditional American conservatives were voicing their concerns in extended critiques of the Bush administration. Prominent among these was Stefan Halper and Jonathan Clarke's *America Alone* (2004) which gained added weight from the fact that both authors, one American and the other British, had extensive experience of government (Halper having served in the Nixon, Ford, and Reagan administrations, Clarke in the British diplomatic service) besides being firmly conservative in outlook. 'Our philosophic anchoring', they announced, 'is a conservative one':

We have lived and worked in the same culture from which many of the neo-conservatives have emerged. As often as not we have been colleagues. We have fought many of the battles that they have fought. We too have locked horns with shadowy emanations of the Soviet Union and seen inside of the beast; we have been on the ground in North Korea and Cuba, stood in the same trenches taking the incoming fire from European protests over Pershing missiles; we too know our way around the wars and revolutions of Central America; we too know how to defend ambitious aims against the counsels of timidity and defeatism.[18]

The rhetoric is significant. It bespeaks a sense of personal as well as political and intellectual affront in the progress of the neoconservative agenda. The casualty in the elevation of military force to the top of the list of policy instruments, the authors declare, is 'America's moral authority'. 'Far from being seen as liberators', America is regarded with hostility by those she professes to want to help. The authors write in the expectation that there will be a 'swing in the pendulum' back to conservatism's 'moderate roots'. More specifically, they embrace 'an alternative based on "the interest-focused centrist policies" that have guided both Republican and Democratic administrations from 1945–2000'.[19]

While it is possible that this is to overstate the element of consensus between Republican and Democratic administrations in postwar America, this statement certainly reveals the depth of the divide which has opened up between traditional and radical or neoconservatives. Particularly telling were the views of Brent Scowcroft, National Security Adviser under George H. W. Bush and before that Deputy National Security Adviser to Henry Kissinger in the Nixon administration. A former air-force general, Scowcroft was a prime mover in the decision to intervene militarily against Saddam Hussein following the invasion of Kuwait. In an interview with *New Yorker* writer Jeffrey Goldberg, published in October 2005, Scowcroft explained at length his turn against the Bush Jr administration and in the process revealed ever more clearly the extent of the gap between neo- and traditional conservatism. At root, it is argued, lies a philosophical difference between idealism and realism. Neoconservatives adopt an element of the liberal internationalism associated with Woodrow Wilson but combine it with an insistence on the centrality of military power as an instrument of foreign policy. Global democracy promotion and the reliance on the unilateral exercise of American force is the neoconservative formula for global stability as well as American security. By contrast, realism's distaste for moralism in international politics is well expressed in Scowcroft's scepticism about the viability of George W. Bush's war in Iraq. Convinced as Scowcroft was of the justification of the use of force in 1991 to punish Saddam Hussein's violation of Kuwait, 'he did not believe', Goldberg notes, 'that Saddam's treatment of his own citizens merited military intervention'. The realist is sceptical of the politics of good intentions on the grounds that human beings are fallible, but also on prudential grounds. How can you anticipate what the practical outcome of your moral purposes might be? Might not democracy, for example, in the hands of those unused to it lead to undemocratic results? The same reasoning placed a question mark over humanitarian interventions where there was no clear national interest, no strategic rationale. 'Before you intervene', Scowcroft declared, 'you have to ask yourself "If I go in, how do I get out?"' Besides, 'there are a lot of places in the world where injustice is taking place, and we can't run around and fix all of them'.[20]

Coming out as they did in Autumn 2005 as support for the war was falling, the insurgency remained at a high level, and no prospect of withdrawal was in sight, Scowcroft's strictures against the Bush administration were headline news. He had after all been mentor to the Secretary of State, Condoleezza Rice, having brought her into the National Security Council in 1989 as a Soviet expert. Goldberg ascribes Rice's defection to the neoconservative camp to her religious faith, which brought her closer to the ideological politics of George W. Bush. The publication of Scowcroft's views brought a predictable response from Charles Krauthammer. In his *Washington Post* column he described Scowcroft's take on the Iraq war as 'cold-blooded and wrong-headed', the product of a realism which prized stability above all and regarded the depredations of dictators such as Saddam Hussein as beyond the consideration of American policy-makers. Scowcroft's insensitivity to the aspiration to democracy in Iraq and the wider Middle East was, Krauthammer suggested, of a piece with the refusal of the Bush Sr administration to deal decisively with Saddam. 'It is not surprising', he concluded, 'that Scowcroft, who gave indecency a twelve-year life extension, should disdain decency's return.'[21]

Other significant fault-lines in American conservatism were exposed by the post-9/11 capture of the foreign-policy agenda by neoconservatism. Anti-government libertarians were also alienated by the way in which the war on terror was waged. Neoconservatism, wrote a member of the Cato Institute, 'is using the threat of terrorism to expand government at home and abroad'. The Patriot Act was indicative of a desire on the part of neoconservatives 'to reshape America and the world through the efforts of a robust federal government'. Furthermore, Bush's domestic agenda, which included federal promotion of faith-based initiatives and an increasing federal role in local education, were 'inconsistent with the concept of limited government and federalism'. Those neoconservatives such as Max Boot who have praised American 'imperialism' and seek to re-order the entire Middle East along neoconservative lines are 'profoundly un-American'. What is needed now, went the libertarian position, was 'for limited government conservatives exemplified by Ronald Reagan and Barry Goldwater to join forces with libertarians and enlightened liberals who respect civil liberties ... [to] speak out in support of America's heritage of liberty'.[22]

There is some irony in this invocation of Ronald Reagan, since his legacy was just as attractive to neoconservatives, though for different reasons. In an article published in *Foreign Affairs* in 1996, William Kristol and Robert Kagan had called, in what is generally seen as an anticipation of the PNAC's agenda, for a 'neo-Reaganite foreign policy' to counter the global weakness into which America was drifting under Clinton.[23] It is evidence of the multi-faceted nature of Reagan's legacy but also of the disarray in American conservatism that his legacy should be so disputed. In fact there were more than two Reagans. Halper and Clarke talk of the 'false histories' of the Reagan years purveyed by neoconservatives. Their own preferred Reagan is essentially a pragmatic optimist who may have made strident ideological noises but combined strong moral convictions with prudence and even caution when it came to the possibility of actual confrontation. In fact, Halper and Clarke claim, neoconservatives forgot or suppressed their own disquiet with the second Reagan term when the expectation of decisive moves against communism failed to materialize and Reagan seemed to embrace a revised version of détente.[24] Thus discussion of the Reagan legacy throws up at least three Reagans: the ur-neoconservative ideologue, the libertarian (as in the Cato Institute's version), and the pragmatic conservative – ample evidence, if it were needed, of serious cracks in the edifice of conservatism.

Much of the above was primarily in the realm of intellectual debate, though Scowcroft's opinions doubtless carried weight in political circles if only as a substantial voice to be countered. Of more immediate consequence to the Bush administration was opposition by Republicans in Congress to measures associated with the war in Iraq and the war on terror more generally. Senators Warner of Virginia, McCain of Arizona, and Graham of South Carolina aroused the ire of Vice-President Cheney in the summer of 2005 with their call for the inclusion in a military appropriations bill of a ban on 'cruel, inhuman or degrading treatment or punishment'. Summoning the three senators to his office, Cheney failed to convince them to withdraw this provision from the bill. They agreed to disagree on the issue.[25] There appeared shortly, however, an even more damaging and contentious issue in the revelation that the CIA had been using secret locations in a variety of countries to interrogate suspected terrorists – the practice, so-called, of 'rendition'. When combined with the growing evidence of disquiet in Congress about the continued insurgency and violence in Iraq itself, it was apparent that administration policy was under severe pressure from erstwhile supporters as well as dyed-in-the-wool opponents. The frontal attack on administration policy by Democratic congressman Murtha, which included the demand for withdrawal of US troops, could possibly have been swatted away as partisan sniping were it not for the fact that Murtha was a an ex-marine and Vietnam veteran, a past supporter of US military ventures, and an acknowledged patriot.[26] Needless to say, Bush's difficulties in justifying the war in Iraq, to many in his own party as well as to his opponents, grew during 2006 as the conflict spun seemingly out of control.

Our concern here, however, is less with tracing in detail the rise of opposition to the war in Iraq than understanding how a particular approach to policy, and indeed an entire philosophical outlook, can move from a position of centrality, comprehensiveness, and pre-eminence to one which looks increasingly marginal, narrowly conceived and highly contested. In retrospect, the transformation of the Republican agenda under Bush since September 11 may look like a neoconservative coup. Indeed, in its October 2002 issue the magazine *The American Conservative*, the organ of traditional American conservatism, quoted with approval Pat Buchanan's observation that 'the conservative movement has been highjacked and turned into a globalist, interventionist, open borders ideology, which is not the conservative movement I grew up with'.[27] How did neoconservatism succeed in achieving such a position? The idea of a coup is attractive to those who seek clear and unequivocal causes for complex events, but there is no conclusive evidence that Bush was the plaything of his aides, inexperienced as he was on entering office in the field of foreign affairs. It is possible that historians in the future will discover evidence that the president was manipulated into initiating the war in Iraq, but as things stand the evidence suggests that in the wake of September 11 he shared neoconservative convictions about foreign policy. More likely is that a subtler process was taking place which involved the employment of certain kinds of rhetoric as a means of convincing others of the case for war. We cannot look inside the head of the president, but it is possible to observe explanations, justifications, and exhortations in the language of presidential speeches which serve to link the 'bully pulpit' of the presidency with the collectivity of the people, policies with national values, and present needs with past events and traditions. The processes involved here are a special case of the broader question of how any political ideology establishes a position of dominance. The critical move is to present a particular policy as the natural and inevitable out-growth not merely of a party position but of consensual national traditions and values. George W. Bush's strategy for achieving this, I would suggest, was based on three closely linked moves: the sanction of history, the rhetoric of freedom, and the invocation of religion.

Rhetoric in the service of policy: history

The first of these requires some preliminary remarks since it is of significance far beyond the present case. Popular wisdom has it that the United States, with its relatively brief history, is an un-historical or even an anti-historical nation. Henry Ford famously said 'history is bunk'. Whatever he actually meant by this – it is most probable that he meant most existing accounts of history, rather than the past itself, were bunk – it has been taken to confirm a self-evident truth: that America has always been more interested in the future than the past, that its aston-ishing speed of growth was based on a willingness to tear up the past in the service of a better future, and that by comparison with other major powers it has in any case a short history. Appearances are deceptive. In fact, America's past is present in a peculiarly active and tangible way. First, despite the Civil War, there is an unusual degree of continuity in American constitu-tional and political structures. American constitutional debate involves continuous dialogue with the eighteenth-century terms and values which originally shaped it. But it is not only strictly constitutional and political debate which demonstrates this continuity. The same is true of social issues. As Tocqueville pointed out in the 1830s, in the United States social and poli-tical issues have a habit of becoming judicial issues.[28] This is a consequence in turn of the written constitution and the power of the Supreme Court to rule on constitutionality. The result is that urgent contemporary social issues such as race relations, abortion, the death penalty, and school prayer are discussed in terms which to a considerable degree are consonant with those of the eighteenth century, not least in relation to the dynamics of federalism. Above all, however, they rest on interpretation of key amendments to the Constitution which are surrounded by an accumulation of exegesis.

A second important reason for the presence of the past in America is the creation of the American state at a particular moment in time, accompanied by documents which gave explicit voice to founding ideals which have remained talismanic presences throughout America's history. It has rightly been remarked that no society is more conservative than one founded in revolution, since the overriding task of successive governments of whatever party is to preserve the institutions and ideals of the revolution. It applied to the Soviet Union and it applies to the United States, with the singular difference that the American idea of revolution proved more flexible and adaptable to change than the Soviet. At any rate the consequence has been that America's past is unusually active in its present. Arguably the issue in America is not the absence of history but the difficulty of separating from it. All presidents, indeed all political movements whether of left or right, seek to associate current policies with founding principles. George W. Bush left the American people in no doubt what he meant by this when he declared in his first inaugural address:

> We have a place, all of us, in a long story – a story we continue but whose end we will not see. It is the story of a new world that became a friend and liberator of the old, a story of a slave-holding society that became a servant of freedom, a story of a power that went into the world to protect but not to possess, to defend but not to conquer ... *I will bring the values of our history to the care of our times.*
>
> (emphasis added)[29]

Such grand gestures are not the only way in which the sanction of history enters into calculations about the present. There are more or less subtle gradations between such broad-canvas legitimations at the level of general principles and the invocation of history to bolster specific policies. We shall turn to the latter shortly. Meanwhile, some way between these poles lies the use of history to support a political orientation which presents itself as politically neutral but in which in actuality tends towards partisanship. In contemporary American conservatism this is signalled by a sequence of connections drawn between condemnation of appeasement in the 1930s, something akin to the idolization of Winston Churchill, and the continuation of this great tradition in the figures of Ronald Reagan and Margaret Thatcher. The dictatorships of Hitler, Stalin, Saddam Hussein and others are identified as enemies of the tradition. The overriding historical analogy for American conservatives in the war on terror, as it was for many in the Cold War, is that of appeasement of the 1930s, the lesson being that it is futile and dangerous to compromise with dictators. They must be resisted at an early stage or they will have to be tackled later under less favourable circumstances. This element is favoured by conservatives of all stamps.

This conclusion leads in turn to a third, and much more specific, element in the sanction of history, as practised by the Bush administration – the search for legitimation for the argument for 'pre-emption' in foreign policy which emerged in the summer of 2002 as the Bush administration prepared the ground for military action against Iraq. It must first be noted that what the Bush administration termed 'pre-emption' should more properly have been called prevention. Pre-emptive action applies to the danger of imminent attack, not the possibility or likelihood of it down the line. By employing the term pre-emption with reference to a relatively remote possibility the Bush administration was in effect exaggerating the immediacy of the threat from Iraq. In the *National Security Strategy* (NSS) of autumn 2002 the argument emerged fully fledged, having been adumbrated in a number of previous speeches. The way in which the strategy was presented indicates an awareness on the part of the administration of certain difficulties in presentation. There was a need to present it both as a necessary innovation and as a policy sanctioned by history. On the first point, the case rested on the inapplicability of the Cold War doctrine of deterrence to a situation in which the enemy took the form of rogue states which did not subscribe to international conventions or values, and shadowy groups of terrorists who might use weapons of mass destruction without warning. In such circumstances the United States must 'be prepared to stop rogue states and their terrorist clients before they are able to threaten or use weapons of mass destruction against the United States and our allies and friends'. Unfamiliar and threatening as this situation was, however, history provided moral and legal support for the policy. 'For centuries', it was noted, 'international law recognized that nations need not suffer an attack before they can lawfully take action to defend themselves against the forces that present an imminent danger of attack.' Admittedly, history was not a complete guide here because the old idea of 'imminent danger' referred to visible armies, navies and air forces preparing to attack and it scarcely covered new forms of aggression by terrorists and rogue states. However, there was the further point, somewhat vaguely and sweeping expressed, that 'the United States has long maintained the option of pre-emptive action to counter a sufficient threat to our national security'.[30]

It was left to others to fill in the historical gaps and indeed to reinterpret American foreign policy in the light of present needs. The fullest account along these lines was by leading US diplomatic historian John Gaddis in *Surprise, Security and the American Experience* (2004). Gaddis' argument involved a delicate balancing act in that he wanted to make two divergent arguments: first that there were good American historical precedents for the Bush revolution in foreign policy (which can be summed up in the terms pre-emption, unilateralism, and hegemony) and second, that Bush's foreign policy was a genuine innovation in American 'grand strategy'. Our concern here is less with the success or otherwise with which Gaddis resolves this contradiction than with the extent to which he is able to provide historical precedents for Bush's grand strategy, particularly with reference to pre-emption. Gaddis' key reference point is John Quincy Adams' supposed plan of seeking security for the United States by expansion, the main example being the process by which the United States acquired Florida from Spain in 1818–19. An incursion into Florida by General Andrew Jackson acting with 'questionable authority' resulted in Jackson's challenge to his government to endorse his action and seize the opportunity to annex the somewhat chaotically governed Florida to the United States. Adams' successful promotion of this ploy, which resulted in a treaty with Spain ceding Florida to the United States, became, so we are told, a model for similar subsequent pre-emptive actions in the war with Mexico in 1846–48, the war with Spain in 1898, and numerous interventions in Latin America in the first two decades of the twentieth century.[31]

This appears to be a case in which the desire to find a consistent pattern of precedents for the Bush administration's argument for pre-emption gets the better of the historian. No quoted sources are offered which would bear out the conclusion that anything like a doctrine of pre-emption was in Adams' mind. Adams supported the acquisition of Florida in 1819, but later opposed the war with Mexico in which there were much larger territorial gains to be made. Furthermore, while there is a common theme of expansion in the events Gaddis refers to, contexts and strategies varied. And, as Gaddis, himself points out, the same John Quincy Adams who advocated the acquisition of Florida also urged America not 'to go in search of monsters to destroy', in recognition of the fact that the quest for security might as often as not require restraint rather than expansion. To be sure, Gaddis does refer to Adams' cautionary remarks about expansionism and the danger of America seeking to become the 'dictatress of the world'. To that extent Gaddis affirms that at this point the Adams legacy and the Bush strategy 'part company'. Nevertheless, the suggestion that such an unambiguous legacy exists and that the Bush strategy is in principle in a clear line with it rests on shaky historical foundations. But it is just this foundation on which the argument for the war in Iraq partly rests. Careful as Gaddis is to enter caveats about the success with which Bush pursued the strategy, the key justificatory move has been made. Gaddis' book becomes a godsend to the policy-maker of the war in Iraq, a boon enhanced by the suggestion that Bush's strategy is 'a redefinition, for only the third time in American history, of what it will take to protect the nation from surprise attack', the other two being those initiated by John Quincy Adams and Franklin Roosevelt's policy of global containment of aggressive powers resulting from the Pearl Harbor attack.[32]

Rhetoric in the service of policy: freedom

The second element in the Bush strategy for associating his foreign policy with national values is the invocation of freedom. This, of course, is intimately bound up with the sanction of history since freedom is the historical value most closely associated with the founding of the United States and its 'mission'. What needs to be emphasized is the incantatory quality of the invocation of freedom in such speeches as Bush's second inaugural address, in which the word freedom, or occasionally its near synonym 'liberty', is used over thirty times in the space of a few pages. It is hard to gauge the precise effect of such insistent repetition but we can estimate from the assumptions which are made by the speaker what the intended effects are on his audience. Evidently freedom is the foundation on which all other American values are based, and it resonates with ideas of freedom in the American Revolution, in biblical history, the struggles against slavery in all its forms, the free market, the first amendment to the US Constitution which guarantees freedom of speech and religion – indeed the whole gamut of political, economic, social, religious, personal and historical values on which the United States is founded.

One section of this address takes the form of effectively three stanzas with the same repeated opening: 'In America's ideal of freedom ... ' In the first instance freedom is associated with economic independence which is the foundation for justice and equality. Second, freedom is linked with 'private character' which in turn supports families and faith communities (including that of Islam); and finally, freedom and its attendant rights are the basis of community-mindedness, including opposition to racism and other divisive attitudes of mind. These paragraphs constitute not so much definitions of freedom or inquiries into its meaning as celebratory affirmations of what are taken to be givens by all Americans. A further important feature of Bush's rhetorical strategy leads on directly from the first: the presumed self-evidence of the value and meaning of freedom. No definition, no inquiry into its meaning, is needed. We know what freedom is and what its means: it is what makes us Americans. The roots of such thinking lie in the mindset of the Jeffersonian Enlightenment, most obviously expressed in the Declaration of Independence. Jefferson's legacy lay not merely in the content of the values he expressed – 'life, liberty, and the pursuit of happiness' – but in his insistence on their presumed givenness: 'we hold these truths to be *self-evident*'. Furthermore these values are global and universal. As the *National Security Strategy* expressed it, on the progress towards political and economic freedom 'this path is not America's alone. It is open to all.' The extension of freedom to others is part of America's 'great mission'.[33] To oppose such a mission and the policies designed to implement it is by implication to oppose the values which underpin it.

In practice, policy-makers have had to concede that honest and well-intentioned Americans have opposed the war in Iraq. Documents such as inaugural addresses are ideologically maximalist consensus-seeking and consensus-generating efforts; they are hardly policy documents as such. They are designed specifically not to invite questioning. They are nevertheless the clothing in which policy typically appears and are important for what they reveal about what the speaker believes in principle to be non-negotiable. And notice the frequency with which the idea of 'non-negotiable values' appears in Bush's speeches.

Rhetoric in the service of policy: religion

As for the invocation of religion, the links between neoconservatism and the Christian right in America have on occasions been peculiarly close, though their origins are quite different. While both rejected the cultural and moral values of the counter-culture of the 1960s, they had different institutional bases and different ends in view. Neoconservatism grew out of the disillusionment of liberals with the political and moral values of the 1960s and in particular a feeling that the counter-culture amounted to, in the words of Jeane Kirkpatrick, 'a wholesale assault on the legitimacy of American society'.[34] Religion was not a central issue for most neoconservatives, and not all were believers. Political ideology was the primary focus of the first generation of neoconservatives; most were intellectuals based in the northeastern United States. As for the Christian right, its roots lay in revulsion against the moral and especially the sexual revolution of the 1960s, and its power base was in the South. The revolt against the moral values of the 1960s and the most powerful impetus for a change in public morals was strongest among evangelical Christians, notably the Southern Baptist church, which in the late 1960s became the largest of the Protestant denominations in the United States. This regional bias in the development of evangelical Christianity was matched by what has been termed the 'southernization' of American politics, particularly the Republican Party.[35] From the late 1960s the Republican Party sought to rebuild its power base, after several decades of effective Democrat dominance in Congress, by targeting the South which had always been socially conservative and which had become politicized in reaction to the civil rights movement. Goldwater's presidential candidacy in 1964, which failed miserably – Johnson's victory was by the largest popular vote in American history – was nevertheless significant for the conservative cause, since Goldwater's majorities in the deep southern states, traditionally Democratic Party territory, showed how deep was the potential for Republican gains in the South. Thereafter, many southern voters switched party allegiance in defiance of the Democratic Party's advocacy of black civil rights and mutliculturalism, while the Republican Party adopted a 'southern strategy'.

The agendas of the Christian right and of the neoconservatives coalesced in the Republican candidacy of Ronald Reagan in 1980. He combined social and moral conservatism with an apparently uncompromising stance towards the Soviet bloc. In practice his presidency proved to be more moderate than the rhetoric suggested. In foreign policy he was noticeably pragmatic despite the colourful rhetoric ('evil empire', etc.), thus disappointing the neoconservatives, and he failed to deliver key items on the Christian right's agenda such as a federal ban on abortion. However, there was a new wave of activity by Christian groups in the 1990s which chimed with the neoconservatives' challenge to the Clinton presidency. The agenda of evangelical Christians, as Halper and Clarke point out, thus became associated with partisan Republicanism, which was similarly the vehicle for the neoconservatives.[36] In George W. Bush the neoconservatives and the Christian right found their champion, and few would dispute the fact that Bush brought religious belief more explicitly to bear on his public office than any other modern president. Jimmy Carter was certainly at least as devout and did not hide his religious belief, but he was careful not to link it too closely with policy-making. In Bush's case, insistent though he was on several occasions to deny that he regarded himself as an instrument of God's will, his choice of rhetoric and the frequency and intensity with which he invoked religious themes, created the impression that this is precisely what he thought.[37] We do not have to accept the accuracy of a report by an Israeli journalist of a claim by President Bush that God had instructed him to invade Iraq to acknowledge the centrality of religious faith to his policy-making. This was apparent even before September 11 in the words of his first inaugural address: 'we are not this story's author, who fills time and eternity with his purpose. Yet his purpose is achieved in our duty.' In his first speech after September 11, Bush declared that 'freedom and fear, justice and cruelty, have always been at war, and we know that God is not neutral between them'. In his 2004 State of the Union Address, Bush concluded that '[freedom] is not carried forward by our power alone. We can trust in that greater power who guides the unfolding of the years. And in all that is to come, we can know that His purposes are just and true.'[38] Nor is it irrelevant that the speech-writer who penned Bush's 2002 State of the Union Address and changed the originally drafted 'axis of hatred' to 'axis of evil' was, as Bob Woodward noted, 'a self-described evangelical Christian and "compassionate conservative" [who] admired the way Bush didn't shy away from injecting his religious convictions and moral conclusions into his speeches'.[39]

Bush's policies, especially those associated with the war on terror which were of high urgency and importance, were clothed in religious imagery which resonated with many Americans. Clearly not all Americans, however. Bush's religiosity attracted much criticism, and not only from atheists, on the grounds that it politicized religion even as it cast religiosity over politics. In so doing it trampled on the deep and difficult divide between church and state which has been an article of political faith since the passage of the first amendment to the Constitution in 1791 – difficult because the high levels of religious belief and church attendance in the United States exert continuous pressure to breach the separation of church and state. For present purposes the point to be emphasized is the extent to which the war on terror was invested with religious significance by implication if not by active design.

The failure of the mission

The argument of this chapter contains an assumption about the trajectory of the neoconservativism; it is presumed to have failed to achieve its goals. Clearly, given the impossibility of predicting the future, this assumption cannot be definitive. Indeed, the judgements made here are inevitably in part political. Others do and will continue to come to other conclusions.[40] It could be argued that the agenda goes forward, despite certain obvious setbacks. At the time of writing (November 2006) the war continues and Congress continues to vote appropriations for it, even if the post-mid-term election Congress is bound to raise sharper questions than ever. War is the new reality, to which the American people and the world at large have become to some extent inured, whatever attitudes are taken towards it. Until the elections of 2008 the full extent of the damage to the neo-conservative agenda will not be known.

However, even if judgements might vary about whether 'fail-ure' is the appropriate word to characterize the fate of the neo-conservative mission, there can be little dispute about the fact that it is under serious challenge. The argument that it has failed is based on a range of evidence, quantitative and qualitative. With some slight variations, the poll data showed a steady fall in approval ratings of President Bush between March 2003 and 2006, for his handling of the situation in Iraq and also in answers to the question of whether the United States made the right decision in using military force against Iraq.[41] Further-more, as we have seen, the fracturing of the right in America has placed neoconservatism firmly on the defensive, and behind that fracturing lies the reality of the failure as yet of the administration's policy to achieve its goal in Iraq and the diffi-culty of knowing when or whether it can. There are several possible measures of this, but among the most compelling is the revision of the administration's estimate of the likely future course of the war on terror, or the 'long war' as it was coming to be called in the early months of 2006. While resisting the conclusion that the long war on terror would mean an indefi-nite commitment of American troops in Iraq and elsewhere, Defense Secretary Rumsfeld affirmed the war on terror itself was likely to be all but open-ended. The war on terror was being redefined in terms of the Cold War.[42] What that meant in terms of American troop deployments in Iraq was not yet clear, but Donald Rumsfeld's departure from the Department of Defense in November 2006 constituted an acknowledgement that whatever time-scale put on the war on terror as a whole, there were powerful reasons for seeking an exit strategy from Iraq. The challenge for policy-makers in the next few years will be how to reduce the American commitment in Iraq without it being taken as a defeat for American policy. The Bush administration seems perilously close to the dilemma Nixon faced in Vietnam, which he sought to resolve with the unfortunately named policy of 'peace with honor'. The neocons' cherished project is seemingly in tatters.

A related measure of the diminishing returns from the prosecution of war in Iraq might be the growing awareness of the extent to which the war in Iraq was consuming America's energies, to the detriment of its interests elsewhere. 'Is Washington Losing Latin America?' asked the president of the Inter-American Dialogue in early 2006. His answer, that 'relations between the United States and Latin America today are at their lowest ebb since the end of the Cold War', and that 'after 9/11, Washington lost interest in Latin America', has relevance to other issues and areas on the US agenda, not least the Palestinian–Israeli conflict.[43] The Middle Eastern Road Map, announced in April 2003, proposed a timetable in which the final phase of a three-stage process, involving the establishment of a Palestinian state, would be completed by the end of 2005. Needless to say, the failure to achieve this goal cannot be put down exclusively or even mainly to the United States, but it is a measure of the all-consuming nature of the war on terror and the Iraq war that so little US energy should have been devoted to this issue. The neoconservative agenda was always sharply focused on the Middle East, but within that its focus was on Iraq, coupled with support of Israel, to which was added a larger but somewhat vaguely formulated goal of promoting democracy in the region. The United States does not share the view of Arab states that resolution of the Palestinian–Israeli conflict is the single most important issue in the region.

These points bear some expansion, but here the emphasis must be on the fragility of the 'neoconservative moment': the revelation that, despite the efforts of the Bush administration to portray its agenda as *the* American ideology, it is evidently only *an* American ideology and a highly partial one at that, riding the crest of the post-9/11 wave. The historical, ideological and religious claims, and the inflated rhetoric in which they are couched, are barely able to hide the confusions, double-standards and deceptions associated with the prosecution of the agenda itself. The US claim to be the liberator of Iraq and of the wider Middle East now looks questionable in light of the virulent opposition which the American presence has aroused. The claim to be standing for freedom similarly looks questionable in the light of the open-ended detention of prisoners without trial Guantanamo Bay and Abu Ghraib, as does the idea that the United States is acting in some sense in line with God's purpose – a claim which many evangelicals find repugnant. In the summer of 2002, a group of evangelical Christian leaders in the United States called for an 'even-handed US policy' towards Israel and the Palestinians, and rejected 'the way some have distorted biblical passages as their rationale for uncritical support' for Israel.[44] In short, the emperor's clothes were by now, if not entirely gone, distinctly threadbare.

What was clear, in conclusion, was the intellectual thinness of neoconservatism, its dogmatic simplicity, its resistance to reality and to evidence, and its denial of values such as prudence, realism, alliance-seeking, and negotiation, which could claim to be as American as those which neoconservatives claimed for themselves. What was also clear, however, was the difficulty of mounting a direct political challenge inside the United States to the neoconservative agenda, driven as it was by the post-9/11 war psychology and couched as it was in a language which possessed appeal beyond the confines of neoconservatism itself. Besides, it is one thing to offer a critique of a political ideology but quite another to mount an alternative. As things stand, such effective opposition as there is comes from American conservatives, not least because they share some of the premises of the neoconservatives and are concerned, as schismatics always are, to mark the differences between themselves and a new orthodoxy. Who knows what a viable liberal agenda would look like in circumstances where liberalism is not so much ineffective or under suspicion as irrelevant? Wherever the challenge comes from, it will need to take the measure not only of neoconservative policies but also of the language in which they are couched and the values which lie behind them. One legacy of the Bush years, which future administrations will have to tackle, will surely be the need to re-address the question of what such terms as democracy and freedom might mean for America in the twenty-first century.

7   The Bush administration and the idea of international community

The 'illusory international community'

In January 2000, as the presidential election got into its stride, Condoleezza Rice published a campaigning article in the influential magazine *Foreign Affairs*. Since she was George W. Bush's foreign-policy adviser, it could be assumed that her views would give an indication of the likely direction of policy under a Bush administration. The subtitle, 'promoting the national interest', told the main story. After a period of rudderless leadership under Clinton, during which (so the argument went) any consistent conception of the national interest had been lost sight of and in which, his most conservative critics jibed, Clinton had pursued 'foreign policy as social work', it was time to reassert America's own interests as the guiding principle of American foreign relations. This was not a matter of selfishness, far less of isolationism. 'Foreign policy in a Republican administration', Rice declared, 'will most certainly be internationalist.' There was no incompatability between the assertion of America's national interest and the promotion of global peace and stability. Indeed, Rice went on, when America exercised power 'without hectoring and bluster ... in concert with those who share its core values, the world becomes more prosperous, democratic and peaceful'. In effect this was a bid to wrest internationalism from the liberal idealists and to marry internationalism with realism. What precisely internationalism might mean at this stage in policy terms was not self-evident. What was clear was that American policy should proceed from 'the firm ground of the national interest, *not from the interests of an illusory international community*' (emphasis added).[1]

Campaign documents are not, of course, policy statements. Simplifications and overstatements are expected, even required. Earlier in the article Rice was somewhat less categorical than in the passage quoted above. In setting the national interest against 'humanitarian' interests and those of the 'international community', she said that there was nothing wrong with doing something which benefited all humanity but this was 'a second-order effect'. The flaw in the Wilsonian tradition, which she said found echoes in the Clinton administration, was to believe that power could only legitimately be exercised on behalf of someone or something else. Many Americans, she wrote, were uncomfortable with the notion of power and appealed instead to 'notions of international laws and norms, and the belief that the support of many states – or even better, of institutions like the United Nations – is essential to the legitimate exercise of power'. It was time to rebalance American foreign policy by placing faith in the legitimacy of the exertion of American power. If Rice conceded something to the 'international interest', the use of the word 'illusory' to describe the international community is nevertheless highly revealing. It suggests a philosophical orientation which goes deeper than policy choices and informs the entire framework in which policy is made. It is this philosophical position which I explore here with a view to establishing how far such notions underpinned the policies of the Bush administration, where such notions came from, and, finally, where the Bush administration can be placed in relation to America's foreign-policy traditions.

The idea of the international community

What is meant by 'the international community' and what does it mean to doubt its existence? In the first place it implies that there is a source of legitimacy for action by states which is larger than or transcends that of national governments. That entity is difficult to define, but doubtless has reference to our common membership of the human race and the idea that the peace and stability of each nation considered individually is more likely to be guaranteed by common action. It implies also that national sovereignty is necessarily limited by reference to the international norms, whether explicitly through international law and other agreements, including treaties, between states or implicitly by means of mutual restraint based on acknowledgement of others' interests. It betokens a belief that there is more to be gained than lost by accepting certain limits to sovereignty. Finally, the idea of an international community rests on a recognition that sovereignty is necessarily diminished by the effects of globalization. There is no need here to rehearse all the familiar arguments. Suffice it to say that the immense growth in the number and rate of cross-border interactions, and flows of goods, information, finance and people in recent decades has rendered national boundaries, if by no means redundant, certainly of diminished significance. In many fields, it is now recognized that there are no purely national solutions to key problems such as global warming, environmental degradation, international trade, population movements, terrorism and many others. Marshall McLuhan's 'global village' is now a reality. Above all, in the hands of its advocates, 'international community' is both a descriptive and a normative term. It describes what the world is really like, or at least what it is becoming, but conveys also a value judgement: communitarian thinking on a global scale is not only pragmatically necessary, it is good in and of itself.

It is, of course, highly doubtful whether, when Condoleezza Rice expressed scepticism about the idea of the international community, she meant to deny that these processes were taking place. Her claim rested surely on the conviction that, despite evident changes in the context of national action, the nation-state remained the primary constituent of the international system. International law was made between governments. The United Nations and other comparable organizations were premised on the existence of sovereign nations as the contracting parties to international agreements. In no sense was the UN a world government, and any suggestion that it might become one should be firmly scotched. Pollution, global warming, and the whole panoply of transnational phenomena might recognize no national boundaries but the economies which produced them operated within national borders and were subject in the first instance to national legal frameworks; moreover the mechanisms for taking action remained in the hands of sovereign governments. Furthermore, individuals generally identified themselves with nations and their associated traditions, languages, symbols, sports teams, and the like. Finally, the primary function of national governments was to ensure the security and well-being of their citizens. Not to do so would be to renege on their fundamental responsibility, besides being a recipe for political suicide. From this point of view the 'international community' was a metaphysical construct beloved of idealists who had little grasp of the real world. In the real world effective power was still wielded by the governments of nation-states, and moreover it was desirable that they should continue to do so.

The Bush adminstration and the international community

How far can Rice's statement be taken as representing that of the Bush administration as a whole? It was made before Bush came into power, before 9/11 and the many changes which resulted from its impact. I asked a high-ranking American official in 2006 whether he thought Secretary Rice still subscribed to the sentiments expressed in the article, and the reply was an embarrassed laugh and 'most certainly not'. America, he responded, had learned in the wake of 9/11 the lesson that it needed allies to secure its global position and must necessarily look beyond its own particular interest. Furthermore, had the United States not at every stage in the war on terror sought to build coalitions and where possible gain the endorsement of international organizations for military and other actions? To these points can be added the invocation of 'the international community' by President Bush himself on a number of occasions. In a speech to American veterans in November 2005, Bush called for the government of Syria to 'do what the international community has demanded: cooperate fully with the Mehlis investigation [into the murder of the former prime Minister of Lebanon] and stop trying to intimidate and de-stabilize the Lebanese government'.[2] At a press conference on 22 August 2006 he called on the 'international community' to come forward with troops to form a peace-keeping force in southern Lebanon following the conflict between Israel and Hizbollah. In his 2005 State of the Union Address, the president spoke of America's 'aim to build and preserve a community of free and independent nations'.[3] Admittedly here the emphasis is on the independent character of the members of the community, but it is nevertheless described as a community.

There is a limit, however, to how far these and comparable instances can carry us. In most cases Bush invoked the international community when the United States sought endorsement of action it wished to pursue. The international community was less often invoked when a situation involved obligations on the part of the United States or when it related to a decision taken by others. While on occasions the Bush administration believed it prudent and valuable to invoke the notion of the international community, in the main it found little favour with his government. This is not to deny that the Bush administration prefers to act in concert with allies when possible. Multilateralism is not incompatible with a belief in the primacy of national sovereignty as the leading principle of international relations. It simply means that for pragmatic reasons it may be best to act with allies where appropriate, even if one has to be prepared to 'go it alone' when it is not. The most trenchant expression of this is to be found in Bush's 2004 State of the Union Address:

from the beginning, America has sought international support for our operations in Afghanistan and Iraq, and we have gained much support. There is a difference, however, between leading a coalition of many nations, and submitting to the objections of a few. America will never seek a permission slip to defend the security of our country.[4]

A more detailed look at the record of the Bush administration confirms first impressions that notions of 'international community' are marginal to American policy. But the case is not of a simple rejection of the idea. While there are examples of a categorical dismissal of internationalist perspectives, in many instances there is a perceived need to placate the internationalist constituency at home and abroad in presumed recognition of its generally high profile and legitimacy. The case of the United States' rejection of the Kyoto Protocol on climate change is one such example. On the one hand, National Security Adviser Condoleezza Rice is reported to have told European leaders at a private function in early 2001 that Kyoto was 'dead', and there seems little doubt that this represented the gut sentiment of the administration.[5] On the other hand, when President Bush made a major speech on this subject during the summer of the same year he took care not merely to speak more diplomatically but to endorse the framework of discussions of climate change. 'The Kyoto Protocol was fatally flawed in fundamental ways', he declared,

but the process used to bring nations together to discuss our joint response to climate change is an important one. That is why I am today committing the United States of America to develop with our friends and allies and nations throughout the world an effective and science-based response to the issue of global warming.

Words, of course, are cheap but it is significant that it was felt necessary to pay court to the global framework in which climate change was being discussed. It was important also to assert

American leadership on this issue despite non-participation in the Protocol. Hence 'America's unwillingness to embrace a flawed treaty should not be read by our friends and allies as any abdication of responsibility. To the contrary, my administration is committed to a leadership role on the issue of climate change.' Arguably, however, the key statement in this speech comes in the paragraph which precedes this one, since it contains the nub of the objection to the Protocol. Not only were the Kyoto targets unrealistic, 'arbitrary and not based upon science' but 'for America, complying with those mandates would have a negative economic impact, with layoffs for workers and price increases for consumers'. Where America's economic well-being was concerned there could be no compromise.

The issue here is not the rights or wrongs of the Bush administration's policy on climate change but the rationale on which it is based. Significantly, Bush does not accept the view, held increasingly by experts in international relations and environmental science alike, that climate change challenges not only our way of life but also common assumptions about international relations, most obviously state-centred theories. While Bush acknowledges that 'the issue of climate change respects no border', there is no recognition that existing models of global politics which privilege states over international institutions might be inadequate to cope with climate change.[6] The Bush administration remains doggedly 'realist' on this question, though one is entitled to ask whether 'realism' is realistic on such a topic. At any rate, national interests dominate. Sovereignty is supreme.

Another case in point is the International Criminal Court (ICC), though here the approach is less conciliatory. The idea of the ICC went back to the 1950s when it was envisaged as a permanent follow-up to the court which had tried Nazi war criminals at Nuremberg. The ICC was to embody the principle, for the first time on a permanent basis, that individuals and not merely states could be tried for crimes against humanity by an international court according to universal standards. The difficulty in arriving at definitions of various key concepts such as 'aggression' had led to regular postponements of the submission of proposals to the UN General Assembly. The end of the Cold War broke the logjam and a text was completed in 1998 after several years of drafting and re-drafting. Sixty countries were required to ratify the proposal for it to come into operation, which was achieved on 1 July 2002. The United States had signed up to the ICC on 31 December 2000, in one of President Clinton's last acts in office. Though harbouring serious doubts about aspects of the treaty, Clinton endorsed the ICC in order to 'reaffirm our strong support for international accountability and for bringing to justice perpetrators of genocide, war crimes and crimes against humanity'. Conservatives in America had long opposed the court, and in May 2002 the Bush administration reversed the earlier decision, writing to the UN that the United States did 'not intend to become a party to the ICC'.

Once again the issue is not whether the United States' specific objections to the ICC's jurisdiction and powers were justified, but the grounds on which the objections were based and the measures used to combat them. The primary objection, as expressed by Under Secretary of State for Arms Control and International Security, John Bolton (later the US representative at the UN) in a speech to the conservative think-tank, the American Enterprise Institute, was that members of American military forces and civilians working for them could be liable to politically motivated prosecution by a court whose jurisdiction lay outside the control of the United States and whose authority the United States could not accept. Furthermore, Americans serving overseas in a country which had ratified the treaty would be subject to prosecution even if the United States were not a member of the court. Thus the ICC, he said, had 'unacceptable consequences for our national sovereignty'. Hence the need for measures to ensure that this could not happen and the chosen instrument was the formation of bilateral 'Article 98' treaties with as many countries as possible which would be legally binding agreements that would 'prohibit the surrender of US persons to this Court'. ('Article 98' refers to a provision of the

Rome Treaty which created the ICC allowing for such arrangements.)[7] There were numerous other objections, including fears that the concept of universal jurisdiction itself was too vague and indiscriminate,[8] but they came down to the charge that the court would remove from American citizens protections which they had a right to expect under the US Constitution.

Legal scholars have debated whether these fears were justified, and not surprisingly there are profound disagreements. What is striking, however, as compared with the Bush administration's justification of its opposition to Kyoto, is the absence of any effort to placate the advocates of the internationalist position. The ICC is unacceptable on any terms because US sovereignty is indivisible. In the face of the universalist claims of the pro-ICC camp, the Bush administration's response is unremittingly particularist. Only scores of individual treaties with each of the parties to the ICC can guarantee the protection of US citizens. And this from a nation whose own constitution and other founding documents set out universalist principles. What the Bush administration apparently could not accept was that, in the words of former Clinton staffer Morton Halperin, the United States had 'a long-term stake in the creation of an international system in which uniform rules are established and enforced'. Halperin drew attention to specific features of the treaty which provided safeguards for American citizens – and to that extent he believed there were good pragmatic grounds for accepting the treaty – but the burden of his argument was longer term and based on principle. The world was changing and the ICC was an opportunity for the United States to participate in those changes and help mould them. Washington must choose, he wrote 'between returning to a world in which all nations pursue their own short-run security and economic interests or a world in which government behavior is subjected to accepted procedures for creating and enforcing international norms'.[9] Even more categorically, the legal scholar Paul Murphy observed that 'for the moment ... the United States has rejected a revolutionary effort to enhance the rule of law in international affairs'.[10]

Sovereignty is especially at play in constitutional and legal questions because these go to the heart of citizenship and the principles of government and indeed of national identity. In the field of national security, sovereignty is equally at issue, if anything more so since defence policy relates to the survival of the nation itself. Measures to secure survival thus trump all others. This does not mean that they do not provoke internal political debate, but it does mean that generally the burden of proof in arguments about the need for this or that new weapons system generally lies with those opposing them. The debate about National Missile Defense (NMD) is a clear case in point. Its origins lie in Reagan's Strategic Defense Initiative (SDI), or 'Star Wars', announced in 1983, which was intended to replace reliance on mutually assured destruction (MAD) as the keystone of America's defense against nuclear attack, with the concept of a defensive shield which would detect and destroy all incoming missiles. Tests were undertaken but the system, which proved politically controversial and fraught with technical difficulties, was not introduced. Among the obstacles to be overcome was the 1972 Anti-Ballistic Missile Treaty with the Soviet Union, which expressly prohibited deployment of missile defence systems by either side. Missile defence became a live issue again in the 1990s when Congress mandated Donald Rumsfeld to chair a commission to examine the threat from ballistic missiles. His 1999 report led to the passage of the National Missile Defense Act of 1999 which was signed somewhat reluctantly by President Clinton. This act provided for research into NMD but left a decision on deployment until later. With Rumsfeld now Secretary of Defense in the new administration, Bush revived the issue in his first months in office, giving a major speech on the subject to the National Defense University in May 2001.

Bush's rationale for NMD was based heavily on the premise that the end of the Cold War had changed the international scene out of all recognition and with it America's defence requirements. In place of a cohesive bloc of hostile nations led by a malevolent Soviet Union, American was faced with an equally dangerous but less predictable world in which 'more nations have nuclear weapons and still more have nuclear aspirations'. These included 'rogue states' such as North Korea and Iran as well as Saddam Hussein's Iraq. In the circumstances new defence concepts and technologies were necessary, and obstacles to their introduction, such as the ABM Treaty, must be removed. NMD was presented as part of the answer to the whole array of technological and military challenges which the new international situation presented to the United States and its allies. Bush made much of the need for cooperation of allies, and indeed he offered NMD in the context of an opportunity to develop a 'new framework' of collective defence which recognized the potential for 'new cooperative relationships' with former antagonists such as Russia as well as existing allies. In short, NMD was heavily packaged as a proposal based on 'common responsibilities and common interests' which looked to the future and not the past.[11]

However, the implicit invocation of community is deceptive. There are broad parallels with the presentation of the Kyoto decision, in that it is recognized that a unilateral decision on a sensitive subject will sit better if it is couched in language which acknowledges the existence of a wider interest than that of the American national interest; or rather, since there is no reason to doubt that Bush is sincere in believing that realization of the American national interest in this sphere will also meet the interests of other, the task is to convince the global audience that America's and the world's interests are as one. Certainly, this is the underlying assumption. In this way, Bush is able both to present an 'internationalist' position which is, however, still consistent with a realist state-centric vision of international relations.

Reaction to the NMD speech indicates that Bush was not successful, at least in the short term, in convincing most of his allies, far less former enemies, that their interests would be served by deployment of the NMD system. Fears included the possibility that NMD would force Russia and China to increase their strategic arms capabilities at a time when there was powerful momentum to reduce them, that abrogation of the ABM treaty would destabilize relations between Russia and America, and that that NMD would lead to the militarization of space. Europeans were concerned that 'a US decision to protect itself with NMD could lead to divergent security systems within NATO – more specifically, a fortress America'. Above all, though, was the perception that the United States had hatched this scheme on her own without consultation with allies. The danger, wrote one American commentator, was that 'missile defense, by exceeding its political tolerances, will become the poster child for multiple complaints about American unilateralism and indifference to concerns of others'.[12] In the event, as is often the case with such decisions, the outcome was less dramatic than many feared. The US abrogation of the ABM Treaty had less dire consequences for US–Russian relations than expected. Once it was clear that the Bush administration was set on this path, the Russians essentially accepted it as a fait accompli. Meanwhile, Britain and other European allies of the United States made agreements with Washington to allow elements of the NMD system on their soil. It is likely that once deployment approaches the issue will re-emerge and could prove once again disruptive. As of the autumn of 2006, however, the issue was quiescent, overshadowed by the more urgent problems of the pacification of Iraq and Afghanistan, and the wrangle with Iran over nuclear power.

As far as the present theme is concerned, nothing could disguise the fact that the NMD decision was of a piece with other key decisions taken in Bush's first months in office. The term 'unilateralism', however, is insufficient to define the full scope of the Bush approach since, as we have seen, the administration was prepared to contemplate joint action where it was deemed possible, and on occasions the language of 'community' was employed. The issue is rather the underlying atomistic concept of the international system which informs the overall approach to policy-making. It is manifested in what one commentator has called America's 'embarrassing practice of treating international agencies and agreements as foreign policy "options" which it can cherrypick or neglect at its own convenience'.[13] Nowhere is this more visible than in policy towards Iraq. There has been extensive commentary on the build-up to the war in Iraq: the move in the autumn of 2002 for the passage of a UN resolution (1441) to condemn Saddam's refusal to comply with UN weapons inspections, the subsequent attempt to achieve a second resolution to provide authority for the use of force against Iraq, the failure of that attempt, and the opening of military action against Iraq on 20 March 2003. It is well known that key figures in the Bush administration, and indeed Bush himself, did not favour seeking a second resolution because they believed that the necessary authority for military action was supplied by 1441 and previous UN resolutions requiring Iraq's compliance with the inspection regime set up after the Gulf War. The decision to go through the bruising process of seeking a second resolution owed much to the influence of British prime minister Tony Blair whom, it is reported, Bush 'absolutely had to have … aboard'. Moreover, once agreed upon, what Bush wanted from the UN route above all, according to reporter Bob Woodward, was an outcome: which is to say, a resolution which would enable him to secure the elimination of Saddam's weapons of mass destruction. 'The commitment', notes Woodward, 'was not to the UN process.'[14]

Significantly, while Blair evidently agreed with Bush's assessment of the threat posed by Saddam, his justifications for action showed a noticeable departure from those of the American administration. In a major speech delivered in March 2004 Blair placed Iraq in the broadest possible context. The new reality of international relations, he suggested, was of interdependence, and there was without doubt such a thing as the 'international community'. Even prior to September 11, said Blair,

> I was already reaching for a different philosophy in inter-national relations from a traditional one that has held sway

since the Treaty of Westphalia in 1648, namely that a country's internal affairs are for it alone, and that you don't interfere unless it threatens you, or breaches a treaty, or triggers an obligation of an alliance.

The combination of the rise of Islamic extremism and the efforts of some highly unstable states to develop weapons of mass destruction, coupled with the September 11 attacks, confirmed and deepened his perception that the 'international community' had a duty to eliminate threats to global stability. International law was no longer adequate to meet the range of threats; international institutions such as the UN must be modified to meet them. 'The doctrine of international community', he concluded,

> is no longer a vision of idealism. It is a practical recognition that just as within a country, citizens who are free, well-educated and prosperous tend to be responsible, to feel solidarity with a society in which they have a stake, so do nations that are free, democratic and benefiting from economic progress tend to be stable and solid partners in the advance of humankind.[15]

The fact that in the case of Iraq the different concepts of international relations held by Bush and Blair should have produced the same policy choice should not itself be a cause for surprise. Theoretical orientations do not automatically dictate particular policies, though they often create family resemblances among them. On the particular question of Iraq, Blair's was by no means the only 'liberal' or 'internationalist' justification for war. Views on Iraq in the United Kingdom did not initially fall strictly along party or ideological lines. Elements of the human rights lobby, for example, pushed strongly for intervention on the grounds of Saddam's vicious record. This seemed an opportunity for internationalism to make a practical difference. What could be more justified than removal of a tyrant and the rebuilding of a society on a democratic basis? Had not the 'international community' failed to fulfil its responsibility in Rwanda, and only belatedly in Bosnia and Kosovo and elsewhere in the 1990s? Besides, on other questions discussed above, the Blair government took different views from the United States. The UK signed up to both the Kyoto Protocol and the ICC. That Blair agreed to the siting of early warning stations for America's NMD system in the UK must be put down to his conviction that the Atlantic connection was essential to British security and global stability, a view which helps also to explain his support for the United States in Iraq. In short, British assumptions bore some similarity to those held by European advocates of 'international community', to be discussed later, while nevertheless maintaining contact with the state-centric realism of the Americans.

The Bush administration's attitude towards the UN, meanwhile, was if anything more sharply revealed in a speech to the General Assembly in September 2004 at a time when the prospect in Iraq was grim. Suicide bombings, many of them directed at applicants to join the new Iraqi army and police force, cast doubt over the possibility of a move towards elections (due to be held in January 2005); the insurgency had led to ferocious fighting with US forces, above all in the attempt by those forces to clear the town of Falluja of insurgents; sectarian conflict was on the rise, and precious little had been achieved towards reliable supply of basic services and utilities. In this context, Bush's speech to the UN seemed not only remarkably sanguine but remote from the realities on the ground in Iraq. He did not address the problems in Iraq, except obliquely, but rather made a pitch to the internationalist constituency, apparently in the hope that the UN would come forward with assistance to the fledgling Iraqi government of Prime Minister Allawi. Bush was evidently not looking for the UN to take a decision-making role in Iraq. He urged rather that 'the UN, and its member nations, must respond to Prime Minister Allawi's request, and do more to help build an Iraq that is secure, democratic, federal, and free'.[16] This vague request is wrapped in a rhetorical package which evinces a somewhat forced effort at consensus with his audience. The repeated refrain of 'because we believe in human dignity ... ', each one followed by a claim of great things achieved or an injunction to undertake new challenges; the inflated and abstract idealism of the language, coupled with the lack of connection of his words with the fierce conflict on the ground in Iraq, indicated, according to one commentator, that Bush was speaking to the American public rather than the international community or, if the latter, then it betrayed a misunderstanding of its expectations and needs. 'There was nothing about that speech', said one observer, 'that was an attempt to convince sophisticated European and African diplomats to go along with the American cause. ... He gave his standard "I have a dream" speech which is "I dream we can spread liberty and secular democracy." That speech works with an American public and not the United Nations.' 'Though speaking to the lofty ideals of American intentions is seen as arrogant to much of the international community', wrote another, 'it resonates with American voters.' Bush's rival in the upcoming 2004 presidential election, John Kerry, admittedly not an unbiased observer, blamed Bush for 'pushing away' America's allies.[17] The *New York Times* referred to 'skeptical foreign leaders and envoys' in Bush's UN audience.[18] In short, in this context Bush's internationalism appeared disingenuous, a device employed out of perceived necessity rather than conviction, designed to restore credibility in an enterprise which was under severe pressure. 'There is an absolute collapse of trust in the intentions of the administration', noted one American Middle Eastern specialist:

> in the international community, one reason they don't cooperate with the [Bush] administration is that they don't believe that its intentions are its stated intentions. And they are fearful that if the administration was helped out of the Iraq mess that it might feel empowered to embark on additional unilateral adventures, which they don't want.[19]

As far as the present theme is concerned, the key point is not so much the cynicism in sections of the international community about American intentions on Iraq, as the tension in the Bush administration between its conviction that real and effective power still lies with nation-states and the recognition that membership of the 'international community' demands public commitment to certain internationalist norms of language and behaviour. The next question must be: how far is this a feature peculiar to the Bush Jr administration and how far a wider feature of American foreign relations? In order to answer this question we must place the Bush administration in the widest possible context.

The idea of the international community in historical context

It must first be acknowledged that the Bush administration's broad approach to international relations is consonant with that of great power diplomacy for the bulk of the modern era. It is based on the bedrock principles of national sovereignty and national interest which form the basis of what international relations theorists called 'realism'. This is not to say that the Bush administration's foreign policy is to be wholly explained in terms of classical realism; no administration or nation is a pure expression of a theory. As is clear from other chapters in this book, there is an ideological drive behind his policy associated in part with the neoconservative agenda and in part with a devotion to the founding values of the American nation. America is thus both a nation-state and a vehicle for certain values. For the purposes of this argument the key feature of what might be called the hyper-realism of the Bush administration is its devotion to a concept of international relations which privileges the nation-state. This notion goes not only beyond party but beyond nation. For most of America's history and for most American policy-makers, as for most European, the following statement by Hans J. Morgenthau, the high priest of the theory of realism, would have been regarded as the common sense of the matter: 'above the national societies', he observed in a book published in 1951, 'there exists no international society so integrated as to be able to define for them the concrete meaning of justice or equality, as national societies do for their individual members'.[20] Nation-states dedicated to the promotion and defence of their national interests were the building blocks of the international system and largely determined the behaviour of the system. Nor was this a new theory. The idea that the pursuit of power and self-interest dictated relations between governments had a pedigree going back to Thucydides. In modern times the theory of realism is associated with the writings of seventeenth-century philosopher Thomas Hobbes and the practice with the Treaty of Westphalia which ended the Thirty Years War and established the idea of national sovereignty as the guiding principle of international relations. In the absence of effective rules at a level above that of national governments, international relations were characterized by 'anarchy', by which was meant not a total absence of order but an absence of government. Such order as did ensue was created by balances of power based on calculations of interest and advantage on the part of governments. Rival concepts based on idealist notions of international law as a regulator of international relations, or the idea of international community founded on religion or Enlightenment ideas of common humanity, had to run the gauntlet of the reality, which was that in the main power was the deciding factor and war the means of making the decisions.

Much has changed, however, even in the relatively short time since Morgenthau asserted his dictum. Theories of international relations have proliferated in the years since the Second World War, along lines which reflect the complexities of global developments themselves as well as associated ideological shifts. To traditional realism and idealist or liberal theories spawned by the Enlightenment must be added neo-realism, Marxist theories, social constructivism, feminism, post-colonialism, etc., etc.[21] However, it must be stressed that these innovations are of relatively recent origin, and while they may have challenged or even displaced traditional theories in the academy, there is a sense in which realism remains the bedrock theory, the common sense of the matter, especially among those who are practitioners rather than theorists, and especially among the larger states who possess the greatest capacity to exert their independent will in international affairs and who continue to rely on traditional instruments of power – military and economic might – to achieve their goals. In the terms used by British diplomat Robert Cooper, America remains a 'modern' nation while others, which are caught in the web of interdependence and naturally seek to achieve their goals through association with groupings of powers, are 'post-modern'.[22] America's apparent devotion to primacy of the sovereign nation-state, so strongly expressed in the Bush administration's stance towards the outside world, is thus a function of its power and its size, and the sense, illusory or not, that it can do without the international community. Some have talked about a 'Bush revolution in foreign policy', but arguably it is a counter-revolution which consists in turning back the clock to an earlier state of international relations.[23]

Sovereignty and the American tradition

Yet it is common knowledge that there is a powerful idealist strain in American foreign policy and indeed in American culture in general. George W. Bush's foreign policy has even been described by some as Wilsonian in its ambition to spread democracy to the rest of the world. How does this fit with the picture we have painted here of a realist bias in his administration's foreign relations? To understand this we need to consider the early history of American foreign policy. America was established at a moment in history when realism largely dictated the practice of international relations but was under challenge by idealist principles drawn from the Enlightenment. Intense debate surrounds the origins of American diplomacy, with some historians emphasizing certain novel Enlightenment features of American diplomatic theory and practice and others the traditional balance of power context which, they claim, largely determined the character of American diplomacy.[24] Without attempting here to resolve this debate, it is worth emphasizing that, whether one interprets key statements of early American policy as realist or idealist, they have in common an insistence on the cardinal principle of American independence of action, American sovereignty. Washington's injunction, echoed soon after by Jefferson, that America must enter 'no entangling alliances' was no isolationist call. While repudiating entangling political relations, which could only lead to war, he insisted that America must have maximum possible trade relations with other nations. Nor should Adams' insistence that America must declare the Monroe Doctrine unilaterally rather than agree to a joint declaration with Britain be regarded as isolationist, but rather a product of the same resistance to entanglement with other powers. A devotion to sovereign independence is the golden thread running through the history of American foreign policy – not supposed dichotomies between idealism and realism, or isolation and involvement, or internationalism and nationalism. Even Woodrow Wilson's idealistic internationalism had an intensely nationalist imprint, bearing the influence of Washington's insistence on 'no entangling alliances' as a cornerstone of American foreign policy. When the United States entered the First World War it did so as an 'associated' not an 'allied' power. In the words of John A. Thompson's fine recent study of Woodrow Wilson,

> whether it was her rights or ideals that she was fighting for, America's purposes were her own. In taking this position, the President was maintaining a more unequivocally nationalist line than such Republicans as Roosevelt and Lodge who saw their country as joining Britain and France, shamefully late, in a common cause. As during the period of neutrality, Wilson held to important aspects of the isolationist tradition even as he was leading the United States into commitments and actions that broke with it.

Furthermore, while Wilson's idealist belief in America's mission to spread its values distinguished him from the realist's emphasis on power, as Thompson notes, the ideals that he generally appealed to were those of 'America's national ideology'.[25] Wilson is a good example of how intensely nationalist American idealism can be, just as Bush's foreign policy is an example of how intensely idealist nationalism can be. Furthermore, however far Wilson was prepared to go in sharing an element of sovereignty with his cherished League of Nations, it was clear in the outcome of the intense debate about American participation that his vision was not shared by a majority of Congress.

Against this must be set the development in the post-World War II period of multiple international institutions in which the United States was not merely a participant but a founding and leading member. These include the United Nations, the International Monetary Fund (IMF), the World Bank, the General Agreement on Trade and Tariffs (GATT), and numerous lesser organizations which together make up the map of interdependence which characterizes the contemporary international world. Clearly, the upheaval caused by the Second World War produced a step-change in America's relations with the international order, as it did for other nations. Recent scholarship on America's relations with international institutions since the Second World War suggests, however, that, for all the apparently turn towards internationalism and a certain softening of the emphasis on national sovereignty, American attitudes towards multilateral rules and institutions remained ambivalent and continued to do so in the post-Cold War period. There were, to be sure, motives for a deepening and a thickening of America's relations with other nations in 1945. John Ikenberry describes what he calls the 'institutional bargain' which lay at the heart of the postwar relationship with Europe:

> in the institutional bargain, the leading state wants to reduce compliance costs and weaker states want to reduce their costs of security protection, or the costs they would

incur trying to protect their interests against the actions of a dominating leading state. This is what makes the institutional deal attractive: the leading state agrees to restrain its own potential for domination and abandonment in exchange for the long-term institutionalized cooperation of subordinate states.[26]

Evidently, the scale of the reshaping of international institutions following World War II was a measure of the shift in balance of power caused by the war. As Ikenberry points out, such changes are characteristic of the aftermaths of great conflicts, and indeed without such a stimulus it is hard to imagine the United States or any other nation entering into such novel arrangements. Furthermore, that such institutional innovations and the corresponding American commitment were sustained after World War II for four decades owed much to the pressure supplied by antagonism with the Soviet Union. Even so, the evidence suggests that the United States was, in Ikenberry's words, 'reluctant to tie itself too tightly to these multilateral institutions and rules'.[27] No doubt this was partly because the United States was happier to maintain such arrangements when it was in a position to control them, or, in Ikenberry's terms, that in a number of spheres the United States could see no concrete gain from participation. There was no working 'institutional bargain'. Hence, when the General Assembly of the United Nations became dominated in the 1970s by the voting power of 'Third World' nations opposed to many United States policies, the US effectively discounted that body and concentrated its energies in the Security Council. When the International Court of Justice condemned America for mining the ports of Nicaragua during the Reagan administration's covert war against the Sandinista government, America ignored the judgement. During the same administration the US withdrew from the UN Economic, Social and Cultural Organization (UNESCO) and also for a short while from the International Labor Organization (ILO) out of dissatisfaction with their pronouncements.[28] A comparable stance was manifested in the 1990s when, as a result of Congressional action, the United States withheld a substantial portion of its contribution to UN funds, only paying the arrears in the days following the terrorist attacks of 9/11.[29]

Indeed the United States' ambivalent attitude towards international institutions deepened in the aftermath of the Cold War. On the one hand, this new postwar situation offered the opportunity for a renegotiation of America's relations with international organizations – new institutional bargains to meet new situations. Not least, in the absence of the automatic Soviet veto in the Security Council, the UN seemed more amenable to the American will, as evidenced by the global reaction to the Iraqi invasion of Kuwait. Nor was this simply a matter of the organization bowing to American will. Collective security, it now appeared, could operate as the organization's founders intended. American interests and the 'new world order' seemed to coincide. Furthermore, there was a wider general will to contemplate using the UN in peacekeeping, peace-making and nation-building roles.[30] Certainly expectations arose in this regard, and a number of urgent situations presented themselves in the disorders resulting from the withdrawal of support to developing nations by the United States and the former Soviet Union as the Cold War receded. Ethiopia and Somalia were among the most damaged in the new category of 'failed states'. The disintegration of Yugoslavia generated a further raft of pressures for the 'international community' to do something to check the destruction of communities.

On the other hand, while these situations cried out for resolution, they were interventions of choice, entered into individually with little overall rationale or consistent criteria. Each raised in peculiarly stark ways the question of the basis on which intervention in the affairs of a sovereign state could be undertaken. In the United States discussion raged about the criteria for intervention without producing any consistent principles.[31] Under what circumstances could a sovereign state's borders be crossed to prevent an obvious evil? Did the UN

Charter, particularly the clause asserting the inviolability of sovereignty, provide sufficient flexibility to cater for the multiplicity of new situations? What connections existed between a humanitarian crisis in a developing nation and the American national interest? What, indeed, did the national interest mean under these circumstances? Did it need to be redefined in order to take account of these situations? The American experience of Somalia in 1992–93 indicated the complexity and dangers of high-minded humanitarian interventions which could easily turn into unmanageable situations. The massacres in Rwanda only a year later indicated the opposite lesson: that not doing anything could spell tragedy. In Bosnia the United States intervened on behalf of the UN following the massacre of Muslims at Srebrenica and oversaw negotiations which led to the Dayton Agreement in 1995. But this intervention was hesitant and belated according to critics both inside and outside the United States. Much damage had been done by the time the accords were finalized. In Kosovo in 1999, in the absence of UN consensus on intervention, under the auspices of NATO the US engaged in bombing of Serbian forces to protect Kosovan Albanians and this time was accused by some of precipitate and unnecessary action. Above all it was difficult to gain domestic consensus for these interventions. Many 'liberals' thought the United States was doing too little; Clinton, it was charged, was failing to seize hold of the opportunity both to educate the American public about its new global responsibilities and to resolve serious crises. Many conservatives believed the United States had no business intervening in situations where it had no obvious or direct interest. From this standpoint, Clinton's foreign policy was derided as legalistic, obsessed with the UN, indecisive and amounting to little more than 'social work', which for the realist was about as far away from the real function of foreign policy as you could get.[32]

The story of the 1990s, if one can risk generalization about such a complex period of time, was of gestures towards developing new ideas and new policy instruments to meet the new world disorder, but few consistent principles and none which lasted beyond the end of the Clinton administration. Despite the charges of some conservatives, there was no wholesale embrace by Clinton of a new philosophy of international relations, far less an abandonment of the idea that American interests must lie at the core of American foreign policy. New terms and phrases appeared. 'Engagement and enlargement' were offered as successors to Cold War 'containment', while 'assertive multilateralism' was intended to convey a blending of enlightened internationalism and hard-nosed realism. However, neither of these terms took on as a label which served to define an overall approach. In short, the end of the Cold War threw existing ideas about international relations and America's place in the world into the melting pot without producing a clear new direction.

There was thus no radical shift from a consistent liberal internationalism under Clinton to conservative nationalism under Bush. America's ambivalence about international institutions and the idea of an international community were present all along, even if they became more explicit and doctrinal under Bush. That tendency to stand back from the kind of commitment which would compromise American sovereignty was an integral part of America's historic stance towards the outside world, a consequence, it has been argued by Edward Luck, of 'a deeply ingrained sense of exceptionalism' which remains 'a defining characteristic of US foreign and security policy'.[33] In short, the issue went beyond foreign relations but extended to the sense that America's self-identity depended on maintaining a certain detachment from the world – indeed independence. It is this which helps to account for what the *Economist* called (before 9/11) 'America's odd attitude to international institutions'.[34] The 'realism' of the Bush administration was in the end ideologically driven.

America's attitude towards international institutions is not so odd, however, if we consider the domestic political context in which American foreign policy is conducted and the consequences this has for attitudes towards international law and international institutions. Overseas observers frequently overlook this context and see in America's resistance to the call of the 'international community' only a perverse refusal to consider wider interests than their own, a refusal which is presumed to result simply from ignorance of the world beyond America's shores. In actuality, there are structural and institutional, as well as cultural, obstacles to the development of a global perspective. One of these obstacles is built into the American federal system of government, though it is an 'obstacle' which Americans regard as vital to their freedom. In the first place, the states of the union retain some leverage over the federal government by virtue of the formal constitutional guarantee that any powers not granted to the federal government are reserved to the states; but more tangibly, as far as foreign policy is concerned, in the requirement that treaties be approved by a two-thirds majority of the Senate. Senators who resent the federal government's negotiation of treaties which tie America to rules and obligations which then lie beyond America's control can exploit the constitutional requirement for a two-thirds majority to block such moves. Or, as in the case of the proposed Bricker Amendment in the early 1950s to limit the president's authority to negotiate treaties, senators can exert powerful political pressure on the executive branch through persuasion and threat. The effect of this pressure was to convince President Eisenhower that it was not politically feasible to push for an international convention against genocide, with consequences which have been chronicled at length in Samantha Power's '*A Problem From Hell': America and the Age of Genocide*.[35] The issue of genocide, moreover, raises the question of the 'international community' in a peculiarly stark fashion, since it sets a moral imperative which is of universal significance against the principle of sovereignty. America's receptivity to universal moral principles is well known and famously expressed in its founding documents. Yet in the practice of its international relations the United States frequently prefers to emphasize its own sovereignty, its own independence.

As far as the domestic context is concerned, it is noteworthy that there is frequently a correlation between suspicion of the federal government and suspicion of international organizations which would restrict American freedom. Indeed, a dislike of concentrated power runs deep in American culture and not only among conservatives. Though the philosophy of 'states' rights' has less salience now than it once had, not least because of its association with the defence of racist legislation and practices in the South until the 1960s, it would be foolish to entirely discount its power to block internationalist projects. Besides, within the federal government itself the separation of powers between the legislative and executive branches can and does have the power to limit presidential action in foreign policy. There are numerous historical examples, from the failure of Woodrow Wilson to gain passage of the Treaty of Versailles to Congress' restrictions on spending in Southeast Asia in the 1970s, but the same dynamic continues. It was a Republican-led Congress in the mid-1990s which voted, against the wishes of the president, to withhold America's UN dues.[36] In the summer of 2006, in the face of a refusal of Congress to back his proposals for a bill covering treatment of terrorist suspects, President George W. Bush was forced to agree to a compromise.[37] In sum, the checks and balances associated with American federalism ensure that American presidents must always be conscious of the domestic dimensions of foreign policy. It means also that foreign leaders and negotiators must be aware that the president does not always have the last word on whatever is agreed over the negotiating table. Above all, it means that America's capacity to participate in international ventures which might involve a perceived compromise of its sovereignty is limited by its political culture and traditions.

The turn towards new ideas of sovereignty

The signs are, however, that there is a change in perception in influential quarters in America. Academic theorists of international relations have long discussed concepts such as 'international society' and related ideas which acknowledge that the environment in which nation-states operate is changing out of all recognition. In recent years, however, such ideas have begun to be discussed by those who are closer to the policy realm. There appears to be movement towards the view propounded by Tony Blair that the 'international community' is not just an idea or an ideal but an emerging reality which has practical consequences. Among the Americans who have seen this most clearly is Francis Fukuyama, whose conversion from a neoconservative in the late 1990s to something approaching a liberal internationalist was under way, if not yet complete, by the time of the intervention in Iraq. 'Americans', he wrote in a book published in 2004, 'tend not to see any source of democratic legitimacy higher than the constitutional democratic nation-state.' Europeans, by contrast, 'tend to believe that democratic legitimacy flows from the will of an international community much larger than any individual nation-state'. Fukuyama made it clear where his intellectual as well as his national allegiance lay when he noted that 'the "international community" is a fiction insofar as any enforcement capability depends entirely on the action of individual nation-states'.[38] Only two years later, however, in the midst of the quagmire of the Iraq war which exposed the limits not only of American power but also of the intellectual basis of American foreign policy, Fukuyama's emphasis had changed. 'The old realist model of international relations that sees the world exclusively organized around sovereign nation-states simply does not correspond to the world that is emerging', he noted, 'and it will not be sufficient to meet the needs of legitimacy and effectiveness in international action in the future.' Being multilateral was not enough in itself if it meant acting in concert only on your terms: 'that is just another form of unilateralism'. What the United States must begin to accept was certain constraints on its freedom in return, of course, for the tangible gain of 'legitimacy', a priceless commodity in international affairs, especially when you were engaging in actions which were bound to be opposed by some parts of world opinion. If the United States were willing to accept this trade-off, then it would have the capacity to shape international institutions much more effectively than was currently the case. Its undoubted multidimensional power would be best served, not through the exercise of military force, but through its ability to shape international institutions.[39]

Fukuyama is not the only influential voice in the United States calling for a revision of basic concepts in American foreign policy. Richard Haass, a career foreign-policy official who has held positions in American administrations from Carter to Reagan, Bush Sr and George W. Bush, has urged a rethink of the concept of sovereignty. 'Americans', he says, 'have traditionally guarded their sovereignty with more than a little ferocity.' What the world now needs, however, is a concept of sovereignty which is 'less than absolute'. He proposes a 'contractual' idea of sovereignty, 'one that recognizes the obligations and responsibilities as well as the rights of those who enjoy it'. The overriding reality was that borders were now porous, and the

> notion that the world is somehow divided into internal and external spheres and that foreign policy and national security policies of the United States (or any country for that matter) need or can only deal with the external and can safely ignore the internal or domestic side of other countries is an anachronism.

Haass offers the notion of 'integration' as the 'natural successor to containment'. At its centre is the creation of a 'cooperative relationship among the world's major powers', the translation of this cooperation into effective institutions and actions, and the extension of these goods to all countries and people. Abstract though it is, it parallels the process of integration in the European Union, and to that extent represents a potential narrowing of the cultural and intellectual gap between Europe and the United States which was made so much of by Robert Kagan and other neoconservatives during the most heated exchanges across the Atlantic about the move to war in Iraq.[40] It is also perhaps of significance that 'integration' was the word adopted by Madeleine Albright to describe the foreign-policy orientation of the Clinton administration. 'Not an exciting term', she acknowledged, 'but one that embodied a process of bringing nations together around basic principles of democracy and open markets, the rule of law and a commitment to peace.'[41] There is no pretence that such an intellectual revolution will suddenly make decisions about intervention easier. What is striking, though, is the awareness that the ground is shifting under America's feet and that the adventure in Iraq has exposed these shifts more clearly than anything else. Haass states baldly that

> launching a preventive war when it was not warranted works directly against the ability of the United States to develop and benefit from the opportunity that exists to bring about a world in which other major powers will work with the United States to promote common objectives.[42]

The conclusion to be drawn from these and other similar arguments which are emerging in the United States is that there is a quiet revolution under way which has the potential to bring a substantial change in America's relationship with the rest of the world. It is currently only a potentiality, however. There remains, as we have seen, a strong predisposition against the idea of the international community which has roots in America's domestic culture and history no less than in foreign policy. Indeed, global calls for integration and greater reliance on international organizations find an America at its most intensely nationalistic. Much depends on how events turn out. If the crisis in Iraq worsens or remains unresolved, it is conceivable that there will be powerful voices in America calling for retrenchment in foreign policy and a return to a narrow conception of the national interest rather than a redirection of the American interest towards 'integration'. On the other hand, the forces making for change are so strong that it is inconceivable that they can be completely ignored. There is even the chance that the structural constraints on America's ability to adopt internationalist positions may be easing. Specifically, states' rights, which in the past has been an issue associated with conservative causes, are now being employed in the service of internationalist causes. In the area of measures to combat climate change, several states, notably California, are pushing for observance of the Kyoto limits on emissions, which is having an impact on the national debate. Moreover, as we have seen, even the Bush administration acknowledges the necessity of taking into account international opinion and institutions, even if only as a formality. Nor is it a matter merely of America changing its mind. International institutions are likely to change too to reflect the changing realities. Pressure is building for revision of the UN Charter to reflect the changing global power distribution, as well as to facilitate the kinds of interventions which are increasingly demanded of the organization, though with what success remains to be seen.[43] Meanwhile, whatever the outlook of any single American administration, it will surely become less and less plausible to speak of the international community as 'illusory'.

Conclusion

American freedom and the war in Iraq

If there is one overriding conclusion which flows from the preceding chapters it is that ideas have consequences. The frameworks with which we interpret the world, the values we hold, the assumptions we make, affect reality and are not merely reflections of it. Viewed from this standpoint, understanding a sequence of events such as the war in Iraq means looking beyond policies themselves to the assumptions which underlie them. There are many reasons for thinking that the war in Iraq was a questionable enterprise but one of them surely is that it was invested from the outset with excessive expectations about the likely impact of American intervention. These expectations, judging by reports of the absence of detailed forethought about the post-conflict period, existed in a realm of their own, virtually independent of the military planning process. It was not that there was no thought about the postwar situation at all – indeed the State Department had compiled a detailed study entitled 'The Future of Iraq' – but that those charged with such planning were marginalized by the principal policy-makers.[1] Expectations, wish-fulfilments, thus filled the gap left by the absence of planning. These in turn were the product of assumptions about the applicability of American values to other nations and cultures, and more specifically about their applicability to Iraq. The war in Iraq was invested with huge American cultural capital. Iraq, it was envisaged, would become a vanguard democratic nation in a Middle East ripe for change; its example would trigger other comparable transformations in the direction of freedom.

The chief problem with relying on such inflated claims is that it blinds policy-makers to evidence which contradicts the adopted assumptions. It makes it difficult to deal with the unexpected, with setbacks of all sorts, indeed with the real world. It also makes it hard to sell the policy to others who may resent the cultural baggage which comes with the policy. The appointment by Congress of an Iraq Study Group in the spring of 2006 under former Secretary of State James Baker, charged with assessing the effectiveness of the occupation and looking for alternative policies which might give promise of an orderly withdrawal within a reasonable time-frame, demonstrated the cul de sac into which the policy had run. It was not, however, simply a failure of policy but an exposure of the inadequacy of the assumptions on which it was based.

Of course the crossroads reached in 2006 was by no means entirely to be explained in terms of the cultural factors discussed in this book but, as expressed by the Bush administration, they bore a large responsibility because they militated against flexibility of thought. This is not to say that there are not some occasions when it is right and proper and even necessary to invest so much of the national capital in a cause and no more so than when the nation is attacked directly. Pearl Harbor and also arguably September 11 are examples of challenges to the core of the nation's being. In that sense the war on terror bears some comparison to World War II even if in most other respects they are quite unlike each other. Part of the difficulty of justifying the war in Iraq arises from the fact that the connection between it and September 11 is not clear. President Bush continued to picture Iraq as a base from which terrorism could have been launched against the United States long after connections between Iraq and al-Qaeda had been shown to be non-existent. And this is leaving aside the question of the existence of weapons of mass destruction. The war was oversold as vital to America's interest, but a growing number of Americans doubt the government's claims to the extent that the credibility of the whole enterprise is undermined. Not only did the repeated assertions that the coalition was winning in Iraq look hollow as military and civilian casualty lists grew and chaotic sectarian fighting spread, but the grandiose claims during 2004 and 2005 that a wave of democracy was sweeping through the Middle East looked increasingly empty by the latter months of 2006. Some sort of exit strategy became essential. Reality could no longer be ignored, as the appointment of the Iraq Study Group showed. The 'state of denial' described by journalist Bob Woodward, whose book appeared in October 2006 just as parts of the Iraq Study Group's report was leaked, could no longer be sustained.[2]

One broad conclusion to be taken from these events is that while many American products are eminently exportable, 'Americanism' as a package of cultural assumptions and doctrines does not travel well. Indeed it can be highly destructive. How does a nation avoid the danger of over-investment of cultural capital in an enterprise which cannot bear its weight? One way is by reconceiving the national mission in a way that takes explicit account of the international context which prevails. It means acknowledging the existence of the 'international community' as a necessary component of any calculation of the 'national interest'. It means asking what democracy might mean in different cultures and societies and possibly accepting that you might have to settle for less than your best definition of democracy. The same applies to 'freedom' which exposes particular challenges for Americans because it lies so close to the centre of its idea of nationhood. At one level we all know what freedom is – it is the opposite of slavery, the absence of restraint (within certain limits defined by the requirement that one person's freedom should not entail the unfreedom of others), the right to express oneself, to be oneself. The American image of freedom is so bound up with the American Revolution, with the Minutemen, with Patrick Henry's 'give me liberty or give me death' and other iconic events and people that it is hard for many Americans to envisage a concept of freedom which has a different starting point – a concept, for example, which starts with the community as opposed to the individual. But even the American notion of freedom, when considered in its own terms, is not a simple one. 'America cannot exist half-free and half-slave', said Abraham Lincoln but actually it did exist half-slave and half-free for many generations (through the colonial period and up to the Civil War) and the legacy of that contradiction still exists in America. The freedom of the many in America was contingent on the slavery of others,[3] with the result that the word freedom could never be used with complete innocence. The grant of freedom to the slaves did not of itself resolve the issue of the meaning of freedom; the debate simply shifted to a different ground. The long history of the Civil Rights movement, from resistance to the discriminatory 'Jim Crow' laws instituted in Southern States after Reconstruction through to the 'Freedom Rides' and the path-breaking Civil Rights legislation in the 1960s is the story in one sense of the struggle to give fuller meaning to the word freedom. But even here there is no completeness, indicating that freedom, in common with other values, is a process rather a completed fact. The awareness that it is an incomplete process brings one always back to the realities on the ground. It also guards one against arrogance and complacency. Though there is no reason to doubt the sincerity of the aspiration to the promotion of freedom in America's post-9/11 operations, was it prudent to call the military action in Afghanistan 'Operation Enduring Freedom' or the war in Iraq 'Operation Iraqi Freedom', given the complexities of rebuilding those shattered nations and the ease with which setbacks could expose them as empty slogans? To think of freedom as a completed fact, as an idea whose meaning is transparent and whole, is to risk losing sight of reality. Thus it is always necessary to ask, when invoking freedom, whose freedom is being talked about, what kind of freedom is meant, are your and my notions of freedom the same? These are not merely philosophical questions but practical ones too.

There will never be a single definition of freedom to which everyone can subscribe and the same goes for other supposed universal values and rights. However, to say that there can be no absolute consensus does not mean that there is no common ground at all which can be shared by people of different cultures. There are already in existence some pointers in the direction of agreement, even if they remain as yet at the level of general principle rather than uniformity of practice. The Universal Declaration of Human Rights (1948) was an attempt to conceive of rights and freedoms to which all members of the United Nations could subscribe. Furthermore, they have strong echoes of the American Declaration of Independence and the US Constitution and indeed were drafted largely by Americans. They are expressions of the Enlightenment values on which America was founded. America thus apparently starts ahead in this task of conceiving of its national interest in relation to international norms. And yet, for reasons which were explored in Chapter 7 of this book, the United States, especially under George W. Bush, has resisted embracing the idea of an international community which the UN Declaration seems to entail because of the constraints it would impose on American independence. We are thus presented with the paradox of a nation that preaches universalist values which, however, are wielded in the service of national rather than international causes. Nothing is more calculated to alienate America from the international community than the exposure of a gap between the claim to universalism and the reality of self-interest. The argument is not that America uniquely acts in its own self-interest. Far from it; self-interest remains the chief driving force for all states and will remain so until the nation-state is no longer the main constituent of the international system. The argument is rather that the United States presents its own particularist vision as of universal applicability. That the language which is used to promote particularism is a language of universals only sharpens the contradiction. That the United States possesses such huge power relative to other states only sharpens it further. That al-Qaeda and other extremist Islamist groups promote their own ideologies as universals and are willing to use any means to spread them only raises the stakes further, serving apparently to validate the kind of response made by the Bush administration.

As far as the American side of this question is concerned, which is all that can be addressed here, there is no simple solution to this dilemma because it lies at the heart of America's conception of itself. What cannot be expected is that America's leaders should turn themselves into political philosophers and spend their time debating the meaning of freedom. Yet some reflection on the meaning of key ideas such as freedom is surely necessary. The Bush administration's assumption that the meaning of freedom is self-evident must be examined as a question which admits of a variety of practical solutions. 'Pragmatism', which, as it happens, is the one philosophical approach which can be said to have originated in America, does not mean an abandonment of principle but it does mean a rigorous testing of principle against changing reality. This too is in the American tradition.

Notes

Introduction

1 The entire letter reads: 'Nottingham [University] is advertising in your Education Supplement for a "Lecturer in American Thought and Culture (Fixed-term)". What do they know that we don't?' *Guardian*, 16 August 2006.

2 Joseph S. Nye, *Bound to Lead: The Changing Nature of American Power*, New York: Basic Books, 1990; and *The Paradox of American Power: Why the World's Major Superpower Can't Go it Alone*, New York: Oxford University Press, 2002.

3 Nye, *The Paradox of American Power*, p. 9.

4 Nye, *The Paradox of American Power*, p. 11.

5 Andrea Elliott, 'More Muslims Arrive in U.S., after 9/11 Dip', *New York Times*, 10 September 2006.

6 Jason Burke, *Al Qaeda: The True Story of Radical Islam*, London: Penguin, 2004, pp. 52–55.

7 Nye, *The Paradox of American Power*, p. 11.

8 Bill Clinton, *My Life*, London: Hutchinson, 2004, p. 421.

1 Anti-Americanism and the clash of civilizations

1 Samuel P. Huntington, 'The Clash of Civilizations?', *Foreign Affairs*, 72, no. 3 (summer 1993) pp. 22–49; and *The Clash of Civilizations and the Remaking of World Order*, New York: Simon and Schuster, 1996.

2 Huntington, 'The Clash of Civilizations?', p. 22.

3 See the two subsequent issues of *Foreign Affairs* for the first bout of critiques and Huntington's response (vol. 72, nos 4 and 5). *Foreign Affairs* has collected these and other commentaries in *Clash of Civilizations: The Debate*, New York: Norton, 1996. Inevitably much of the debate has focused on the West's relations with Islam. See John L. Esposito, *The Islamic Threat: Myth or Reality?*, New York: Oxford University Press, 1995, especially ch. 6; Malise Ruthven, *A Fury for God: The Islamist Attack on America*, London: Granta, 2002; Fawaz A. Gerges, *America and Political Islam: Clash of Cultures or Clash of Interests?*, Cambridge: Cambridge University Press, 1999.

4 *National Security Strategy of the United States of America*, September 2002, 19, at www.whitehouse.gov/nsc/ (accessed 18/9/2003).

5 Bush, speech to Congress, 20 September 2001, www.msnbc.com/news/ 631906.asp (accessed 18/5/2002); Bush, State of the Union Address, 29 January 2002, www.whitehouse.gov/news/releases/2002/01/ (accessed 25/6/03); Bush, State of the Union Address, 28 January 2003, www.whitehouse.gov/news/releases/2003.01 (accessed 22/1/04); Bush, State of the Union Address, 20 January 2004, www.whitehouse.gov/ news/releases/2004/01/ (accessed 22/1/2004); *National Security Strategy of the United States*, 1.

6 For a discussion of Toynbee and the Cold War see Richard Crockatt, 'Challenge and Response: Arnold Toynbee and the United States During the Cold War', in Dale Carter and Robin Clifton (eds) *War and Cold War in American Foreign Policy, 1942–1962*, Houndmills, UK: Palgrave, 2002, pp. 108–30.

7 See Raymond Williams, *Keywords*, London: Fontana, 1976, pp. 48–50.

8 For all his debt to Toynbee, however, Huntington does not allow for the complexity and variety of interconnections between civilizations which is present in Toynbee's scheme.

9 For a recent example see Mehdi Mozaffari (ed.) *Globalization and Civilizations*, London: Routledge, 2002.

10 Huntington, *Clash of Civilizations*, pp. 54–55.

11 Charles A. Beard and Mary R. Beard, *The Rise of American Civilization*, New York: Macmillan, 1930, p. vii.

12 Note debate over Western civilization courses in the US. Gilbert Allerdyce, 'The Rise and Fall of the Western Civilization Course', *American Historical Review*, 87, June 1982, pp. 695–725, followed by comments and author's rejoinder.

13 The term is used by Samuel Huntington; see *Clash of Civilizations*, pp. 266–72, but was employed much earlier by John Dewey in his *Individualism Old and New*, New York: Capricorn Books, 1962 (first published 1930), ch. II.

14 Huntington discusses the definitional problems associated with culture and civilization in 'The Clash of Civilizations?', pp. 40–44.

15 Arnold Toynbee, *A Study of History*, London: Oxford University Press, 1934, vol. 1, pp. 44–45; Huntington, 'The Clash of Civilizations?', p. 24.

16 Raymond Williams explores the many meanings and usages of the term culture in *Keywords*, pp. 80–81. Useful discussions of culture in international relations which contain many important cautionary principles are Fred Halliday, *The World at 2000: Perils and Promises*, Houndmills, UK: Palgrave, 2001, ch. 8; and Michael J. Mazarr, 'Culture in International Relations', *Washington Quarterly*, 19, no. 2, spring 1996, pp. 177–97.

17 Max Lerner, *America as a Civilization: Life and Thought in the United States Today*, New York: Simon and Schuster, 1957, pp. 3, 58, 61–62, 65. For a discussion of the rise of 'Americanism' in the context of a discussion of anti-Americanism, see Richard Crockatt, *America Embattled: September 11, Anti-Americanism and the Global Order*, London: Routledge, 2003, pp. 46–51.

18 Robert Kagan, *Of Paradise and Power: America and Europe in the New World Order*, London: Atlantic Books, 2003, pp. 1, 2.

19 Thomas Paine, *Political Writings*, ed. Bruce Kuklick, Cambridge: Cambridge University Press, 1989, p. 23.

20 Will Hutton, *The World We're In*, revised edn, London: Abacus, 2003.

21 Bush, State of the Union Address, 20 January 2004, at www.whitehouse. gov/news/releases/2004/01/ (accessed 22/1/2004).

22 The best recent study of the ideology of American nationalism is Anatol Lieven's *America Right or Wrong: An Anatomy of American Nationalism*, London: HarperCollins, 2004. See especially ch. 2, 'Thesis: Splendor and Tragedy of the American Creed'.

23 Jedediah Purdy, 'Universal Nation', in Andrew Bacevich (ed.) *The Imperial Tense: Problems and Perspectives of American Empire*, Chicago: Ivan Dee, 2003, pp. 102–10.

24 William Kristol and Robert Kagan, 'Toward a Neo-Reaganite Foreign Policy', *Foreign Affairs*, 75, July/August 1996, p. 32. The major recent study of American exceptionalism is Seymour Martin Lipset, *American Exceptionalism: A Double-edged Sword*, New York: Norton, 1996.

25 See John Higham, *Strangers in the Land: Patterns of American Nativism*, New York: Atheneum, 1963.

26 Samuel P. Huntington, *Who Are We? America's Great Debate*, New York: Free Press, 2004.

27 This is the title of a book by Joseph S. Nye, *Bound to Lead: The Changing Nature of American Power*, New York: Basic Books, 1990.

28 See, for example, Geir Lundestad's suggestion that the growth of American empire was 'by invitation' rather American design. *The American 'Empire' and Other Studies of US Foreign Policy in a Comparative Perspective*, Oxford: Oxford University Press, 1990.

29 Niall Ferguson, *Colossus: The Rise and Fall of the American Empire*, London: Allen Lane, 2004, p. 29. Among the other recent works on American empire are Andrew Bacevich, *American Empire: The Realities and Consequences of U.S. Diplomacy*, Cambridge, MA: Harvard University Press, 2002; and Andrew Bacevich (ed.) *The Imperial Tense: Problems and Perspectives of American Empire*, Chicago: Ivan Dee, 2003.

30 See Paul Kennedy, 'Maintaining American Power: From Injury to Recovery', in Strobe Talbott and Nayan Chanda (eds) *The Age of Terror: America and the World After September 11*, Oxford: Perseus Press, 2001, pp. 58–60.

31 See Hutton, *The World We're In*, chs 5 and 6.

32 Richard Haass, *Intervention: The Uses of American Military Force in the Post-Cold War World*, 2nd edn, Washington, DC: Carnegie Endowment, 1999, usefully outlines the debates as well as providing a good deal of detail on particular interventions.

33 *The 9/11 Commission Report: Final Report of the National Commission on Terrorist Attacks upon the United States*, New York: Norton, 2004, p. 51.

34 Quoted in Gilles Kepel, *The War for Muslim Minds: Islam and the West*, Cambridge, MA: Harvard University Press, 2004, pp. 123–24.

35 Bush, State of the Union Address, 2002. At www.whitehouse.gov/news/ releases/2002/01/2002129-11.html (accessed 25/6/2003).

36 Niall Ferguson, *Colossus*, pp. 126–27.

37 For an early example of the Bush administration's insistence that the war against terror was not a war against Islam, see Bush's speech of 20 September 2001. For a perspective on the experience of American Muslims since 9/11 see Muqtedar Khan, 'Putting the American in "American Muslim,"' *New York Times*, 7 September 2003.

38 Note the significance accorded to NSC-68 by neoconservatives William Kristol and Robert Kagan in 'Toward a Neo-Reaganite Foreign Policy', pp. 28–30.

39 There is now a large and fast growing literature on Anti-Americanism, especially with regard to Europe. See Paul Hollander, *Anti-Americanism: Critiques at Home and Abroad, 1965–1990*, New York: Oxford University Press, 1992; Crockatt, *America Embattled*, ch. 2; David Ellwood, *Anti-Americanism in Western Europe: A Comparative Perspective*, Baltimore, MD: Johns Hopkins University, Bologna Center, 1999; Denis Lacorne, Jacques Rupnik and Marie-France Toinet (eds) *The Rise and Fall of Anti-Americanism: A Century of French Perception*, New York: St Martin's Press, 1990; Philippe Roger, *L'ennemi américain: généalogie de l'antiaméricanisme français*, Paris: Editions du Seuil, 2002; Stefan Halper and Jonathan Clarke, *America Alone: The Neoconservatives and the Global Order*, Cambridge: Cambridge University Press, 2004, ch. 8; Nur Bilge Criss, 'A Short History of Anti-Americanism and Terrorism: The Turkish Case', in Joanne Meyerowitz (ed.) *History and September 11*, Philadelphia, PA: Temple University Press, 2003, pp. 56–72. For a view of anti-Americanism in the Arab world which plays down the 'civilizational' element, see Usama Makdisi, '"Anti-Americanism" in the Arab World: An Interpretation of a Brief History', in Meyerowitz (ed.) *History and September 11*, pp. 131–56; Brendon O'Connor and Martin Griffiths (eds) *The Rise of Anti-Americanism*, London: Routledge, 2006.

40 One popular answer to this question is Ziauddin Sardar and Merryl Wyn Davies, *Why Do People Hate America?*, Cambridge: Icon Books, 2002.

41 See Crockatt, *America Embattled*, ch. 2, 'How the World Sees America: The Roots of Anti-Americanism'.

42 Among the most substantial contributions is Halper and Clarke, *America Alone*. Of particular value in charting the impact of neoconservatism on Bush's policies towards the Islamic world is Kepel, *The War for Muslim Minds: Islam and the West*, ch. 2.

43 Yvonne Yazbeck Haddad, 'Islamist Perceptions of US Policy in the Middle East', in David W. Lesch (ed.) *The Middle East and the United States: A Historical and Political Reassessment*, 3rd edn, Cambridge, MA: Westview Press, 2003, p. 481.

44 Werner Weidenfeld, *America and Europe: Is the Break Inevitable?*, Gütersloh, Germany: Bertelsmann Foundation Publishers, 1996, pp. 9–10.

45 See Sergio Fabbrini, 'Layers of Anti-Americanism: Americanization, American Unilateralism and anti-Americanism in a European Perspective', *European Journal of American Culture*, 23, no. 2, 2004, pp. 79–94.

46 The Pew Research Center, *A Year After the Iraq War: Mistrust of America in Europe Ever Higher, Muslim Anger Persists*, people-press.org/reports/display.php3?PageID=796 p. 2 (accessed 6/2/04).

47 Klaus Larres, 'Mutual Incomprehension: US–German Value Gaps beyond Iraq', *The Washington Quarterly*, 26, no. 2, spring 2003, pp. 23, 30, 31.

48 Marshall Fund, *Transatlantic Trends*, p. 5; Pew Research Center, *A Year after the Iraq War*, p. 7.

49 See Crockatt, *America Embattled*, p. 149.

50 *New York Times*, 13 May 2004.

51 Quentin Peel, in 'Analysis: The Sheriff and the Posse', BBC Radio 4, 1 November 2001, broadcast transcript, p. 5; Tony Judt, 'The War on Terror', *New York Review of Books*, 20 December 2001, p. 102.

52 Robert Cooper, *The Breaking of Nations: Order and Chaos in the Twenty-first Century*, London: Atlantic Books, 2003, pp. 127, 136.

2 The role of culture in international relations

1 Stefan Halper and Jonathan Clarke, *America Alone: The Neo-Conservatives and the Global Order*, Cambridge: Cambridge University Press, 2004, pp. 198–99.

2 Edmund Burke, *Reflections on the Revolution in France* [1790]; and Thomas Paine, *The Rights of Man* [1791 and 1792], Garden City NJ: Dolphin Books, 1961, pp. 45, 281.

3 Abdullah Ahmed An-Na'im, 'Upholding International Legality Against Islamic and American *Jihad*', in Ken Booth and Tim Dunne (eds) *Worlds in Collision: Terror and the Future of Global Order*, Houndmills, UK: Palgrave, 2002, p. 164.

4 Amitav Acharya, 'State–Society Relations: Asian and World Order After September 11', in Booth and Dunne (eds) *Worlds in Collision*, p. 195.

5 Amin Saikal, *Islam and the West: Conflict or Cooperation?*, Houndmills, UK: Palgrave, 2003, p. 9.

6 Fouad Ajami, 'The Summoning', *Foreign Affairs*, 72, no. 4 (September/October 1993), p. 9.

7 Albert L. Weeks, 'Do Civilizations Hold?', *Foreign Affairs*, 72, no. 4 (September/October 1993), p. 25.

8 Edward Said, *From Oslo to Iraq and the Roadmap*, London: Bloomsbury, 2004, p. 124. The essay from which the quotation is taken was first published in *Al-Ahram*, *Al-Hayat*, and *The Nation* in October 2001.

9 See Ashley Montague (ed.) *Toynbee and History*, Boston MA: Porter Sargent, 1956.

10 Including especially *Islam and the Myth of Confrontation: Religion and Politics in the Middle East*, London: I. B. Tauris, 1996; and *The World at 2000: Perils and Promises*, Houndmills, UK: Palgrave, 2001, ch. 8.

11 Fred Halliday, *The Middle East in International Relations: Power, Politics and Ideology*, Cambridge: Cambridge University Press, 2005, pp. 46–47.

12 Edward Said, *Orientalism*, Harmondsworth, UK: Penguin, 1978, pp. 1, 2, 3.

13 See, for example, Robert W. Cox, 'Civilizations and the Twenty-first Century: Some Theoretical Considerations', in Mehdi Mozaffari (ed.) *Globalization and Civilizations*, London: Routledge: 2002, p. 9; Halliday, *Islam and the Myth of Confrontation*, ch. 7; Steve Smith and Patricia Owens, 'Alternative Approaches to International Theory', in John Baylis and Steve Smith (eds)

The Globalization of World Politics: An Introduction to International Relations, 3rd edn, Oxford: Oxford University Press, 2005, p. 289.

14 Samuel P. Huntington, 'The Clash of Civilizations?', *Foreign Affairs*, 72, no. 3 (summer 1993), p. 48.

15 Edward Said, *Culture and Imperialism*, London: Vintage, 1994, pp. xv, 59.

16 Edward Said, *Peace and Its Discontents: Gaza-Jericho 1993–1995*, London: Vintage, 1995; *The End of the Peace Process*, revised and updated edn, London: Granta, 2002; *From Oslo to Iraq and the Roadmap*, London: Bloomsbury, 2004.

17 Among the chief items are: Michael Hardt and Antonio Negri, *Empire*, Cambridge, MA: Harvard University Press, 2000; Atilio A. Boron, *Empire and Imperialism: A Critical Reading of Michael Hardt and Antonio Negri*, London: Zed Books, 2005; Chalmers Johnson, *Blowback: The Cost and Consequences of American Empire*, New York: Henry Holt, 2000; Andrew Bacevich, *American Empire: The Realities and Consequences of U.S. Diplomacy*, Cambridge MA: 2002; Andrew Bacevich (ed.) *The Imperial Tense: Prospects and Problems of American Empire*, Chicago: Ivan R. Dee, 2003; Niall Ferguson, *Colossus: The Rise and Fall of the American Empire*, London: Allen Lane, 2004.

18 See Bernard Lewis' recent books: *What Went Wrong?: Western Impact and Middle Eastern Response*, London: Phoenix Books, 2002; *The Crisis of Islam: Holy War and Unholy Terror*, London: Weidenfeld and Nicolson, 2003. For Huntington's 'bloody borders' statement see *The Clash of Civilizations and the Remaking of World Order*, New York: Simon and Schuster, 1996, pp. 254–58. It was Bernard Lewis who coined the term 'clash of civilizations' in an article entitled 'The Roots of Muslim Rage', *Atlantic Monthly*, September 1990. For a discussion of the impact of this article see John L. Esposito, *The Islamic Threat: Myth or Reality?*, 2nd edn, New York: Oxford University Press, 1995, pp. 195–98.

19 Said, *Orientalism*, pp. 300–1.

20 Said, *From Oslo to Iraq*, pp. 245–46.

21 Halliday, *Islam and the Myth of Confrontation*, pp. 201, 210–11.

22 Said's memoir *Out of Place*, London: Granta Books, 2000, is moving testimony of his own location in between the cultures of the Orient and the Occident.

23 Akira Iriye, 'Culture and Power: International Relations as Intercultural Relations', *Diplomatic Relations*, 3 (spring 1979), p. 115.

24 Simon Murden, 'Culture in World Affairs', in John Baylis and Steve Smith (eds) *Globalization and World Politics: An Introduction to International Relations*, 3rd edn, Oxford: Oxford University Press, 2005, p. 540.

25 Benjamin Barber, *Jihad vs McWorld: Terrorism's Challenge to Democracy*, New York: Ballantine Books, 1995, p. 17.

26 Morrell Heald and Lawrence S. Kaplan, *Culture and Diplomacy: The American Experience*, Westport, CT: Greenwood Press, 1977, p. ix.

27 On national character see Rupert Wilkinson, *The Pursuit of American Character*, New York: Harper and Row, 1988. The classic critique of American moralism and idealism in foreign policy is George F. Kennan, *American Diplomacy 1900–1950*, Chicago: University of Chicago Press, 1950. On ideology see Michael H. Hunt, *Ideology and U.S. Foreign Policy*, New Haven, CT: Yale University

Press, 1987. Two more recent historical interpretations of American foreign policy which draw heavily on cultural sources are W. McDougall, *Promised, Land, Crusader State: The American Encounter with the World Since 1776*, Boston, MA: Houghton Mifflin, 1997; and Walter Russell Mead, *Special Providence: American Foreign Policy and How It Changed the World*, London and New York: Routledge, 2002.

28 See Eric Hobsbawm, *Nations and Nationalism Since 1780*, Cambridge: Cambridge University Press, 1990.

29 Liah Greenfeld, *Nationalism: Five Roads to Modernity*, Cambridge, MA: Harvard University Press, 1992, pp. 3–4.

30 Benedict Anderson, *Imagined Communities: Reflections on the Origins and Spread of Nationalism*, revised edn, London: Verso, 1991, pp. 6, 12.

31 Reprinted in Fred Halliday, *Two Hours That Shook the World: September 11, Causes and Consequences*, London: Saqi Books, 2002, pp. 217–19.

32 See Ussama Makdisi, '"Anti-Americanism in the Arab World": An Interpretation of a Brief History', in Joanne Meyerowitz (ed.) *History and September 11*, Philadelphia, PA: Temple University Press, 2003, pp. 131–56.

33 Malise Ruthven, *A Fury for God: The Islamist Attack on America*, London: Granta Books, 2002, p. 76. See pp. 74–98 for a detailed account of this visit and the writings which made Qutb a seminal force in modern Islamism.

34 See Fawaz Gerges, *America and Political Islam: Clash of Cultures or Clash of Interests?*, Cambridge: Cambridge University Press, 1999, pp. 74–76; Esposito, *The Islamic Threat*, pp. 173–79.

35 In Esposito, *The Islamic Threat*, p. 177.

36 Esposito, *The Islamic Threat*, p. 220.

37 Michael J. Mazaar, 'Culture and International Relations', *Washington Quarterly*, spring 1996, pp. 177–96.

38 See Barber, *Jihad vs McWorld*; and Anthony Giddens, *Runaway World: How Globalisation is Reshaping our World*, London: Profile Books, 1999, especially ch. 3.

3 No common ground?: Islam, anti-Americanism and the United States

1 *The Great Divide: How Westerners and Muslims View Each Other*, at www.pewglobal.org/reports/display.php?ReportID=253 accessed 5/10/2006.

2 See, for example, Ziauddin Sardar and Merryl Wyn Davies, *Why do People Hate America?*, Cambridge: Icon Books, 2002.

3 Fred Halliday, *Islam and the Myth of Confrontation: Religion and Politics in the Middle East*, London: I. B. Tauris, 1996, p. 43.

4 F. A. Gerges, *America and Political Islam: Clash of Cultures or Clash of Interests?*, Cambridge: Cambridge University Press, 1999, p. 126.

5 I am, of course, aware that a majority of the world's Muslim population does not live in the Middle East, but I focus on this region because it is there that the relationship between Islam and the United States expresses itself most explosively.

6 For the State Department's figures see its Fact Sheet on Islam in the US at www.usinfo.state.gov/usa/islam/fact2.htm (7 November 2003). There

are numerous difficulties in establishing reliable figures. The US Census does not ask individuals to declare their religious affiliation, though it records numbers of congregations and some other related data. In these circumstances establishing a figure is often subject to political motives. Some estimates go as high as 8 million while others are as low as 1.8 million.

7 See Felicia R. Lee, 'A Sketch of Arab-Americans: Who Should Study Whom?', New York Times, 15 November 2003.

8 Daniel Benjamin and Steven Simon, The Next Attack: The Failure of the War on Terror and a Strategy for Getting it Right, New York: Times Books, 2005, pp. 118–19.

9 Scott Bohlinger, 'First Museum Devoted to Islam Based in Jackson, Mississippi', US Department of State: International Information Programs, 27 March 2003. www.usinfo.state.gov/usa/islam/a032703.htm (16/4/2003).

10 Speech to Congress, 20 September 2001, www.whitehouse.gov/news/releases/2001/09/print/20010920–28.html (25/6/2003).

11 US Department of State, International Information Programs. usinfo.state.gov/usa/islam/s120402.htm (16/4/2003).

12 Quoted in Anatol Lieven, America Right or Wrong: An Anatomy of American Nationalism, London: HarperCollins, 2004, pp. 143–44.

13 Published by the Council on American–Islamic Relations at www.cairnet.org/html/911statements.html (16 April 2003). See also the results of a survey of the American Muslim community based on a questionnaire which suggests that they are a highly educated group: 58 per cent reported that they had college degrees. John Zogby, In Sh'allah: Meet America's Muslim Community (reprinted by permission from The Public Perspective), US Department of State: International Information Programs, www.usinfo.state.gov/usa/islam/ashallah.htm (16/4/2003).

14 Andrea Elliott, 'More Muslims Arrive in U.S., after 9/11 Dip', New York Times, 10 September 2006.

15 See Richard Crockatt, America Embattled: September 11, Anti-Americanism and the Global Order, London: Routledge, 2003, p. 88.

16 A useful brief account of the course of the Iranian Revolution since 1979 is Amin Saikal, Islam and the West: Conflict or Cooperation?, Houndmills, UK: Palgrave Macmillan, 2003, pp. 69–88. Fuller accounts of Iranian developments published since 9/11 are Shahram Chubin, Whither Iran? Reform, Domestic Politics and National Security, International Institute for Strategic Studies, Adelphi Paper 342, 2002; Mark Downes, Iran's Unresolved Revolution, Aldershot, UK: Ashgate, 2002; Dilip Hiro, Iran Today, London: Politico's Publishing, 2006. As I was finishing this manuscript Ali Ansari published Confronting Iran: The Failure of American Foreign Policy and the Next Great Conflict in the Middle East, New York: Basic Books, 2006. This offers an unusually rich analysis of American–Iranian relations which focuses on the existence on both sides of tenacious myths which shape the relationship.

17 Karen Armstrong in the Guardian, 8 May 2003, p. 23.

18 On Khatami see John L. Esposito, Unholy War: Terror in the Name of Islam, Oxford: Oxford University Press, 2002, pp. 136–39; Hiro, Iran Today,

pp. 171ff.; and Ansari, *Confronting Iran*, ch. 5. See BBC news report on Iran, 25 September 2006, www.newsvote.bbc.co.uk/l/hi/world/middle (accessed 2/10/2006) for an account of demonstrations in sympathy with the victims of 9/11; and Ansari, *Confronting Iran*, pp. 181–84.

19 Hiro, *Iran Today*, p. 394.

20 Afshin Molavi, 'Our Allies in Iran', *New York Times*, 3 November 2005.

21 Ansari, *Confronting Iran*, p. 239.

22 Hiro, *Iran Today*, p. 362.

23 Armstrong, op. cit. On Soroush see Ruthven, *Islam*, pp. 373–75; and Hiro, *Iran Today*, pp. 320–24.

24 Olivier Roy, *The Failure of Political Islam*, London: I. B. Tauris, 1999, p. 7.

25 See Esposito, *Unholy War*, pp. 50–51, 133–41.

26 On the meaning of jihad see Malise Ruthven, *A Fury for God: The Islamist Attack on America*, London: Granta Books, 2002, ch. 2, esp. pp. 60–61.

27 James Piscatori, 'Order, Justice, and Global Islam', in Rosemary Foot, John Lewis Gaddis and Andrew Hurrell (eds) *Order and Justice in International Relations*, Oxford: Oxford University Press, 2003, p. 273.

28 John L. Esposito, *The Islamic Threat: Myth or Reality?*, 2nd edn, New York: Oxford University Press, 1999, pp. 217, 219.

29 See Piscatori, 'Order, Justice, and Global Islam', pp. 283–84.

30 Despite what some of his critics have said, Huntington is not an advocate of confrontation. In his concluding paragraph he writes that the West must 'develop a more profound understanding of the basic religious and philosophical assumptions underlying other civilizations and of the ways in which people in those civilizations see their interests'. This in turn requires an 'effort to identify elements of commonality between western and other civilizations' ('The Clash of Civilizations?', *Foreign Affairs*, 72, no. 3, summer 1993, p. 49). The framework of the argument, however, places the emphasis on the conflictual elements in international relations, and it is for this reason that I invoke it.

31 Huntington, 'Clash of Civilizations?', p. 28.

32 Samuel Huntington, *The Clash of Civilizations and the Remaking of World Order*, New York: Simon and Schuster, 1996, pp. 217, 218.

33 Huntington, *Clash of Civilizations*, p. 318.

34 Esposito, *Unholy War*, pp. 52–53.

35 Esposito, *Unholy War*, pp. 56–61. See also R. Scott Appleby, 'History in the Fundamentalist Imagination', in Joanne Meyerowitz (ed.) *History and September 11*, Philadelphia, PA: Temple University Press, 2003, pp. 157–74. This latter piece makes a convincing case for defining 'fundamentalism' in terms of an apocalyptic view of history.

36 See Huntington, *Clash of Civilizations*, 109–20. He remarks (p. 109n.) that the Islamic 'Resurgence' is as important as the American, French, or Russian Revolutions. Bernard Lewis examines the impact of the West on Islam in two books: *What Went Wrong?: Western Impact and Middle Eastern Response*, London: Phoenix Books, 2002; and *The Crisis of Islam: Holy War and Unholy Terror*, London: Weidenfeld and Nicolson, 2003. The latter contains a

chapter on 'Discovering America' which concludes, on the basis of a discussion of Qutb's famous reaction to a visit to the United States and its subsequent influence on his own development and the rise of Islamism, that the most powerful accusation against the United States was 'the degeneracy and debauchery of the American way of life, and the threat that it offers to Islam' (p. 61).

37 The most extreme case was surely the murder in Arizona of a Sikh petrol station owner by a crazed individual on a shooting spree intended to avenge the September 11 attacks. The murderer was sentenced to death. *Guardian*, 11 October 2003, p. 17.

38 See, for example, Bhikhu Parekh, 'Terrorism or Intercultural Dialogue', in Ken Booth and Tim Dunne (eds) *Worlds in Collision: Terror and the Future of the Global Order*, London: Palgrave, 2002, p. 272.

39 'Muslim Opinion sees Conspiracy', *Christian Science Monitor*, 6 November 2001. Accessed 15 March 2004 at www.csmonitor.com/2001/1106/. Conspiracy theories were not confined to Muslims. It is a growth industry among a wider public. Among the most sophisticated is David Ray Griffin's *The New Pearl Harbor: Disturbing Questions about the Bush Administration and 9/11*, Moreton-in-the-Marsh, UK: Arris Books, 2004.

40 The fact that the caliphate was abolished by the Turkish leader Kemal Ataturk did not stop it being a disaster in the Muslim calendar. In a statement on 7 October 2001, bin Laden seems to be referring to these events when he said that 'our Islamic nation has been tasting the same for more than 80 years, of humiliation and disgrace, its sons killed and their blood spilled, its sanctities desecrated'. Printed in full in Fred Halliday, *Two Hours That Shook the World: September 11, 2001, Causes and Consequences*, London: Saqi Books, 2002, p. 233.

41 Michael Slackman, 'Bin Laden Says West is Waging War Against Islam', *New York Times*, 24 April 2006.

42 Ussama Makdisi, '"Anti-Americanism" in the Arab World: An Interpretation of a Brief History', in Joanne Meyerowitz (ed.) *History and September 11*, Philadelphia, PA: Temple University Press, 2003, pp. 131–56.

43 The literature on this topic is now huge. Among the many contributions, I have found the following most useful: Gilles Kepel, *The War for Muslim Minds*, Cambridge, MA: Harvard University press, 2004; Esposito, *The Islamic Threat: Myth or Reality?*; Olivier Roy, *The Failure of Political Islam*, London: I. B. Tauris, 1999; Olivier Roy, *Globalized Islam: The Search for a New Umma*, New York: Columbia University Press, 2004; Fred Halliday, *Islam and the Myth of Confrontation: Religion and Politics in the Middle East*, London: I. B. Tauris, 1999; Malise Ruthven, *Islam in the World*, London: Penguin, 2000.

44 See Ivo Daalder and James D. Lindsay, *America Unbound: The Bush Revolution in Foreign Policy*, Washington, DC: Brookings Institution Press, 2003, esp. chs 1 and 2.

45 Americanism and Americanization as targets for 'anti-Americanism' are discussed in Crockatt, *America Embattled*, pp. 46–57, and in Chapter 4 of this book.

46 Excellent discussions of terrorism by Islamic groups are Malise Ruthven, *A Fury for God: The Islamist Attack on America*, London: Granta Books, 2002; and Esposito, *Unholy War*. See also John Burns, 'Bin Laden Stirs Struggle on the Meaning of Jihad', *New York Times*, 27 January 2002.

47 Parekh, 'Terrorism or Intercultural Dialogue', p. 275.

48 Michael Ignatieff has made the case for seeing ethnic conflict in the former Yugoslavia as the result rather than the cause of political failure. See *The Warrior's Honor: Ethnic War and the Modern Conscience*, London: Vintage, 1999, pp. 39–46, esp. p. 45.

4 Americanism: a short history

1 Nora Jacobson, 'Before You Flee to Canada, Can We Talk?', *Washington Post*, 28 November 2004; Marie-France Toinet, 'Does Anti-Americanism Exist?', in Denis Lacorne, Jacques Rupnik and Marie-France Toinet (eds) *The Rise and Fall of Anti-Americanism: A Century of French Perception*, New York: St Martin's Press, 1990, pp. 230–31.

2 Brendon O'Connor, 'What is Anti-Americanism: Tendency, Prejudice or Ideology?', paper delivered at the Institute for the Study of the Americas, University of London, 21 October 2005, p. 18.

3 Among the major works on American character are David Potter, *People of Plenty: Economic Abundance and the American Character*, Chicago, IL: University of Chicago Press, 1954; and Daniel Boorstin, *The Genius of American Politics*, Chicago: University of Chicago Press, 1953. On consensus history see John Higham, 'Beyond Consensus: The Historian as Moral Critic', *American Historical Review*, 67 (1962) pp. 609–25; and Peter Novick, *That Noble Dream: The 'Objectivity Question' and the American Historical Profession*, Cambridge: Cambridge University Press, 1988.

4 This essay was completed before I became aware of a multi-authored book entitled *Americanism: New Perspectives on the History of an Ideal*, edited by Michael Kazin and Joseph A. McCartin, Chapel Hill, NC: University of North Carolina Press, 2006. This is a rich collection of essays on a variety of topics related to the theme of Americanism. The editors usefully describe Americanism as meaning 'both what is distinctive about the United States . . . and loyalty to that nation, rooted in defense of its political ideals'. These ideals include self-government, equal opportunity, freedom of speech and association, and a belief in progress (p. 1). My own purpose is rather narrower, though certainly complementary, which is to trace specific usages of the term 'Americanism' with the aim of establishing its various inflections and the precise ways in which the term has been wielded by a range of writers and politicians. I believe that this helps to give more concreteness to the discussion of Americanism which otherwise can become somewhat amorphous. The editors urge American progressives and liberals to reclaim Americanism from the conservatives. My own analysis is concerned less with this political agenda than with showing the process by which conservatives have managed to establish such ascendancy over the term.

Indeed, I am not persuaded that it is a good thing for American leftists to seek to compete with the right in claiming the mantle of Americanism.

5 See H. L. Mencken, *The American Language: An Inquiry into the Development of English in the United States*, 2nd edn, New York: Alfred A. Knopf, 1921, pp. 38–44, ch. V.

6 W. T. Stead, *The Americanization of the World*, New York: Garland, 1972 (first published London: Horace Markley, 1901).

7 Julius Streicher, 'What is Americanism?', *Der Stürmer*, no. 23, 1944, accessed on 26/04/2006 at www.calvin.edu/academic/cas/gpa/ds1.htm

8 Richard Ruland, preface to *A Storied Land: Theories of American Literature*, edited with notes and commentary by Richard Ruland, New York: E. P. Dutton, 1976, volume II, p. xv.

9 Thomas Wentworth Higginson in Ruland (ed.) *A Storied Land*, pp. 15–16.

10 There he asked the question 'What then is the American, this new man?', to which he gave the answer:

> The American is a new man, who acts upon new principles; he must entertain new ideas, and form new opinions. From involuntary idleness, servile dependence, penury and useless labor, he has passed to toils of a very different nature, rewarded by ample subsistence – This is an American.
>
> > (J. Hector St John de Crêvecoeur, *Letters from an American Farmer*, London: Dent, 1973, p. 43)

11 Henry James, *The American Scene*, Harmondsworth, UK: Penguin, 1994, pp. 262–63.

12 'Den Vereinigten Staaten', in *Werke, Kommentare und Register*, Hamburger Ausgabe, Band I, Munich: Verlag CH Beck, 1981, p. 333.

13 James Russell Lowell, *Abraham Lincoln*, at manybooks.net/pages/lowelljaetext971lncn/29.html (accessed 3/6/2006), p. 30.

14 Alexis de Tocqueville, *Democracy in America*, translated, edited and with an introduction by Harvey Mansfield and Delba Winthrop, London: The Folio Society, 2002 (first published by the University of Chicago Press, 2000), vol. 2, part II, ch. 2, p. 482.

15 See, for example, *Democracy in America*, vol. 2, part II, ch. 4, 'How Americans Combat Individualism with Free Institutions'.

16 Grover Cleveland, inaugural address, 1893, www.yale.edu/lawweb/avalon/pesiden/inaug/cleve2.htm (accessed 4/6/2006).

17 Ayn Rand, *Textbook of Americanism* (published as a series of articles in *The Vigil* in 1946), available at laissez-fairepublic.com/textbook.htm (accessed 26/4/2006).

18 Her testimony can be found in Eric Bentley (ed.) *Thirty Years of Treason: Excerpts from Hearings Before the HCUA, 1938–1968*, New York: Viking Press, 1971, pp. 111–19.

19 Theodore Roosevelt, 'True Americanism', *Forum* (1894).

20 *Public Papers of Woodrow Wilson*, ed. Arthur S. Link *et al.*, Princeton, NJ: Princeton University Press, 1947–, vol. 33, p. 148.

21 *The Writings of Theodore Roosevelt*, ed. William H. Harbaugh, Indianapolis and New York: Bobbs-Merrill, 1976, pp. 382–83.

22 Henry James, review of Roosevelt's *American Ideals and Other Essays Social and Political*, in Christopher Ricks and William L. Vance (eds) *The Faber Book of America*, London: Faber, 1990, pp. 252–53. (Originally published in *Literature*, 23 April 1898.)

23 Randolph Bourne, 'Trans-National America', in Carl Resek (ed.) *War and the Intellectuals: Essays by Randolph Bourne, 1915–1919*, New York: Harper and Row, 1964, pp. 107, 108, 114, 115, 115–16, 119 (first published in the *Atlantic Monthly*, July 1916). Jonathan Hansen discusses Bourne and also other pluralists such as Horace Kallen in a fine essay on 'True Americanism: Progressive Era Intellectuals and the Problem of Liberal Nationalism', in Kazin and McMartin (eds) *Americanism*, pp. 73–89.

24 Of particular value on the Klan, as far as the theme of this essay is concerned, is David M. Chalmers, *Hooded Americanism: The First Century of the Ku Klux Klan, 1865–1965*, Garden City, NJ: Doubleday, 1965.

25 Hiram Evans, 'The Klan's Fight for Americanism' (1926), in Richard Hofstadter (ed.) *Great Issues in American History: From Reconstruction to the Present Day, 1864–1969*, New York: Vintage Books, 1969, pp. 326–27, 327, 328.

26 Evans, 'The Klan's fight Against Americanism', p. 330.

27 Evans, 'The Klan's fight Against Americanism', p. 325.

28 Evans, 'The Klan's fight Against Americanism', p. 329.

29 Constitution of the American Legion, at www.legion.org (accessed 1/6/2006).

30 *Isms: A Review of Alien Isms, Revolutionary Communism and Their Active Sympathizers in the United States*, compiled by the National Americanism Commission of the American Legion, National Headquarters, Indianapolis, IN, 1937, p. 13.

31 Arthur Schlesinger Jr, *The Vital Center: The Politics of Freedom*, New Brunswick NJ: Transaction Publishers, 1998 (first published by Riverside Press, 1949).

32 For the view that Truman was ultimately responsible for McCarthyism, see Richard Freeland, *The Truman Doctrine and the Origins of McCarthyism*, New York: Knopf, 1972.

33 Gary Wills, introduction to Lillian Hellman, *Scoundrel Time*, New York: Bantam Books, 1976, p. 16.

34 J. Edgar Hoover, testimony before the HUAC, 26 March 1947, in Ellen Schrecker (ed.) *The Age of McCarthyism: A Brief History with Documents*, Boston, MA: Bedford Books of St Martin's Press, 1994, p. 119.

35 Maurice Isserman, *Which Side Were You On?: The American Communist Party During the Second World War*, Middletown, CT: Wesleyan University Press, 1982, pp. 10–11.

36 Claud Cockburn, 'Rackets Strictly on American Lines', in Ricks and Vance (eds) *The Faber Book of America*, pp. 378–79.

37 Harold Laski, *American Democracy*, New York: Viking Press, 1948, p. 748.

38 Max Lerner, *America as a Civilization*, New York: Simon and Schuster, 1957, pp. 456, 506.

39 Louis Hartz, *The Liberal Tradition in America*, New York: Harcourt Brace, 1955, p. 11.

40 Carl Schurz, 'Address delivered to the Chamber of Commerce of the State of New York', 2 January 1896, at www.library.wisc.edu/etext/wireader/WER1027.html (accessed 5/6/2006).

41 John Dewey, *Individualism Old and New*, New York: Prometheus Books, 1990, pp. 10–11 (first published 1930).

42 There is, of course, a question about whether Theodore Roosevelt could be described as a conservative, not least because he embraced what were termed 'progressive values' during his presidency and indeed ran as candidate for the Progressive Party in the presidential election of 1912. Without entering into the debate about the nature of progressivism, it should be pointed out that Roosevelt's version of progressivism was premised on an intense nationalism, American 'exceptionalism', and a willingness to wield the big stick in foreign policy, qualities which have made him extremely attractive to the neoconservatives of post-Cold War America. For a good example of Roosevelt's appeal to neoconservatives, see William Kristol and Robert Kagan, 'Toward a Neo-Reaganite Foreign Policy', *Foreign Affairs*, July/August 1996, p. 32.

43 *Common Sense Americanism*, www.csamericanism.org (accessed 14/12/2005).

44 See www.americanism.org/pages/other/purpose.htm (accessed 26/4/2006); www.legion.org (accessed 11/6/2006); www.srmason-sj.org/library/collections/Americanism/6.htm (accessed 12/6/2006).

45 David Michael Green, 'The War on Americanism', at www.truthout.org/cgi-bin/artman/exec/view.cgi/48/1731 (accessed 12/6/2006). This article was originally published in the *Albany Times Union*.

46 George W. Bush, first inaugural address, at www.whitehouse.gov/news/inaugural-address.html (accessed 5/10/02).

47 For this reason I am suspicious of the idea, put forward by Michael Kazin and Joseph A. McCartin, that 'Americanism should be revived and practiced as the foundation of a new kind of progressive politics' (Kazin and McCartin (eds) *Americanism*, p. 16).

5 What's the big idea? Models of global order in the post-Cold War world

1 Adam Watson, *The Evolution of International Society: A Comparative Historical Analysis*, London: Routledge, 1992, ch. 17.

2 Barry Buzan and Richard Little, 'Beyond Westphalia? Capitalism after the "Fall"', *Review of International Studies*, 25, December 1999, p. 93.

3 John Baylis and Steve Smith (eds) *The Globalization of World Politics: An Introduction to World Politics*, 3rd edn, Oxford: Oxford University Press, 2005, pp. 2–3.

4 See J. N. Rosenau, *Turbulence in World Politics: A Theory of Change and Continuity*, Hemel Hempstead, UK: Harvester/Wheatsheaf, 1990.

5 'Hegemony' was a term adopted by Marxist analysts, following Gramsci, but soon became familiar among international relations theorists in the form of 'hegemonic stability theory'. It is now routinely used by empirical

scholars as well as theorists to describe the United States in the contemporary international system. See, for example, Rosemary Foot, S. MacFarlane and Michael Mastanduno (eds) *US Hegemony and International Organizations*, Oxford: Oxford University Press, 2003. A comparable evolution has been followed by 'empire'. This is discussed below.

6 See Richard Crockatt, 'Challenge and Response: Arnold Toynbee, the United States and the Cold War', in Dale Carter and Robin Clifton (eds) *War and Cold War In American Foreign Policy, 1942–1962*, Houndmills, UK: Palgrave, 2002, pp. 108–30.

7 Noam Chomsky, *World Orders Old and New*, London: Pluto Press, 1997.

8 Andrew Bacevich, *American Empire: The Realities and Consequences of U.S. Diplomacy*, Cambridge, MA: Harvard University Press, 2002, pp. 1–6.

9 George H. W. Bush, State of the Union Address, 29 January 1991, at www.bushlibrary.tamu.edu/research/papers/ (accessed 9/3/2007).

10 See Ian Clark, *The Post-Cold War Order: The Spoils of Peace*, Oxford: Oxford University Press, 2001.

11 See Joseph S. Nye, *Bound To Lead: The Changing Nature of American Power*, New York: Basic Books, 1990.

12 See, for example, *Guardian Studies, New World Order?: Seven Writers in Search of an Ideal*, London: 1991.

13 Francis Fukuyama, 'The End of History?', *National Interest*, summer 1989, pp. 3–18.

14 *Guardian*, 3 May 1989, p. 26.

15 Anthony Lake, 'Remarks to Johns Hopkins School of Advanced International Studies', United States Information service, US Embassy, London, 22 September 1993, 22 pp.

16 Samuel P. Huntington, 'The Clash of Civilizations?', *Foreign Affairs*, 72, no. 3, summer 1993, pp. 22–49; and *The Clash of Civilizations and the Remaking of World Order*, New York: Simon and Schuster, 1996.

17 Huntington, *Clash of Civilizations*, pp. 183, 183–84, 193.

18 Huntington, *Clash of Civilizations*, pp. 305–8; and *Who Are We? America's Great Debate*, New York: Free Press, 2004.

19 Huntington, 'The Clash of Civilizations?', p. 22.

20 National Security Council, 'Security Strategy of the United States', September 2002, at www.whitehouse.gov/nsc/ (accessed 18/9/2003).

21 Charles Krauthammer, 'The Unipolar Moment', *Foreign Affairs*, 70, 1990–91, pp. 23–33.

22 Charles Krauthammer, 'The Unipolar Era', in Andrew J. Bacevich, *The Imperial Tense: Prospects and Problems of American Empire*, Chicago: Ivan R. Dee, 2003, p. 60 (first published in *The National Interest*, winter 2003).

23 John Mearsheimer, 'Back to the Future: Instability After the Cold War', *International Security*, 15, no. 2, 1990, pp. 191–222.

24 George Friedman and Meredith Lebard, *Coming War with Japan*, New York: St Martin's Press, 1991.

25 Madeleine Albright, *Madam Secretary: A Memoir*, New York: Macmillan, 2003, pp. 139–40.

26 See Jan Aart Scholte, *Globalization: A Critical Introduction*, Basingstoke, UK: Palgrave, 2000; and Anthony Giddens, *Runaway World: How Globalisation is Reshaping Our Lives*, London: Profile Books, 1999.

27 See Giddens, *Runaway World*; Hans-Henrik Holm and George Sorensen (eds) *Whose World Order? Uneven Globalisation and the End of the Cold War*, Boulder, CO: Westview Press, 1995; and Benjamin R. Barber, *Jihad vs McWorld: Terrorism's Challenge to Democracy*, New York: Ballantine Books, 2001.

28 Joseph S. Nye, *The Paradox of American Power: Why the World's Only Superpower Can't Go it Alone*, New York: Oxford University Press, 2002, pp. 77–81.

29 John L. Gaddis, 'Towards the Post-Cold War World', *Foreign Affairs*, 70, no. 2, spring 1991, p. 122.

30 Joseph S. Nye, 'What New World Order?' *Foreign Affairs*, 71, no. 2, spring 1992, pp. 95–96.

31 G. J. Ikenberry, 'Liberalism and Empire: Logics of Order in the American Unipolar Age', *Review of International Studies*, 30, no. 4, 2004, p. 609.

32 See William Appleman Williams, *The Roots of American Empire: A Study of the Growth and Shaping of Social Consciousness in a Marketplace Society*, New York: Random House, 1969; and *The Tragedy of American Diplomacy*, New York: Dell, 1972 (first published 1959).

33 Deepak, Lal, 'In Defense of Empires', in Bacevich, *The Imperial Tense*, p. 45.

34 Niall Ferguson, *Colossus: The Price of America's Empire*, London: Allen Lane, Penguin Books, 2004, p. 294.

35 There is now a large literature on American empire. A useful guide to the range of issues involved is a forum in the *Review of International Studies*, 30, no. 4 (2004), with contributions by Michael Cox, G. John Ikenberry and Michael Mann.

36 James Chace, 'In Search of Absolute Security', in Bacevich, *The Imperial Tense*, p. 119.

37 Martin Walker, 'An Empire Unlike Any Other', in Bacevich, *The Imperial Tense*, p. 135.

38 Victor Davis Hanson, 'What Empire?', in Bacevich, *Imperial Tense*, p. 147.

39 Michael Cox, 'Empire, Imperialism and the Bush Doctrine', *Review of International Studies*, 30, no. 4, 2004, pp. 598–99.

40 Ikenberry, 'Liberalism and Empire', p. 619.

41 R. Keohane and Joseph S. Nye, *Power and Interdependence: World Politics in Transition*, Boston, MA: Little, Brown, 1977, p. 24.

42 Robert Cooper, *The Breaking of Nations: Order and Chaos in the Twenty-first Century*, London: Atlantic Books, 2003, pp. 16–18, 21–22, 26ff.

43 See Elliott Cohen, 'A Revolution in Warfare', *Foreign Affairs*, 75, no. 2, March/April 1996, pp. 37–54.

44 Ferguson, *Colossus*, pp. 296–98.

45 Anatol Lieven, *America Right or Wrong: An Anatomy of American Nationalism*, London: HarperCollins, 2004; Michael Lind, *The Next American Nation: The New Nationalism and the Fourth American Revolution*, New York: Free Press, 1996.

46 See Hans Kohn, *American Nationalism: An Interpretive Essay*, New York: Collier, 1961 (first published 1957); Liah Greenfeld, *Nationalism: Five Roads to Modernity*,

Cambridge, MA: Harvard University Press, 1992; Lieven, *America Right or Wrong*; Lind, *The Next American Nation*.

47 See Richard Crockatt, *America Embattled: September 11, Anti-Americanism and the Global Order*, London: Routledge, 2003, chs 1–2.

48 Thomas G. Paterson and Dennis Merrill (eds) *Major Problems in American Foreign Relations*, vol. 1, Boston, MA: D. C. Heath, 2000, p. 38.

49 Menzies Campbell, *Independent on Sunday*, 7 November, 2004, p. 29.

50 John L. Sullivan in Paterson and Merrill (eds) *Major Problems in American Foreign Relations*, p. 250.

51 Bush, George W. second inaugural address, 20 January 2005, at www.whitehouse.gov/news/releases/2005/01/20050120-1.html (accessed 9/3/2007).

6 The emperor's clothes: the failure of the neoconservative mission

1 L. Paul Bremer, *My Year in Iraq: The Struggle to Build a Future of Hope*, New York: Simon and Schuster, 2006. See also George Packer, *The Assassins' Gate: America in Iraq*, New York: Farrar, Straus and Giroux, 2006. Daniel Benjamin and Steven Simon place Iraq in the wider context of the war on terror in *The Next Attack: The Failure of the War on Terror and a Strategy for Getting it Right*, New York: Times Books, 2006.

2 *Independent*, 9 March 2006, pp. 1–2.

3 Irving Kristol, *Reflections of a Neoconservative*, New York: Basic Books, 1983, p. xii. A good account of the early phase of neoconservatism is Peter Steinfels, *The Neoconservatives: The Men Who Are Changing America's Politics*, New York: Simon and Schuster, 1979. An exceptionally useful tool for students of neoconservatism is a collection of writings edited by Irwin Stelzer, *Neoconservatism*, London: Atlantic Books, 2004. Stelzer is an unashamed advocate of neoconservatism, but his collection demonstrates the wide range of views coming under that label.

4 Irvin Kristol, 'The Neoconservative Persuasion', in Stelzer (ed.) *Neoconservatism*, p. 35. First published in the *Weekly Standard*, 25 August 2003.

5 See Mario Del Pero, 'The Historical and Ideological Roots of the Neo-Conservative Persuasion', in Sergio Fabbrini (ed.) *The United States Contested: American Unilateralism and European Discontent*, Abingdon: Routledge, 2006, pp. 33–53.

6 Kristol, 'The Neoconservative Persuasion', pp. 36–37. For an account of the influence of neoconservatism on Bush's foreign policy, see Douglas T. Stuart, 'The Neo-Conservatives as a Continuation and an Aberration in American Foreign Policy', in Fabbrini (ed.) *The United States Contested*, pp. 54–68.

7 Stefan Halper and Jonathan Clarke, *America Alone: The Neo-Conservatives and the Global Order*, Cambridge: Cambridge University Press, 2004, pp. 76ff.

8 Ivo Daalder and James D. Lindsay, *America Unbound: The Bush Revolution in Foreign Policy*, Washington, DC: Brookings Institution Press, 2003, p. 47.

9 John Mickelthwait and Adrian Wooldridge, *The Right Nation: Why America Is Different*, London: Allen Lane, 2004, p. 203.

10 Pierre Hassner quoted in G. John Ikenberry, 'The End of the Neo-Conservative Moment', *Survival*, 46, no. 1, spring 2004, p. 20.

11 PNAC Statement of Principles, at www.newamericancentury.org/statementofprinciples.htm (accessed 21/10/2004); PNAC Open Letter to President Clinton, at newamericancentury.org/iraqclintonletter.htm (accessed 21/10/2004).

12 Francis Fukuyama quoted in Robert S. Boynton, 'The Neocon Who Isn't', *The American Prospect* (online edition) 5 October 2005, p. 2.

13 Francis Fukuyama, 'The Neoconservative Moment', *The National Interest*, summer 2004.

14 Francis Fukuyama, 'Invasion of the Isolationists', *New York Times*, op-ed section, 31 August 2005.

15 Interview of Secretary Wolfowitz with Sam Tannenhaus, *Vanity Fair*, May 2003, at www.defenselink.mil/transcripts, pp. 17–18.

16 Francis Fukuyama, comment column, *Guardian*, 22 February 2006, p. 27. This argument was developed at greater length in *After the Neocons: America at the Crossroads*, London: Profile Books, 2006.

17 Ikenberry, 'The End of the Neo-Conservative Moment', *passim*.

18 Halper and Clarke, *America Alone*, p. 5.

19 Halper and Clarke, *America Alone*, pp. 7, 8.

20 Jeffrey Goldberg, 'Letter from Washington: Breaking Ranks', *New Yorker*, 31 October 2005. www.newyorker.com/printables/fact/051031fa_fact2 (pp. 11–12) (accessed 6/11/2005).

21 Charles Krauthammer, 'Cold-blooded and Wrong-headed on Iraq', *Washington Post*, 28 October 2005.

22 Edward H. Crane and William A. Niskanen (for the Cato Institute) 'September 11th – Upholding Liberty in America', www.cato.org/pub_display.php?pub_id=3159 (accessed 9/3/2007).

23 William Kristol and Robert Kagan, 'Toward a Neo-Reaganite Foreign Policy', *Foreign Affairs*, July/August 1996, pp. 18–32.

24 Halper and Clarke, *America Alone*, pp. 164–81.

25 Sheryl Gay Stolberg, 'In the Senate, a Chorus of Three Defies the Line', *New York Times*, 21 November 2005.

26 See Elisabeth Bumiller, 'Cheney Sees "Shameless" Revisionism on War', *New York Times*, 22 November 2005.

27 *The American Conservative*, 21 October 2002, contents page, www.amconmag.com/2002/2002_10_21.html (accessed 13/5/05).

28 Alexis de Tocqueville, *Democracy in America*.

29 George W. Bush, first inaugural address, www.whitehouse.gov/news/inaugural-address.html (accessed 5/10/02).

30 *National Security Strategy of the United States of America* (2002), pp. 8, 9, 10. www.whitehouse.gov/nsc/print/nsall.html (accessed 18/09/2003).

31 John Lewis Gaddis, *Surprise, Security and the American Experience*, Cambridge, MA: Harvard University Press, 2004, pp. 17, 18–22.

32 Gaddis, *Surprise*, pp. 110, 85.

33 *National Security Strategy*, p. 32.

34 Jeane Kirkpatrick, 'Neoconservatism as a Response to the Counter-Culture', in Stelzer (ed.) *Neoconservatism*, p. 239.

35 Anatol Lieven, *America Right or Wrong: An Anatomy of American Nationalism*, New York: HarperCollins, 2004, p. 127.

36 Halper and Clarke, *America Alone*, pp. 196–97.

37 See Daalder and Lindsay, *America Unbound*, pp. 88–89; Bob Woodward, *Plan of Attack*, New York: Simon and Schuster, 2004, p. 379.

38 Text of 20 September speech available at www.msnbc.com/news/ 629271.asp (accessed 5/18/02); 2004 State of the Union Address at www.whitehouse.gov/news/releases/2004/01/20 (accessed 1/22/04).

39 Woodward, *Plan of Attack*, p. 86.

40 Notably Irwin Stelzer in his anthology of neoconservative writings. See Stelzer, *Neoconservatism*, preface to the paperback edition, pp. xii–xv.

41 See www.pollingreport.com/iraq/htm for a range of polls from several polling organizations, including Pew, ABC News/Washington Post and CNN/USA Today covering the period March 2003–February 2006.

42 Department of Defense News Briefing with Secretary Rumsfeld and Admiral Giambastiani, 1 February 2006, at www.defense.link.mil/cgi-bin (accessed 17/2/2006).

43 Peter Hakim, 'Is Washington Losing Latin America?', *Foreign Affairs*, 85, no. 1, January/February 2006, p. 39.

44 Quoted in Jane Lampman, 'New Scrutiny of Role of Religion in Bush's policies', *Christian Science Monitor*, 17 March 2003, www.csmonitor. com2003/0317/p01s01-uspo.htm (accessed 17/2/2006).

7 The Bush administration and the idea of international community

1 Condoleezza Rice, 'Campaign 2000: Promoting the National Interest', *Foreign Affairs*, January/February 2000.

2 George W. Bush, Veterans Day speech, 11 November 2005, at www. whitehouse.gov/news/releases/2005/11 (accessed 18/8/06).

3 George W. Bush, State of the Union Address, 2005, www.whitehouse.gov/ news/releases/2005/02 (accessed 24/1/05).

4 George W. Bush, State of the Union Address, 20 January 2004, at www.whitehouse.gov/news/releases/2004/01 (accessed 1/22/04).

5 Quoted in Ivo H. Daalder and James M. Lindsay, *America Unbound: The Bush Revolution in Foreign Policy*, Washington, DC: Brookings Institution Press, 2003, p. 65,

6 George W. Bush, speech, 11 June 2001, at www.whitehouse.gov/news/ releases/2001/06/2001 (accessed 5/24/02).

7 John R. Bolton, 'American Justice and the International Criminal Court', at www.state.gov/t/us/rm/25818.htm (Note that, while the speech was delivered at the American Enterprise Institute, it appears on the US State Department website.)

8 See Henry Kissinger, 'The Pitfalls of Universal Jurisdiction', *Foreign Affairs*, July/August 2001, pp. 86–96. For further discussion of the ICC see John F. Murphy, *The United States and the Rule of Law in International Affairs*,

Cambridge: Cambridge University Press, 2004, pp. 317–18; and an exchange between Morton Halperin and Gary Dempsey in *Insight on the News*, 7 September 1998, at www.findarticles.com (accessed 13/9/2006).

 9 Halperin in *Insight on the News*, 7 September 1998.

10 Murphy, *The United States and the Rule of Law in International Affairs*, p. 318.

11 George W. Bush, speech to National Defense University, 1 May 2001, at www.clw.org/archive/coalition/bushnmd (accessed 14/9/2006).

12 John Newhouse, 'The Missile Defense Debate', *Foreign Affairs*, July/August 2001, pp. 107, 108–9.

13 Tony Judt, 'America and the War', *New York Review of Books*, 15 November 2001, p. 6.

14 Bob Woodward, *Plan of Attack*, New York: Simon and Schuster, 2004, pp. 162, 180.

15 Text of speech delivered by Tony Blair on 5 March 2004, *Guardian*, 6 March 2004, p. 6.

16 George W. Bush, speech to the UN, 21 September 2004, at www. whitehouse.gov/news/releases/2004/09 (Accessed 15/9/06).

17 CBS News Report by David Paul Kuhn, 21 September 2004 at www.cbsnews.com/stories/2004/09/21/politics/printable644849.shtml (accessed 15/9/2006).

18 Steven R. Weisman, 'Bush, at the UN, Calls for Action to Widen Liberty', *New York Times*, 22 September 2004.

19 CBS News Report by Kuhn, 21 September 2004.

20 Quoted in Martin Wight, *International Theory: The Three Traditions*, eds Gabriele Wight and Brian Porter, London: Leicester University Press for the Royal Institute of International Affairs, 1991, p. 31.

21 The range of theories is conveniently described in John Baylis and Steve Smith (eds) *The Globalization of World Politics: An Introduction to International Relations*, 3rd edn, Oxford: Oxford University Press, 2005, part II.

22 Robert Cooper, *The Breaking of Nations: Order and Chaos in the Twenty-first Century*, London: Atlantic Books, 2003, ch. 2, esp. pp. 44–50.

23 See Daalder and Lindsay, *America Unbound: The Bush Revolution in Foreign Policy.*

24 The work which set the terms for the debate is Felix Gilbert, *To the Farewell Address*, Princeton, NJ: Princeton University Press, 1961. Gilbert's book takes the form of a contextual analysis of George Washington's 1796 'Farewell Address' which, Gilbert concludes, reveals the basic issue of the American attitude toward foreign policy: 'the tension between Idealism and Realism' (p. 136). John Hutson disputes Gilbert's conclusion that the French Enlightenment had a significant influence on the American Founding Fathers, arguing instead that America's founders were out and out realists. See James H. Hutson, 'Intellectual Foundations of Early American Diplomacy', *Diplomatic History*, I (1977) pp. 1–19; and *John Adams and the Diplomacy of the American Revolution*, Lexington, KY: University of Kentucky Press, 1980.

25 John A. Thompson, *Woodrow Wilson*, London: Longman, 2002, pp. 152–53, 250.

26 G. John Ikenberry, 'State Power and the Institutional Bargain: America's Ambivalent Economic and Security Multilateralism', in Rosemary Foot,

S. Neil MacFarlane and Michael Mastanduno (eds) US Hegemony and International Organizations, Oxford: Oxford University Press, 2003, p. 50.

27 Ikenberry, 'State Power and the Intsitutional Bargain', pp. 55–57, 49.

28 Rosemary Foot, S. Neil MacFarlane and Michael Mastanduno, 'Introduction', in Foot et al. (eds) US Hegemony and International Organizations, p. 6.

29 It is important to note, however, that the US Senate had already voted prior to 9/11 to pay the arrears to the UN, though the House dragged its heels until after the terrorist attacks. See Luck, 'American Exceptionalism and International Organization: Lessons from the 1990s', in Foot et al. (eds) US Hegemony and International Organizations, pp. 45–46.

30 Madeleine Albright notes in her memoirs that

> now, with the explosion in the need for international peace-keeping, coupled with the end of the security Council's paralysis, the UN's role was expanding. During the four years of the Bush presidency and the first of Bill Clinton's, the council authorized more new peacekeeping operations than the UN had attempted in its previous forty-five years. In 1990, there were less than fourteen thousand UN peacekeepers. In 1993, the number would peak at more than seventy-eight thousand. For decades in the past the Security Council had rarely met. During my four years we convened almost daily.
>
> (Madame Secretary: A Memoir, London: Macmillan, 2003, p. 135)

31 Richard Haass, Intervention: The Use of American Military Force in the Post-Cold War World, Washington, DC: Carnegie Endowment for International Peace, 1994; and 2nd edn 1998.

32 See especially Charles Krauthammer, 'The Unipolar Era', in Andrew J. Bacevich (ed.) The Imperial Tense: Prospects and Problems of American Empire, Chicago: Ivan Dee, 2003, pp. 47–65 (first published in The National Interest, winter 2003). 'The 1990s were marked by an obsession with "international legality"', suggests Krauthammer. Instead of safeguarding American interests, the liberal internationalists embraced the 'erosion of sovereignty' in the service of a vision of 'goo-goo one-worldism' (pp. 57, 59).

33 Edward C. Luck, 'American Exceptionalism and International Organization: Lessons from the 1990s', in Foot et al. (eds) US Hegemony and International Organizations, p. 25.

34 Economist, 1 September 2001, p. 41.

35 Samantha Power, 'A Problem from Hell': America and the Age of Genocide, London: Flamingo, 2003, pp. 69–70. See also Murphy, The United States and the Rule of Law, pp. 81–82.

36 Edward Luck, 'American Exceptionalism and International Organization', in Foot et al. (eds) US Hegemony and International Organizations, pp. 42–46. Luck shows that the issue is a complicated one. It was closely linked with demands for reform of the UN, with which Clinton had some sympathy, but there is no disguising the basic point that Congress acted in defiance of Clinton's wishes. In his memoirs Clinton writes that 'I thought the refusal

to pay our back dues was irresponsible and damaging to both the UN and the United States, but I agreed that reform was imperative' (My Life, London: Hutchinson, 2004, p. 739).

37 See 'Bush Untethered', New York Times, 17 September 2006.

38 Francis Fukuyama, State Building: Governance and World Order in the Twenty-first Century, London: Profile Books, 2004, pp. 148, 149, 157.

39 Francis Fukuyama, After the Neocons: America at the Crossroads, London: Profile Books, 2006, pp. 157, 173, 174, 190–91.

40 See Robert Kagan, Paradise and Power: America and Europe in the New World Order, London: Atlantic Books, 2003.

41 Albright, Madam Secretary, p. 140.

42 Richard Haass, The Opportunity: America's Moment to Alter History's Course, New York: Public Affairs, 2005, pp. 41–42, 190.

43 See Paul Kennedy, The Parliament of Man: The United Nations and the Quest for World Government, London: Allen Lane, 2006.

Conclusion: American freedom and the war in Iraq

1 See Bob Woodward, State of Denial: Bush at War, Part III, New York: Simon and Schuster, 2006, pp. 120–34.

2 Woodward, State of Denial.

3 This is the thesis of Edmund Morgan's American Slavery, American Freedom: The Ordeal of Colonial Virginia, New York: Norton, 1975.

Select bibliography

Note: References to individual newspaper articles, speeches, and websites are not listed here but are given in full in the notes to the chapters.

Acharya, Amitav, 'State–Society Relations: Asian and World Order After September 11', in Ken Booth and Tim Dunne (eds) *Worlds in Collision: Terror and the Future of Global Order*, Houndmills, UK: Palgrave, 2002, pp. 194–204.

Ajami, Fouad, 'The Summoning', *Foreign Affairs*, 72, no. 4 (September/October 1993) pp. 2–9.

Albright, Madeleine, *Madam Secretary: A Memoir*, New York: Macmillan, 2003.

Allardyce, Gilbert, 'The Rise and Fall of the Western Civilization Course', *American Historical Review*, vol. 87, June 1982, pp. 695–725.

Amanat, Abbas, 'Empowered Through Violence: The Reinventing of Islamic Extremism', in Strobe Talbott and Nayan Chanda (eds) *The Age of Terror: America and the World After September 11*, Oxford: Perseus Press, 2001, pp. 23–52.

American Legion, *Isms: A Review of Alien Isms, Revolutionary Communism and their Active Sympathizers in the United States*, compiled by the National Americanism Commission of the American Legion, National Headquarters, Indianapolis, IN, 1937.

Anderson, Benedict, *Imagined Communities: Reflections on the Origins and Spread of Nationalism*, revised edn, London: Verso, 1991.

An-Na'im, Abdullahi Ahmed, 'Upholding International Legality Against Islamic and American Jihad', in Ken Booth and Tim Dunne (eds) *Worlds in Collision: Terror and the Future of Global Order*, Houndmills, UK: Palgrave, 2002, pp. 162–71.

Ansari, Ali M., *Confronting Iran: The Failure of American Foreign Policy and the Next Great Conflict in the Middle East*, New York: Basic Books, 2006.

Appleby, R. Scott, 'History in the Fundamentalist Imagination', in Joanne Meyerowitz (ed.) *History and September 11*, Philadelphia, PA: Temple University Press, 2003, pp. 157–74.

Bacevich, Andrew, *American Empire: The Realities and Consequences of U.S. Diplomacy*, Cambridge, MA: Harvard University Press, 2002.

Bacevich, Andrew (ed.) *The Imperial Tense: Problems and Perspectives of American Empire*, Chicago, IL: Ivan Dee, 2003.

Barber, Benjamin, *Jihad vs McWorld: Terrorism's Challenge to Democracy*, New York: Ballantine Books, 1995.

Baylis, John and Steve Smith (eds) *The Globalization of World Politics: An Introduction to International Relations*, 3rd edn, Oxford: Oxford University Press, 2005.

Beard, Charles A. and Mary R. Beard, *The Rise of American Civilization*, New York: Macmillan, 1930.

Benjamin, Daniel and Steven Simon, *The Next Attack: The Failure of the War on Terror and a Strategy for Getting it Right*, New York: Times Books, 2005.

Boorstin, Daniel, *The Genius of American Politics*, Chicago, IL: University of Chicago Press, 1953.

Booth, Ken and Tim Dunne (eds) *Worlds in Collision: Terror and the Future of Global Order*, Houndmills, UK: Palgrave, 2002.

Bremer, L. Paul, *My Year in Iraq: The Struggle to Build a Future of Hope*, New York: Simon and Schuster, 2006.

Bull, Hedley, *The Anarchical Society: A Study of Order in World Politics*, London: Macmillan, 1977.

Burke, Edmund, *Reflections on the Revolution in France* [1790] Garden City, NJ: Dolphin Books, 1961.

Burns, John, 'Bin Laden Stirs Struggle on the Meaning of Jihad', *New York Times*, 27 January 2002.

Buzan, Barry and Richard Little, 'Beyond Westphalia? Capitalism after the "Fall"', *Review of International Studies*, vol. 25, December 1999, pp. 89–104.

Chace, James, 'In Search of Absolute Security', in Andrew Bacevich (ed.) *The Imperial Tense: Problems and Perspectives of American Empire*, Chicago, IL: Ivan Dee, 2003, pp. 119–33 (first published 2002 in *World Policy Journal*).

Chalmers, David M., *Hooded Americanism: The First Century of the Ku Klux Klan, 1865–1965*, Garden City, NJ: Doubleday, 1965.

Clark, Ian, *The Post-Cold War Order: The Spoils of Peace*, Oxford: Oxford University Press, 2001.

Cohen, Elliott, 'A Revolution in Warfare', *Foreign Affairs*, 75, no. 2, March/April 1996, pp. 37–54.

Cooper, Robert, *The Breaking of Nations: Order and Chaos in the Twenty-first Century*, London: Atlantic Books, 2003.

Cox, Michael, 'Empire, Imperialism and the Bush Doctrine', *Review of International Studies*, 30, no. 4 (2004) pp. 585–608.

Cox, Robert, 'Civilizations and the Twenty-first Century: Some Theoretical Considerations', in Mehdi Mozaffari (ed.) *Globalization and Civilizations*, London: Routledge, 2002, pp. 1–23.

Criss, Nur Bilge, 'A Short History of Anti-Americanism and Terrorism: The Turkish Case', in Joanne Meyerowitz (ed.) *History and September 11*, Philadelphia, PA: Temple University Press, 2003, pp. 56–72.

Crockatt, Richard, *America Embattled: September 11, Anti-Americanism and the Global Order*, London and New York: Routledge, 2003.

Daalder, Ivo and James D. Lindsay, *America Unbound: The Bush Revolution in Foreign Policy*, Washington, DC: Brookings Institution Press, 2003.

Del Pero, Mario, 'The Historical and Ideological Roots of the Neo-conservative Persuasion', in Sergio Fabbrini (ed.) *The United States Contested: American Unilateralism and European Discontent*, London: Routledge, 2006, pp. 33–53.

Dewey, John, *Individualism Old and New*, New York: Capricorn Books (first published 1930) 1962.

Ellwood, David, *Anti-Americanism in Western Europe: A Comparative Perspective*, Baltimore, MD: Johns Hopkins University, Bologna Center, 1999.

Esposito, John L., *The Islamic Threat: Myth or Reality?*, 2nd edn, New York: Oxford University Press, 1995.

——*Unholy War: Terror in the Name of Islam*, Oxford: Oxford University Press, 2002.

Fabbrini, Sergio, 'Layers of Anti-Americanism: Americanization, American Unilateralism and anti-Americanism in a European Perspective', *European Journal of American Culture*, 23, no. 2, 2004, pp. 79–94.

Fabbrini, Sergio (ed.) *The United States Contested: American Unilateralism and European Discontent*, London: Routledge, 2006.

Ferguson, Niall, *Colossus: The Rise and Fall of the American Empire*, London: Allen Lane, 2004, p. 29.

Foot, Rosemary, S. MacFarlane and Michael Mastanduno (eds) *US Hegemony and International Organizations*, Oxford: Oxford University Press, 2003.

Freeland, Richard, *The Truman Doctrine and the Origins of McCarthyism*, New York: Knopf, 1972.

Fukuyama, Francis, 'The End of History?', *The National Interest*, summer 1989, pp. 3–18.

——*The End of History and the Last Man*, London: Hamish Hamilton, 1992.

——*State Building: Governance and World Order in the Twenty-first Century*, London: Profile Books, 2004.

——*After the Neocons: America at the Crossroads*, London: Profile Books, 2006.

Gaddis, John L., 'Towards the Post-Cold War World', *Foreign Affairs*, 70, no. 2, spring 1991, pp. 102–22.

——*Surprise, Security and the American Experience*, Cambridge, MA: Harvard University Press, 2004.

Gerges, Fawaz A., *America and Political Islam: Clash of Cultures or Clash of Interests?*, Cambridge: Cambridge University Press, 1999.

Giddens, Anthony, *Runaway World: How Globalisation is Reshaping Our Lives*, London: Profile Books, 1999.

Greenfeld, Liah, *Nationalism: Five Roads to Modernity*, Cambridge, MA: Harvard University Press, 1992.

Griffin, David Ray, *The New Pearl Harbor: Disturbing Questions about the Bush Administration and 9/11*, Moreton-in-the-Marsh, UK: Arris Books, 2004.

Haass, Richard N., *Intervention: The Use of American Military Force in the Post-Cold War World*, 2nd edn, Washington, DC: Carnegie Endowment, 1999.

——*The Opportunity: America's Moment to Alter World History*, New York: Public Affairs, 2005.

Haddad, Yvonne Yazbeck, 'Islamist Perceptions of US Policy in the Middle East', in David W. Lesch (ed.) *The Middle East and the United States: A Historical and Political Reassessment*, 3rd edn, Cambridge, MA: Westview Press, 2003, pp. 467–90.

Hakim, Peter, 'Is Washington Losing Latin America?', *Foreign Affairs*, 85, no. 1, January/February 2006, pp. 39–53.

Halliday, Fred, *Islam and the Myth of Confrontation: Religion and Politics in the Middle East*, London: I. B. Tauris, 1999.

——*The World at 2000: Perils and Promises*, Houndmills, UK: Palgrave, 2001.

——*Two Hours That Shook the World: September 11, 2001, Causes and Consequences*, London: Saqi Books, 2002.

——*The Middle East in International Relations: Power, Politics and Ideology*, Cambridge: Cambridge University Press, 2005.

Halper, Stefan and Jonathan Clarke, *America Alone: The Neoconservatives and the Global Order*, Cambridge: Cambridge University Press, 2004.

Hanson, Victor Davis, 'What Empire?', in Andrew Bacevich (ed.) *The Imperial Tense: Problems and Perspectives of American Empire*, Chicago: Ivan Dee, 2003, pp. 146–55.

Heald, Morrell and Lawrence S. Kaplan, *Culture and Diplomacy: The American Experience*, Westport, CT: Greenwood Press, 1977.

Higham, John, 'Beyond Consensus: The Historian as Moral Critic', *American Historical Review*, 67 (1962) pp. 609–25.

——*Strangers in the Land: Patterns of American Nativism, 1860–1925*, New York: Atheneum, 1973.

Hobsbawm, Eric, *Nations and Nationalism Since 1780*, Cambridge: Cambridge University Press, 1990.

Hollander, Paul, *Anti-Americanism: Critiques at Home and Abroad, 1965–1990*, New York: Oxford University Press, 1992.

Holm, Hans-Henrik and Georg Sorenson (eds) *Whose World Order? Uneven Globalization and the End of the Cold War*, Boulder, CO: Westview Press, 1995.

Hunt, Michael, *Ideology and US Foreign Policy*, New Haven, CT: Yale University Press, 1987.

Huntington, Samuel P., 'The Clash of Civilizations?', *Foreign Affairs*, 72, no. 3, summer 1993, pp. 22–49.

——*The Clash of Civilizations and the Remaking of World Order*, New York: Simon and Schuster, 1996.

——*Who Are We? America's Great Debate*, New York: Free Press, 2004.

Hutton, Will, *The World We're In*, revised edn, London: Abacus, 2003.

Ikenberry, G. J., 'Liberalism and Empire: Logics of Order in the American Unipolar Age', *Review of International Studies*, 30, no. 4, 2004, pp. 609–30.

——'The End of the Neo-Conservative Moment', *Survival*, 46, no. 1, spring 2004.

——'State Power and the Institutional Bargain: America's Ambivalent Economic and Security Multilateralism', in Rosemary Foot, S. MacFarlane and Michael Mastanduno (eds) *US Hegemony and International Organizations*, Oxford: Oxford University Press, 2003, pp. 49–70.

Iriye, Akira, 'Culture and Power: International Relations as Intercultural Relations', *Diplomatic History*, 3 (spring 1979), pp. 115–28.

Isserman, Maurice, *Which Side Were You On?: The American Communist Party During the Second World War*, Middletown, CT: Wesleyan University Press, 1982,

James, Henry, *The American Scene*, Harmondsworth, UK: Penguin, 1994.

Johnson, Chalmers, *Blowback: The Cost and Consequences of American Empire*, New York: Henry Holt, 2000.

Kagan, Robert, *Of Paradise and Power: America and Europe in the New World Order*, London: Atlantic Books, 2003.

Kazin, Michael and Joseph A. McCartin (eds) *Americanism: New Perspectives on the History of an Ideal*, Chapel Hill, NC: University of North Carolina Press, 2006.

Kennan, George F., *American Diplomacy 1900–1950*, Chicago, IL: University of Chicago Press, 1950.

Kennedy, Paul, *The Parliament of Man: The Quest for World Government*, London: Allen Lane, 2006.

Keohane, R. and Joseph S. Nye, *Power and Interdependence: World Politics in Transition*, Boston, MA: Little, Brown, 1977.

Kepel, Gilles, *The War for Muslim Minds: Islam and the West*, Cambridge, MA: Harvard University Press, 2004, pp. 123–24.

Kirkpatrick, Jeane, 'Neoconservatism as a Response to the Counter-Culture', in Irwin Stelzer (ed.) *Neoconservatism*, London: Atlantic Books, 2004, pp. 233–40.

Kissinger, Henry, 'The Pitfalls of Universal Jurisdiction', *Foreign Affairs*, July/August 2001, pp. 86–96.

Kohn, Hans, *American Nationalism: An Interpretive Essay*, New York: Collier, 1961 (first published 1957).

Krauthammer, Charles, 'The Unipolar Moment', *Foreign Affairs*, 70, 1990–91, pp. 23–33.

——'The Unipolar Era', in Andrew Bacevich (ed.) *The Imperial Tense: Problems and Perspectives of American Empire*, Chicago, IL: Ivan Dee, 2003, pp. 47–65.

Kristol, Irving, *Reflections of a Neoconservative*, New York: Basic Books, 1983.

——'The Neoconservative Persuasion', in Irwin Stelzer (ed.) *Neoconservatism*, London: Atlantic Books, 2004, pp. 31–38.

Kristol, William and Robert Kagan, 'Toward a Neo-Reaganite Foreign Policy', *Foreign Affairs*, 75, July/August 1996.

Lal, Deepak, 'In Defense of Empires', in Andrew Bacevich (ed.) *The Imperial Tense: Problems and Perspectives of American Empire*, Chicago: Ivan Dee, 2003, pp. 29–46.

Larres, Klaus, 'Mutual Incomprehension: US–German Value Gaps beyond Iraq', *The Washington Quarterly*, 26, no. 2, spring 2003, pp. 23–42.

Laski, Harold, *American Democracy*, New York: Viking Press, 1948.

Lerner, Max, *America as a Civilization: Life and Thought in the United States Today*, New York: Simon and Schuster, 1957.

Lewis, Bernard, *What Went Wrong?: Western Impact and Middle Eastern Response*, London: Phoenix Books, 2002.

——*The Crisis of Islam: Holy War and Unholy Terror*, London: Weidenfeld and Nicolson, 2003.

Lieven, Anatol, *America Right or Wrong: An Anatomy of American Nationalism*, London: HarperCollins, 2004.

Lind, Michael, *The Next American Nation: The New Nationalism and the Fourth American Revolution*, New York: Free Press, 1996.

Lipset, Seymour Martin, *American Exceptionalism: A Double-edged Sword*, New York: Norton, 1996.

Luck, Edward, 'American Exceptionalism and International Organization: Lessons from the 1990s', in Rosemary Foot, S. MacFarlane and Michael Mastanduno (eds) *US Hegemony and International Organizations*, Oxford: Oxford University Press, 2003, pp. 25–48.

Makdisi, Usama, ' "Anti-Americanism" in the Arab World: An Interpretation of a Brief History', in Joanne Meyerowitz (ed.) *History and September 11*, Philadelphia, PA: Temple University Press, 2002, pp. 131–56.

Mazarr, Michael J., 'Culture in International Relations', *Washington Quarterly*, 19, no. 2, spring 1996, pp. 177–97.

McDougall, Walter, *Promised Land, Crusader State: The American Encounter with The World Since 1776*, Boston, MA: Houghton Mifflin, 1997.

Mead, Walter Russell, *Special Providence: American Foreign Policy and How It Changed the World*, London and New York: Routledge, 2002.

Mearsheimer, John, 'Back to the Future: Instability After the Cold War', *International Security*, 15, no. 1, 1990, pp. 5–56.

Mencken, H. L., *The American Language: An Inquiry into the Development of English in the United States*, 2nd edn, New York: Alfred A. Knopf, 1921.

Mickelthwait, John and Adrian Wooldridge, *The Right Nation: Why America is Different*, London: Allen Lane, 2004.

Mozaffari, Mehdi (ed.) *Globalization and Civilizations*, London: Routledge, 2002.

Murphy, John F., *The United States and the Rule of Law in International Affairs*, Cambridge: Cambridge University Press, 2004.

National Security Strategy of the United States of America, September 2002, 19 at www.whitehouse.gov/nsc/ (accessed 18/9/2003).

Newhouse, John, 'The Missile Defense Debate', *Foreign Affairs*, July/August 2001, pp. 97–109.

The 9/11 Commission Report: Final Report of the National Commission on Terrorist Attacks upon the United States, New York: Norton, 2004.

Nye, Joseph, *Bound To Lead: The Changing Nature of American Power*, New York: Basic Books, 1990.

——'What New World Order?', *Foreign Affairs*, 71, no. 2, spring 1992, pp. 83–96.

——*The Paradox of American Power: Why the World's Only Superpower Can't Go it Alone*, New York: Oxford University Press, 2002.

O'Connor, Brendon, 'What is Anti-Americanism: Tendency, Prejudice or Ideology?', paper delivered at the Institute for the Study of the Americas, University of London, 21 October 2005.

O'Connor, Brendon and Martin Griffiths (eds) *The Rise of Anti-Americanism*, London: Routledge, 2006.

Parekh, Bhikhu, 'Terrorism or Intercultural Dialogue', in Ken Booth and Tim Dunne (eds) *Worlds in Collision: Terror and the Future of Global Order*, Houndmills, UK: Palgrave, 2002, pp. 270–83.

Piscatori, James, 'Order, Justice, and Global Islam', in Rosemary Foot, John Lewis Gaddis and Andrew Hurrell (eds) *Order and Justice in International Relations*, Oxford: Oxford University Press, 2003, pp. 262–86.

Potter, David, *People of Plenty: Economic Abundance and the American Character*, Chicago, IL: University of Chicago Press, 1954.

Power, Samantha, *'A Problem from Hell': America and the Age of Genocide*, London: Flamingo, 2003.

Purdy, Jedediah, 'Universal Nation', in Andrew Bacevich (ed.) *The Imperial Tense: Problems and Perspectives of American Empire*, Chicago: Ivan Dee, 2003, pp. 102–10.

Rice, Condoleezza, 'Campaign 2000: Promoting the National Interest', *Foreign Affairs*, January/February 2000, pp. 45–62.

Roy, Olivier, *The Failure of Political Islam*, London: I. B. Tauris, 1999.

——*Globalized Islam: The Search for a New Umma*, New York: Columbia University Press, 2004.

Ruthven, Malise, *Islam in the World*, 2nd edn, London: Penguin Books, 2000.

——*A Fury for God: The Islamist Attack on America*, London: Granta, 2002.

Said, Edward, *Orientalism*, Harmondsworth, UK: Penguin, 1978.

——*Culture and Imperialism*, London: Vintage, 1994.

——*Peace and Its Discontents: Gaza-Jericho 1993–1995*, London: Vintage, 1995.

——*Out of Place*, London: Granta Books, 2000.

——*The End of the Peace Process*, revised and updated edn, London: Granta, 2002.

——From Oslo to Iraq and the Roadmap, London: Bloomsbury, 2004.

Saikal, Amin, *Islam and the West: Conflict or Cooperation?*, Houndmills, UK: Palgrave, 2003.

Sardar, Ziauddin and Merryl Wyn Davies, *Why Do People Hate America?*, Cambridge: Icon Books, 2002.

Scholte, Jan Aart, *Globalization: A Critical Introduction*, Basingstoke, UK: Palgrave, 2000.

Stead, W. T., *The Americanization of the World*, New York: Garland, 1972 (first published London: Horace Markley, 1901).

Stelzer, Irwin (ed.) *Neoconservatism*, London: Atlantic Books, 2004.

Thompson, John A., *Woodrow Wilson*, London: Longman, 2002.

Tocqueville, Alexis de, *Democracy in America*, trans., ed. and with an introduction by Harvey Mansfield and Delba Winthrop, London: The Folio Society, 2002 (first published by the University of Chicago Press, 2000).

Toynbee, Arnold, *A Study of History*, London: Oxford University Press, 1934, vol. 1.

Walker, Martin, 'An Empire Unlike Any Other', in Andrew Bacevich (ed.) *The Imperial Tense: Problems and Perspectives of American Empire*, Chicago, IL: Ivan Dee, 2003, pp. 134–45.

Watson, Adam, *The Evolution of International Society: A Comparative Historical Analysis*, London: Routledge, 1992.

Weeks, Albert, 'Do Civilizations Hold?', *Foreign Affairs*, 72, no. 4, September/October 1993, pp. 24–25.

Weidenfeld, Werner, *America and Europe: Is the Break Inevitable?*, Gütersloh, Germany: Bertelsmann Foundation Publishers, 1996, pp. 9–10.

Wight, Martin, *International Theory: The Three Traditions*, eds Gabriele Wight and Brian Porter, London: Leicester University Press for the Royal Institute of International Affairs, 1991.

Williams, Raymond, *Keywords*, London: Fontana, 1976.

Woodward, Bob, *Plan of Attack*, New York: Simon and Schuster, 2004.

——State of Denial, New York: Simon and Schuster, 2006.

Index